A BEGINNER'S GUIDE TO DANTE'S
Divine Comedy

A BEGINNER'S GUIDE TO DANTE'S *Divine Comedy*

Jason M. Baxter

Baker Academic

a division of Baker Publishing Group
Grand Rapids, Michigan

Published by Baker Academic
a division of Baker Publishing Group
PO Box 6287, Grand Rapids, MI 49516-6287
www.bakeracademic.com

Printed in the United States of America

Library of Congress Cataloging-in-Publication Data
Names: Baxter, Jason M., 1981– author.
Title: A beginner's guide to Dante's Divine comedy / Jason M. Baxter.
Description: Grand Rapids : Baker Academic, 2018. | Includes bibliographical references and index.
Identifiers: LCCN 2017041942 | ISBN 9780801098734 (pbk. : alk. paper)
Subjects: LCSH: Dante Alighieri, 1265–1321. Divina commedia. | Dante Alighieri, 1265–1321—Criticism and interpretation. | Christianity in literature. | Religion and literature.
Classification: LCC PQ4390 .B48 2018 | DDC 851/.1—dc23
LC record available at https://lccn.loc.gov/2017041942

Scripture quotations are from the King James Version of the Bible.

18 19 20 21 22 23 24   7 6 5 4 3 2 1

Contents

Acknowledgments

Almost every thought, almost every sentence in what follows was born in conversation with my wife, my teachers, my friends, or my students. I read each one of the chapters below to little groups of students or friends in my home, over wine and cheese and bread, and the remarks made in the conversations that followed found their way into this book. For this reason I am deeply grateful to my present and past students (who are now my friends), especially Cody Lee, Trevor Lontine, Claire D'Agostino, Hannah Gleason, Jacob Terneus, Joe and Rachel Turner, Scott Sargeant, Isaac Owen, and my fellow *dantista* Carolyn De Salvo. I am grateful to my South Bend friends (Kirk, Maggie, Steve, and Sue) who were my very first audience, anesthetized by Rioja. Heartfelt gratitude goes out to my advisors and professors at Notre Dame, especially Ted Cachey, Christian Moeves, Zyg Baranski, Stephen Gersh, Ann Astell, and especially Vittorio Montemaggi, who more than anyone else taught me what it means to study Dante. My friend Colum Dever invited me to Duke, where I gave two lectures that serve as the basis for two of the chapters below. Another friend from Notre Dame, Tommy Clemmons, was the inspiration to ask Baker Academic if they would publish this book. Over a beautiful summer in Ischia and in the Pincio of the Villa Borghese, my friends James and Judiann listened to revision after revision and provided me with poignant suggestions for improvement. I would like to thank my parents, Bob and Pauletta, and my brother, Josh, for their support, which goes deeper than I can identify. And, finally, to my best friend, my most challenging interlocutor, most fastidious editor, and source of encouragement and inspiration, Jodi. We made it. This book is dedicated to you.

Introduction

Dante as Poet, Prophet, and Exile

Dante's Cathedral: Reading the *Comedy* on Multiple Levels

The *Comedy* (*Divine Comedy* is a title created by Dante's Renaissance admirers) is the greatest work by the Florentine poet Dante Alighieri (1265–1321)—some would say the greatest work of the Western imagination.[1] Whether or not this is true, Dante indubitably keeps company with Homer, Virgil, Sophocles, Shakespeare, and Dostoyevsky. And yet, although the *Comedy* is an undisputed masterpiece, it has a peculiar medieval flavor to it, which makes it taste quite different from a Homeric epic, a tragedy for the stage, or a realistic novel. And this strong medieval flavor can sometimes spoil our appreciation. I have had students confess to me that they had eagerly looked forward to the *Comedy*, but when they actually got to it, they were put off by the work's difficulty and confused by its poetic form. I would like, then, to mention some of the obstacles that the *Comedy*'s medieval form poses to first-time readers.

More than once, the *Comedy* has been likened to a medieval cathedral.[2] If you've ever stepped into an old-world Gothic cathedral, then you know that the vault soars overhead, rising sometimes to 150 feet, and that everywhere you look your eye finds harmony and graceful order. Medieval cathedrals have a sweeping grandeur as well as an all-encompassing design: every part has a place, and every part has a corresponding part across the aisle. The face of the church, the façade, is divided into hierarchical

Figure 1. The vault of the Laon Cathedral.

layers and orderly portals.³ In a similar way, Dante's poem is famous for its architectural order.

At the most basic level, the *Comedy* relates the story of a man lost in a dark wood and saved by the ancient Roman poet Virgil, who had been commissioned by a whole hierarchy of saints. The pilgrim—Dante himself—travels through hell, climbs the mountain of purgatory, and rises through the spheres of heaven on his way to see (and be seen by) God. All of these realms and landscapes through which the pilgrim passes are neatly ordered. Each terrace or descending level corresponds to and gives flesh to the moral philosophical principles of Dante's day.⁴ In fact, one of the great readers of Dante in our time, Roberto Antonelli, has argued that Dante had the basic blueprint of the whole work in his mind even before he began writing!⁵ The poet spent almost fifteen years working on the poem, but he was able to write lines for *Inferno* that would anticipate verses he would write over a decade later for *Paradiso*, because he had a framework for his imaginative world provided to him by the moral philosophy of his day. It is this palpable and concrete architecture of the afterlife that Florentine artists for centuries after Dante loved to try to map out as accurately as they could.⁶

Figure 2. Botticelli's *Map of Hell* (1480–95).

But it's not just Dante's imaginary landscape of the afterlife that is so well ordered; Dante also meticulously crafted the formal structure of his poem. After the gripping first canto of the *Comedy*, thirty-three more canti come in *Inferno*; we then get thirty-three more for *Purgatorio*, and the same number for *Paradiso*, for a total of three sets of thirty-three "little songs" (canti) plus an introductory canto, adding up to a perfect one hundred. It's not just the number of canticles (three) and canti (one hundred) that displays Dante's obsession with the harmonic perfection of his formal craft, though; he also used a complex and fascinating rhyme scheme, the so-called *terza rima* (which English translators after Dorothy Sayers do not try to reproduce). What you will see if you look at the Italian page are groups of three-line stanzas (each known as a *terzina*). The first line of the terzina rhymes with the third line: *vita* in *Inferno* 1.1 rhymes with *smarrita* (*Inf.* 1.3). The middle line of the terzina introduces a new rhyme, which will be repeated twice in the following terzina: thus, *oscura* (1.2) / *dura* (1.4) / *paura* (1.6). But then at the end of 1.5, we have a new rhyme (namely, *forte*), which will again be repeated at the end of verse 7 (*morte*) and verse 9 (*scorte*). The rhyme scheme, then, is a/b/a, b/c/b, c/d/c, in which the unrhymed word in the middle line of each terzina becomes the outside rhymes in the following terzina. This forms a chain of rhymes, in which each terzina is linked to the previous and following stanzas. Thus, from the very beginning of the poem we have stepped into a world of extraordinary mathematical beauty. All of the drama, all of the action to come, all of the individual personalities will unfold in the midst of this linguistic world, regulated by patterns of threes and tens. For Dante, this order was a clear and evocative sign of the Trinity. God is, as it were, everywhere present within the literary cosmos of the poem.[7]

The action unfolds not just within sacred space but also within sacred time. Through his periphrastic allusions, Dante establishes with exactitude when his journey takes place. His descent into hell begins precisely on Good Friday, 1300, and continues until he arrives on the shores of Mount Purgatory at dawn, Easter Sunday. The pilgrim will spend three nights in purgatory until he rises to see the souls of heaven. In the very liturgical season in which the medieval church celebrated Christ's descent into hell and resurrection as a pattern for the Christian life, so too does the pilgrim—seemingly not entirely aware of the sacred time in which he moves—undertake his own journey of descent and rising to renewed life.[8] Thus, the pilgrim passes through an imaginary landscape mapped out into dozens of distinct regions, terraces, and circles, on a journey divided into distinct phases that have been carefully synchronized with liturgical time. And the *poet* narrates each step of this journey in particular canti, all of which have a specific place carefully assigned to them within the numerical ordering of the poem. Indeed, Dante's world is so architectural that the *Comedy* has been called "the last Gothic Cathedral."[9]

And yet there is more to a medieval cathedral than its geometrical order. Indeed, over the walls, ceilings, and floors we can watch a riotous variety of forms at play within the sober, governing architectural patterns: carved stones (of saints, flora, and fauna), interlacing rib vaults, bundles of differently sized stone columns, ornate friezes, windows of different sizes, polychromatic stained glass, and intricate patterns laid into marble floors.[10] Analogously, the pilgrim does not just journey from region to region but holds conversations with a bewildering number of very particular, very different, historical and mythological people. And so, in addition to the well-ordered architectural space, all readers of the *Comedy* are struck—perhaps even overwhelmed and confused—by the poem's extraordinary abundance. In fact, there are nearly 1,500 proper names throughout the *Comedy*: names of rivers in obscure parts of Italy; names of geographical regions (woods, mountains, cities, neighbor-hoods) from history and mythology; classical heroes; mythological beasts; and a host of medieval Florentines (Guido Cavalcanti, Brunetto Latini, Pier della Vigna, Guido da Montefeltro, Cacciaguida, and on and on). Dante intentionally employs a huge cast of characters, drawn from every era of history, right back to Adam and the biblical patriarchs and up to Dante's contemporary Italy. There are 210 characters who make an appearance in *Inferno* alone! Try to imagine a play or a film that contained so many actors.[11]

Both Dante's *Comedy* and the medieval cathedral, then, are constructed analogously to the cosmos created by God. On the one hand, you have constellations, stars, and seasons that move in recurring patterns; you have seas and oceans and continents that stay put within their assigned boundaries. On the other hand, you have millions of unique faces, people, minds, languages, and local histories that live and die within the midst of that governing architecture of time and space. Even though I said that Dante stands in the company of Shakespeare, Dostoyevsky, and Homer, it's understandable why he's difficult to get into.

This rich complexity, which calls forth such ardent admiration, can also account for why this poem is so difficult to appreciate on a first or even second read. It is also for this reason that this book has been written: to build a bridge from where we are, over the difficulties, so that we can enter into the poem with greater appreciation. In chapter 1, I will talk about how Dante zooms out to give his readers a view of the architectural whole (using a kind of poetic telescope), but only after he has zoomed in to give a close-up of particular human beings (a literary microscope). In the remainder of this introduction, though, I want to explore how these key features of the poem have their roots in the author's biography. In particular, I will focus on two major moments in Dante's life: his early love poetry (produced when he was in his twenties) and his failure in politics (the experience of his early thirties). Both of these experiences shaped the horizons for the book he would later write.

Dante before the Dark Wood (1): Love Poet

Dante was born into a minor aristocratic family.[12] Scholars think that in the early 1280s—that is, when Dante was the equivalent of a freshman in college—he began to write his first poems, which he deferentially sent around to the established poets of Florence. These poems were not like the poetry he would later write in the *Comedy*—that is, they were not narrative poems but rather sonnets or *canzoni* ("little songs" of around one hundred verses). All of Dante's youthful poems dealt, in one form or another, with falling in love, being in love, suffering when the one you love doesn't return your love, and so forth. The young poet's short, powerful, melodious verses quickly gained the admiration of the aristocratic, practicing poets of Florence.

Of course, we all know something about the experience of love: those first exciting and awkward moments when you were attracted to someone and that person was attracted to you (or not); how you worried and talked endlessly about it to anyone who was interested (or even to those who weren't); the pain of being dumped. Similarly, medieval love poets for centuries before Dante had written about these things, but they had also tried to get all of these phases and elements of the experience of love down to a precise, poetic science.[13] Each lyric poet had his trademark specialty. Some wrote on the pain of love (e.g., Guido Cavalcanti); Guinizelli specialized in praise of beauty. But all these "faithful servants of love" (*fideli d'amore*) agreed that the experience of love, even when one of sweetness, is so psychologically intense that it can best be described in terms of violence: it is an aching or longing that is so passionate it threatens death; it is an arrow that shatters the heart; it is a hurricane gale that breaks a stone tower. The experience of earthly love outweighed any other possible experience; thus, the man or woman in the servitude of love had a quality of "knowledge" higher than that of ordinary existence. In his sonnet "Tanto gentile," Dante states the ineffability of love concisely: referring to the unspeakable sweetness that comes from Beatrice's eyes, he says that "none can understand but he who experiences it" (v. 11).[14]

Although every stage of love is marked by such intensity, it remains true that the experience of unreciprocated love is the most painful experience of all; or, as a friend of Dante's once put it, "He who loves unloved has the greatest pain; for this pain holds sway over all others and is called the chief one: it is the source of all the suffering that love brings" (Dante da Maiano).[15] Thus, love poets also had a particular interest in discovering the mechanics of the process by which one is infected by the contagion of love, because, if you could figure out the physiological process by which you were struck by love, then you could reverse engineer it and make the lady you fell in love with love you in return. The lyric poet thus tried to create a reading experience that would make his reader sigh, weep, feel warmth, and eventually show compassion. The reader is made to enter into the poet's experience of messiness, confusion, or rage, or of melting, burning, sweetness, and peace. In other words, lyrical poems are "performative"; they are the poet's tool for creating in you what is happening in me.

By the time he was in his late twenties, Dante had already written several dozen such poems. However, around the year 1293, Dante gathered up thirty-one of these poems and arranged them in a little anthology of his own work. He also did something unprecedented: he added an autobiographical and theological commentary to explain the occasions of the poems and hint at their deeper meaning. He called his work *Vita Nuova*, or *The New Life*. The reason this strange, experimental little book (you can read it in under two hours) is so interesting is that it shows Dante's early desire to elevate a popular form of writing—the vernacular love song—to the level of a theological treatise. Dante did not use the learned language of law, science, or the university (Latin), but rather he took the ordinary language of Italian (although highly stylistically refined) and the common experience of love as the tools for looking for something of that philosophical depth that had largely been the pursuit of the learned, Latinate literary culture.[16] And so, the story of how he came to compose these poems takes on powerful overtones.

Dante's poetic story of his "new life" begins with a description of a childhood experience, in the ninth hour, of the ninth day, of his ninth year, when he first laid eyes on Beatrice. Recalling this event almost eighteen years later, Dante writes:

> At that very moment, and I speak the truth, the vital spirit, the one that dwells in the most secret chamber of the heart, began to tremble so violently that even the most minute veins of my body were strangely affected; and trembling, it spoke these words: "Ecce deus fortior me, qui veniens dominabitur michi [Here is a god stronger than I who comes to rule over me]." (*Vita Nuova* II, 3–4)[17]

As Dante explains, he knew from that moment that he had been elected the servant of love and that he would remain in servitude forever. There would never be a moment in which he would try *not* to be in love. In the medieval courtly tradition (for example, in *The Romance of the Rose* or

Chaucer's *Troilus and Criseyde*), the experience of love is as enlivening as it is terrifying. Everything else now seems flat, boring, and dull. In love, you are braver and see the world with a new vigor, but the experience of love can also be extremely dangerous and, as we have seen, painful. For instance, it just so happened that the next time Dante saw Beatrice was exactly nine years later: "She greeted me so miraculously that I seemed at that moment to behold the entire range of possible bliss. . . . I became so ecstatic that, like a drunken man, I turned away from everyone and I sought the loneliness of my room, where I began thinking of this most gracious lady" (III, 5). From then on, Dante nervously anticipated these encounters. When he did see Beatrice, his heart was so full of love that "[he] could not have considered any man [his] enemy" (XI, 16). And yet, at one point in his narration, Dante says that seeing his beloved almost killed him, because as he stared at the miraculous apparition of beauty in front of him, his other vital functions began to fail. Dante plays on the Italian pun of *amore* (love) and *amaro* (bitter) to evoke how such intense joy was painful.

And so things might have continued, but Dante, as he relates, had an epiphany, which began the second phase of his "new life." In the exact middle of *Vita Nuova*, Dante says he realized that all his previous poetry had merely focused on his response to Beatrice when he received her greeting, but then he "felt forced to find a new theme, one nobler than the last" (XVII, 30). This new theme was not his own suffering and rapturous condition in love but the praise of the beauty of his lady, even if he didn't feel ready to sing this praise yet. Beatrice was too great for his words at that time, and so he wrote a poem about how he wished he could write an adequate poem. In this famous poem, which will be explicitly cited in the *Comedy* ("Ladies who have understanding of love"), the young Dante wrote that, wherever his lady goes, "love drives a killing frost into vile hearts / that freezes and destroys what they are thinking; / should one insist on looking at her, / he is changed to something noble or he dies" (XIX, 30). Beatrice, then, is a kind of "burning bush," an epiphany that causes conversion or freezes the hearts of the wicked on sight.

We can see how Dante is trying to unite the two literary cultures of his day: the secular, chivalric court culture, which wrote about romance and this-worldly love; and the theological and monastic culture, which wrote about a joy you had to wait for. But in the *Vita Nuova*, Dante is trying to overcome this division, and for this reason his story, although similar

to other stories of courtly love, is nevertheless adorned with rich theological language. For example, in his dreams, love speaks to him in Latin,
the medieval language of the Bible. Dante calls the times he saw Beatrice
on the street not "meetings" but rather Beatrice's "apparitions" to him.
Those moments in which he is caught up and overwhelmed by the strong
feelings of love are "transfigurations." Even Beatrice's name means "she
who Beatifies." Thus, the poet uses a language steeped in theology to
describe his experience of earthly love.

If Dante's poetic career had ended here, he would be admired, but
read only by a few graduate students at an Ivy League university, like any
one of his largely forgotten contemporaries (Guido Guinizelli or Guido
Cavalcanti). Rather, a disaster took place that changed everything. In the
early 1290s (just a few years before Dante began to write the *Vita Nuova*),
the woman he had written about, who he thought was a physical sign of
the presence of God in Florence, died; that is, in Dante's words, Florence
was deserted and orphaned of this transcendent beauty. Dante uses the
strongest possible language, quoting what the prophet Jeremiah had said
about Jerusalem (Lam. 1:1): "How doth the city sit solitary, that was full of
people! She that was mistress of the nations is now become as a widow!"
(XXVIII, 60). The language is heightened all the more because this text
was chanted in the liturgy of Holy Week to describe man's orphaned state
without the presence of Christ!

In the months that followed Beatrice's death, Dante sought consolation
through writing about his grief and, later, in writing love poems to other
women (XXXI–XXXIX), but nothing served as an adequate substitute.
Dante's disconsolate "waylessness" continued until, one night, he had a
visionary dream in which he saw his soul leave his body, pass through the
heavenly spheres, past the stars, until it came to heaven and saw Beatrice
among the saints of heaven. There Dante was struck by the radiance of
Beatrice, more beautiful now than she had been in life. After relating this
extraordinary dream, Dante concludes his *Vita Nuova* with an exceptional
promise that, after a period of intense study, he would write something
about Beatrice that no man had ever said about a woman before—or in
his words:

> After I wrote this sonnet there came to me a miraculous vision in which I saw
> things that made me resolve to say no more about this blessed one until I would

be capable of writing about her in a nobler way. To achieve this I am striving as hard as I can, and this she truly knows. Accordingly, if it be the pleasure of Him through whom all things live that my life continue for a few more years, I hope to write of her that which has never been written of any other woman. (XLII, 86)

It seems clear that this dream is the distant ancestor of what would become the *Comedy*, although we don't know what form it would have taken if Dante had had the leisure and libraries of Florence, and the next decade, to work on it. Although it's fun to speculate about what this poem would have been like (perhaps just a canzone?), it doesn't matter, because Dante's goals and plans were rather interrupted.

Dante before the Dark Wood (2): Failed Politician

If Dante spent his early twenties writing love poems, he spent his early thirties as a soldier and a politician in Florence. By the year 1300, Dante's political career in his republican city was advancing nicely, and had he spent the rest of his life engaged in Florentine political affairs, he never would have made an attempt to fulfill that promise at the end of the *Vita Nuova*, in which case you would not be reading this book. But something happened to cut Dante's political career short and make him return to the poetry of his youth. In fact, it was the single worst thing that happened to him after the death of Beatrice: he was exiled from Florence (from wife and children, family, friends, and possessions) by his political enemies, for life. In 1302, while Dante was away on a diplomatic mission, the pro-papal faction seized control of the government (assisted by the politically savvy Pope Boniface VIII) and took their chance to get rid of a number of enemies in the opposing faction. Dante received news on the road that if he returned, he would be executed.

In some ways Dante was the victim of large, powerful, international political movements, which had been grinding against one another for centuries, like two huge tectonic plates. I will try to summarize these world events very quickly, to give a sense of how deep the problem went. After the fall of Rome, the Roman Empire was carved up into little bits, which were managed by local chieftains. And yet, over the next several centuries, these chieftains slowly began to consolidate power, adding surrounding regions to their control through marriage and war, until the point that a descendant of one of these tribes had put together a big chunk of land on the borders of modern France and Germany. His name was Charlemagne. On Christmas Day, 800, he was in Rome, and he was crowned the Roman emperor by Pope Leo III. Then he went back up north of the Alps and continued to rule the newly reconstituted "Roman Empire" from his palace at Aachen. This practice of a German emperor, nominally head of the Roman Empire but ruling from north of the Alps, with exceptions and interruptions continued down to Dante's day. These Holy Roman emperors, as they were later called, really thought that they were the rightful successors to Caesar Augustus, Trajan, and Constantine, but they remained physically absent from Italy. As a result, the Italian city-states grew accustomed to ruling themselves, and the church, which had to weather centuries of cultural instability, also grew accustomed to being the center of orderly society.

Thus, it is not too great of a surprise that when the Holy Roman emperors began creeping back down into Italy in the 1200s, there was conflict. Frederick II, grandson of Frederick Barbarossa, moved his court to Palermo, Sicily, and thus had a foothold on the Italian peninsula. His illegitimate son, Manfred (mentioned in *Purg.* 3), tried to continue the legacy of his father. He began moving into central Italy, to bring it under more direct control, but the Italian city-states allied with the pope; together, they in turn invited Charles of Anjou from France to counter Manfred. Manfred was defeated at the battle of Benevento in 1266, the year after Dante was born. Thus, in a way similar to how Southerners for years lived with the memory of the Civil War, even if they had not experienced it, or how my kids know about 9/11, even though they were not alive when it took place, Dante was born into a world that had been shaped by these long-term, international forces that served as a framework even for local politics. Just as politicians of even a small city in the United States will still ally themselves with either Democrats or Republicans, so too did the local political disputes in Dante's day sort themselves out into factions of imperial supporters (Ghibellines, mainly aristocratic families) and papal supporters (Guelphs, mainly new-moneyed, mercantile families).

What does all of this have to do with Dante? Clearly, Dante became the victim of these old disputes, like one caught up in the middle of some immense, indifferent machine, and his exile was the great unjust calamity of his life. What is extraordinary is that Dante himself later described this disaster as one of the secrets of his success as a poet, because this was the event that transformed him from politician to prophet. Being in political exile meant that he had to become "a party unto himself," or, in other words, he was forced to leave the polarizing world of politics. He was forced to ask questions not about short-term solutions but about the long-term conditions of why partisanship existed in the first place.[18]

From Politician to Prophet

Against this background of his exile and early love poetry, we can begin to appreciate the unique intensity of Dante's great poem, as well as its desire to encompass the totality of the world. If you've ever spent a long time away from home in a foreign country, then you know that, even if that place is as delightful as Tuscany, after a while you start aching for home. You miss the effortlessness of life, ease of conversation, shared memories. Similarly, but with much more intensity, Dante ached for home the whole of his adult life. Even years later, when writing the *Comedy*, Dante had this sorrowful sense of the wayfarer in exile (for example, see *Par.* 25.1–9). At the same time, though, when Dante returned to writing after his tumultuous political years (1295–1305), he increasingly wanted to fulfill that old promise at the end of the *Vita Nuova*, the promise to write a love poem that would be greater than anything that had been written before. But now his understanding of love had been forced to get deeper and broader. Now he was writing not for himself and a few Florentine friends but for the world—a world that was so bruised, broken, and divided that it might not even be able to hear a love poem. But what if, just what if, he could write a poem that, by drawing on his own sense of pained exile, could awaken a spiritually sleepy world to what it chooses to forget? What if he could make people feel that they too were in exile, in exile from the Source of Love? What if he could shock, startle, scandalize, and violently shake them wide awake? And then, what if he could give a picture of love that was so beautiful, so stirring, and so deep that they would desire once again to know that love?

Thus, to put it starkly, Dante did not think he was writing literature for entertainment, like a novel, but rather that he was writing a kind of prophetic, visionary treatise—like a Jonah or Jeremiah who came into the city from the desert to rebuke and condemn the inhabitants. His own political exile turned out to be the key to discovering humanity's spiritual exile. This discovery of spiritual exile, in turn, proved to be the key to writing a vision of love ever so much bigger—indeed, cosmic—than even what he had hoped to undertake at the end of *Vita Nuova*. To this end, Dante set about to develop a prophetic sensibility, the power to look down into the root causes of society's problems. And so the wayfarer (the man with the pilgrim's spirit, who lived his life in longing for home, knowing that he would never return), the politician (who labored for a just society), and the poet (who lost sleep at night in the lovesick effort to get just the right music into his language) united to write an intense and ambitious poem that would transform the world: the *Comedy*.

Part 1

INFERNO

1

Zooming In and Zooming Out: How to Read *Inferno*

(*Inferno* 1–2)

From Architecture to Nightmare: Reflecting on *Inferno* 1

Although the *Comedy* is, as I have argued, a poem of impeccable order, the poet is careful to make sure that our first impression is not of the poem's architecture but of its emotional power. In *Inferno* 1 we are immediately seized and carried away by some of the most gripping and dramatic imagery of the *Comedy*. Later, Dante will get philosophical (*Purg.* 25), talk about the moral principles that make up the boundary lines within hell (*Inf.* 11), and argue fine points of doctrine (*Par.* 2). But the reader of *Inferno* 1 doesn't feel he has stepped into a classroom; he has walked into the world of dreams.

The whole of *Inferno* 1 is an extraordinary poetic achievement in its ability to create the feeling of a nightmare. The reader feels the pilgrim's irrational fear, as if both were locked in a terrible dream. And yet the poet insists that his pilgrim is *not* sleeping. In fact, it was sleep that got him into the dark wood in the first place:

> I cannot well recall how I came there.
> I was so full of sleep at the time,
> I abandoned the true way. (*Inf.* 1.10–12)

How he got there, he does not know, but he can remember clearly the disoriented terror that came over him, like a child who has woken up from a bad dream and can't remember where she is. The poem dramatically begins by recalling the memory of that restless and disorienting experience:

> Midway in the journey of our life
> I found myself in the midst of a dark wood—
> the true way was lost.
>
> Ah! How hard to tell!
> How savage, harsh, and difficult was this wood,
> so much so that in my mind my fear returns.
>
> It is so bitter that death is barely worse.
> But to treat the good that I found there
> I will speak about the other things I saw. (*Inf.* 1.1–9)

After the introductory lines, the dreamlike narration continues: the pilgrim wanders through a vague landscape; he sees a hill that is illumined by sunlight on its crown; he stoutly resolves to climb the hill, but then his way is blocked by three strange beasts who refuse to give way; and, finally, having come to the point of absolute desperation, he sees a stranger walk out of the shadows and begs him for help. Again, like a story unfolding within a dream, the narrative seems so rich and full of meaning that it's difficult to pin it down to a single interpretation, and this elusiveness of meaning is in part how Dante gives *Inferno* 1 its psychological power. Meaning keeps slipping through your fingers.

Dante also uses harsh words to reinforce rhetorically this sense of fear and confusion. For example, listen to the Italian words in verses 4–5: *esta selva selvaggia* (a wood "savage, dense, and harsh") has a roughness communicated by sibilant syllables, but then the poet stacks up a number of adjectives (the wood is *selvaggia e aspra e forte*, 1.5). This is a rhetorical device called "polysyndeton," the stacking up of conjunction upon conjunction, as if rhetorically approximating a breathless description: "It was savage and dense and harsh . . ."

Dante also uses two similes to help convey the desperation of the pilgrim's first moments:

> And like one who, with labored breath,
> just escaped from the sea onto the shore,
> turns toward the dangerous waters and stares,
>
> just so did my mind, still in flight,
> turn back to gaze at the pass
> that never yet let out a man alive. (*Inf.* 1.22–27)

Many of my readers will have had a brush with death, perhaps in a car, in which you saw how close you were to having your life ended. Likewise, Dante describes a swimmer immersed in water so rough and stormy that he doubts he will escape drowning. But somehow, against all odds, the swimmer makes it to shore, completely drained of all energy and strength. He stands up wearily and looks back at the raging water. In this way, the poet says, the pilgrim turned to look back at the wood that "never yet let out a man alive" (1.27).

When the weary pilgrim slowly turns and looks up, he sees the "mountain of delight" (*Inf.* 1.77). Along with him, the reader feels a momentary surge of hope. The pilgrim sees the peak, whose "shoulders / [are] now clothed by the rays of the sun" (1.16–17). His fear is momentarily calmed, and he resolves to climb to safety: "I took up the way again through the deserted slope, / in this way: the firm foot was always lower down" (1.29–30). Commentators explain that the mountain is covered in shale-like scree: every time the pilgrim takes a step up, his planted foot slides down. And so, though the pilgrim has good aspirations, the way up is not easy. Then he meets a wild beast: a leopard, which refuses to give way. You can imagine the pilgrim yelling at it, intimidating it, trying to frighten it away, but the beast simply refuses to move. Then a lion appears and roars so loud that "it seemed that the air trembled because of him" (1.48). Finally, a skinny, mongrel wolf, hungry and mangy, forces the pilgrim back down the hill. This is when Dante's second simile comes. The pilgrim is like

> he who wins with joy,
> but then the moment arrives, and he loses all,
> and then is miserable and weeps in all his thoughts. (*Inf.* 1.55–57)

Anyone who has experienced bitter loss knows the feeling. Dante was on the verge of achieving, through sweat and labor, a real good that his heart desired, the radiance and bliss of a mountaintop experience—and just as he thought he was near enough to grasp it, it slips through his fingers and is gone. His heart burns for the memory of what could have been.

And so we have a dreamlike landscape, with action described with the psychological intensity of a nightmare; we hear about the pilgrim's fear, good intentions, obstacles, and failure. We feel Dante's poetry deeply. But in terms of what it means, Dante has left us in the dark: What is this wood? What is the "mountain of delight"? What are the three beasts? Why can't Dante overcome them? And why is it Virgil who comes to save the pilgrim? Why not Saint Patrick? Or Aristotle? Or an angel? Dante's poem is like a journey whose horizons continually recede even as you approach them.

Dante and Wonder: How to Read *Inferno*

Although many of the details are meant to initially elude us, we can still note that, even from the first canto, Dante has begun to coach us in how to read his poem. There are at least two lessons. The first is that the reading experience of the *Comedy* works on multiple levels; we can, for example, get inside the poem and see with the pilgrim's eyes, or we can zoom out, considering the scene from the author's perspective. When these two views overlap, as in *Inferno* 1, we sense a distinct dramatic irony. The very words of the lost pilgrim in *Inferno* 1, unbeknownst to him, are expressed and framed in those groups of threes and tens the author built into his poetry. Thus, from the author's perspective, God is very close and present through the fabric of the poem, even if the character speaking within that poetry is blind to him in whom he lives and moves and has his being (Acts 17:28).

The second lesson is that, although we can consider the poem from that zoomed-out perspective, we have to begin with our immediate reading experience—that is, how Dante's rich and sensuous poetry evokes in us a complicated range of responses (horror, awe, pity, contempt, glee, relief, dread, reverence, and fear). For this reason, it would have been a great mistake to have begun an introduction to the *Comedy* by outlining the moral system that accounts for the architecture of Dante's imaginative world. Beginning with an explanation of the "system" would erect a philosophical or theological scaffolding that could obscure the experience of reading the poetry. Indeed, Dante's most original achievement lies not so much in coming up with that hierarchical order of sins and virtues as in his ability to give flesh to that system of thought, to create a series of individual literary experiences to illustrate those thoughts. This insight should guide how we read the *Comedy*: we have to begin by being moved by the sensible and the sensuous in Dante's poem, and then proceed to a discussion of the tradition of thought that, like a skeleton, informs it.

On a similar note, scholars have had a lot to say about the role of allegory in the *Comedy*,[1] and it is certainly true that you find many allegorical moments: like the three beasts in *Inferno* 1, the tempestuous winds in *Inferno* 5, or the highly symbolic dreams of *Purgatorio* (all discussed below). Allegorical figures are scattered throughout the poem. At the same time, Dante wants the poem to feel real, intense, and personal. The pilgrim is not an allegorical figure but a man who has powerful interior responses. This is what is meant by Dante's "realism."

The *Comedy* (and *Inferno* in particular) is the great poem of interiority, and it is this interiority that popular culture overlooks. In the popular imagination, *Inferno* is a place of fire with a bunch of demons with pincers. The truth is, Dante himself identifies *interiority* as the essential component of his pilgrim's journey: "And I, I alone, / was there, arming myself to endure the war, / both of the way and of the pity of it" (*Inf.* 2.3–5). Dante's language here is powerful: he, he alone (*e io sol uno*), was making interior preparations for the "war" (*la guerra*). Here, he prepares himself not just for the hardships of the journey but also for a war of *pietate* (pity). Obviously, along the way, the pilgrim will encounter difficult landscapes and malicious demons. Along the way, he will suffer extreme fatigue, breathless from arduous climbs. He will experience fear when he thinks he has been abandoned. He will suffer despair when the demons block his forward progress. He will be lied to, chased, screamed at, insulted, threatened, and confused. In the end, he will emerge from hell, his face covered with grime and stained by tears (*Purg.* 1.95–99, 127–29). But even more than these physical trials, the pilgrim will have to undergo feats of the interior life. He will have to undertake a journey of interiority: something he, and he alone, must do. This explains the mystery of why the poet says, "Io sol uno," even though Virgil is standing right next to him, having just rescued him from miserable isolation!

Inferno, then, is the poem of interiority. It aims to crack the crusty shell of the heart and gain access to its secret, guarded places. It aims to use horror, wonder, and terror as ways to create afresh the possibility for transformation; or, to change the image, Dante's poetic violence is meant to melt down the hard heart so that it can be reforged into something new. Not surprisingly, then, the *Comedy* is packed full of "wonder" words: the pilgrim has visions of the *nuovo* and *novitade* (the frightfully new and bizarre); that which is *strano*, *orribile*, and full of *stupore* (strange, horrifying, and that which causes stupor); the pilgrim stops to *ammirare* (wonder) and stare at the *mirabile* and *maraviglia* (the miraculous and the marvelous). Words like this appear hundreds of times throughout the poem.[2] In Dante, these "wonder" words refer to instances of the bizarre, the harrowing, the unexpected, the previously inconceivable: severed heads, disemboweled bodies, backs broken by huge rocks. There are poisonous forests made up of "eerily strange," gnarled trees (*Inf.* 13.15), which resound with whispers; there is the "strange" experience (31.30) of the looming giants, who fill the pilgrim with fear; and there are the mangled bodies of the schismatics, or the headless Bertrand de Born. All of these visions are so startling that Dante can barely believe his eyes (28.113–20). The pilgrim, because his heart is opened up by these phenomena of surprise and fear, desires to stare fixedly (21.22) and to "inebriate" his eyes (29.2). These scenes of wonder are important for Dante, because *admiratio* (wonder) produces the desire to "look closely at" (*mirari*). As Mary Carruthers has pointed out, in the ancient world, rhetoricians worried that their audiences could become "sated," which could lead to *taedium* (boredom); that is, if the speech grew too predictable, then the audience could start to tune out.

In the Middle Ages, these rhetorical concerns were fused with spiritual concerns: monastic writers worried that the soul itself could arrive at a dangerous point of *satietas* (being sated) or *taedium*. And thus medieval spiritual masters recommended a vigorous reading program to keep the heart fresh. For this reason, they illustrated their books lavishly, built cathedrals with all kinds of surprising side chapels and variously colored marbles inlaid in the floor, and constructed cloisters with capitals carved with wildly exuberant images of monsters and fishes. Such diversity, color, and grotesque artistic wonders "surprise us—they did then, they do now. Their very diversity and discord shocks one from the temptation to *taedium*. . . . Experiencing them in itself routs the noonday devil, for the variety they produce relieves tedium and refreshes a wearied mind. They may even strengthen the virtue of inner *hilaritas* [joy], healing a dangerous sadness or melancholy."[3] Thus, getting the blood flowing again through wonder or even horror could heal the spiritual heart. As Gregory of Nyssa put it, "Tears are like blood in the wounds of the soul." Carruthers explains that they are "hot, moist, and restorative of cold, deadened, scarred flesh."[4]

Thus, Dante does not just describe the wonder the pilgrim experiences on his "way"; as a poet, he also tries to produce it, in *you*. Such *admiratio* temporarily destabilizes the mind, shakes its usual certainty, and in this moment of suspended judgment, the one caught up in wonder (the *admirans*) has an opportunity to take in the familiar, as if for the first time. The wondering "reader" becomes what I would call "affectively vulnerable," because in a moment of suspended judgment his or her reason—that impulse to categorize, to put something in its appropriate box, without taking the time to marvel at it—has temporarily let down its guard.

But how does the poet use his craft to make this happen? Among other things, he uses what scholars call "deictic rhetoric"—that is, the language of "pointing." Indeed, Dante pokes and prods us with his words, frequently addressing us and telling us, "Now look here" or "Note that, over there." Many spiritual treatises in Dante's day tried to paint vivid pictures in the mind, so that the reader could "see" and "hear" the suffering of Christ and "feel" the sorrow of Mary. Such writers, too, used deictic rhetoric, saying, "And now imagine that . . ." or "Look, now, how the blood flows from the wounds . . ."[5] In a similar way, we hear Virgil, at one point, yell at Dante: "Drizza la testa, drizza e vedi" ("Raise your head! Raise it and look," *Inf.* 20.31). Just as Virgil directs the pilgrim's attention, so Dante the poet becomes *our* guide. The narrator's voice interrupts the story to poke at us and tell us to look deeper into a matter: "Look deeply for that teaching that lies hidden / underneath the veil of these strange and wonderful lines" (9.62–63). This isn't an isolated case. Rather, the poet constantly tries to involve the reader, addressing him, begging him to look: "Think now, reader," he says early on in *Inferno* (7.94); "Be sharp now, reader," he says later in *Purgatorio* (8.14); "Now, reader, remember," he patiently pleads (*Purg.* 17.1); "Reader, I promise you . . ." (*Inf.* 16.128; see also 25.46; 34.23). Dante never forgets his reader.

In addition to this deictic rhetoric, the poet often tries to get his reader not just to pay attention but also to enter the text and look through the pilgrim's eyes. For example, in *Inferno* 20 Dante says:

> Of strange, shocking, new punishments I now must make verses. . . .
>
> I saw a people, coming through the rounded valley:
> silent and lamenting, moving at the pace
> that stately processions move in our world.
>
> And as I let my gaze descend down upon them,
> it struck me that, wondrously, each one was wrenched around—
> between the chin and the base of the chest,
>
> because the face had been twisted around toward the kidneys,
> and thus they had to make their way backwards. . . .
>
> Maybe, at some point, by some paralysis
> someone has become this wrenched about;
> but I, at least, have never seen it, nor do I think it could it be.
>
> Reader, so that God can let you gather fruit
> from this reading, think, now, think for yourself:
> How I could possibly have kept my cheeks dry?
>
> When from up close I saw our image
> so twisted . . .
>
> Yes, I wept. (*Inf.* 20.1–25)

We see, then, an extraordinary sight: badly deformed human beings, more terribly mangled than any person you might see begging on the streets. This horrifies the pilgrim, causes him to freeze and stare. They appear to him *mirabilmente* (miraculously, 20.11). But then Dante the poet asks us to borrow the eyes of the pilgrim for ourselves: "Pensa per te stesso" ("Think now, think for yourself," 20.20). Look within your own imagination and see if *you* could refrain from weeping. Dante does not just paint a Claude Lorraine–like panel, with characters scattered throughout a sweeping landscape, but aims to get his readers to see and feel as if they had become characters within the painting. Or, to use a metaphor from cinema, Dante asks readers to look through the point-of-view shot, that camera angle you would see if the actor himself were holding the camera. On a couple of occasions, the poet only describes the sounds of hell, so that, like a film when the screen has gone blank, the reader has to focus on the mere acoustic experience of the staccato words. In this way Dante gives the reader a kind of firsthand experience.

One last example. In *Inferno* 17, when Dante climbs on top of Geryon, the beast that will ferry him through the air from upper hell down into its depths, the poet gives us an extraordinary description, as if inviting us, once again, to look through the pilgrim's eyes for ourselves:

> I saw that I was
> in the air—it was all around—and I saw that
> every view of anything but the beast was gone.
>
> It keeps on moving, swimming slowly, slowly,
> wheeling and descending, but I notice nothing
> but a breeze from below on my face. (*Inf.* 17.112–17)

Notice that the poet begins by narrating the event about the pilgrim in the past tense but then switches suddenly into the present, using a series of rich, descriptive words for the flight, but momentarily without reference to the pilgrim, as if trying to create a brief poetic space for us to move into the poem and feel, palpably, the twisting turns of the descent. He wants us to feel ourselves in the saddle, with the wind in our hair. The poet also lyrically evokes the rolling, rocking rhythm of the flight through the internal rhymes and assonance of the line: "Ella sen va notando lenta lenta; / rota e discende" (17.115–16). In moments like this, we are meant momentarily to look through the pilgrim's eyes as if they were our own. In sum, it is this sensitivity to the imaginary power of the poet that we have to bring, first and foremost, to the poem. Once we have done that, we can ask questions about the structure and the symbols. With this in mind, we are now in position to return to our questions about *Inferno* 1.

The Wood and the Beasts

If Dante had wanted us to decode with ease what it was that blocked his way, or what he was looking for, he could have told us! For some reason, the poet has chosen to leave these things veiled. In part he must have done so in order to allow a more universal application to his poetry. Keep in mind how the poem opens: "Midway in the journey of *our* life . . ." (*Inf.* 1.1). That is, although this journey does imaginatively take place precisely in the year 1300, beginning on Good Friday and moving into Eastertide, and although the journey involves a real historical person, Dante Alighieri, the poet still wants us to recognize that the pilgrim's journey is also *ours*. We can all relate to the experience of being morally and spiritually lost, or of suddenly coming to our senses and wondering why we do what we do. You keep a routine, you go to work, you play with the kids, and then all of a sudden you wake up and ask why. Sometimes these periods of questioning and confusion can extend over days or months. We often call them periods of depression, but it's a kind of spiritual "waylessness." For so many writers, from classical antiquity to the Brothers Grimm, being lost in the forest is one of the most frightening experiences imaginable, because you don't know if you are making progress. Have you already walked here? Are you going away from your destination? Are you walking in circles? You don't know, if you have no path to guide you. In a similar way, we can sometimes wake in our lives and wonder why we are pursuing the goods we have committed ourselves to. Whatever happened to the big dreams? Those impossibly heroic goals? How did you get stuck in this dark wood?

One of the greatest Italian scholars of Dante, Guglielmo Gorni, has said that this is how we should understand Dante's *selva oscura* (dark wood): as "the public life in which it is easy to lose the sense of true values, easy to lose that 'hope from on high.'" Gorni continues, "Virgil saves Dante from an existence dominated by the contingent, by accidents, by the vanity of things."[6] In other words, being lost in the dark wood is not necessarily connected to sinful living or neglecting duties. It's a loss of the deep, inspiring memory of why you are doing those things you must do. It's a forgetfulness of the big dream and the clarity of the way to achieve it. If you further remember the imaginary date of the poem, 1300, then note that the story is set five years after Dante had written those impassioned words at the end of the *Vita Nuova*, in which he promised to say something about Beatrice that had never been uttered by a man about a woman. Gorni suggests, then, that this failure to begin the poem promised at the end of the *Vita Nuova* is associated with the dark wood: Dante had lost that vision, the animation, the inspiration to do it. He had lost the vision of love, the sense of the palpable nearness of God.

The deserted landscape of the poem also helps us visualize this area as a spiritual wasteland, devoid of the presence of God. In fact, Dante builds in a powerful reference to the prophet Jeremiah. In Jeremiah 5:3, 6, the prophet laments that, try as you might, you cannot find a righteous man in the world:

> O LORD, are not thine eyes upon the truth? thou hast stricken them, but they have not grieved; thou hast consumed them, but they have refused to receive correction. . . .
>
> Wherefore a lion out of the forest shall slay them, and a wolf of the evenings shall spoil them, a leopard shall watch over their cities: every one that goeth out thence shall be torn in pieces: because their transgressions are many, and their backslidings are increased.

Dante's own beasts seem to come directly from Jeremiah, with an important difference. In Jeremiah they are agents of destruction: violent and bloodthirsty animals, which creep back into the semideserted city when it begins to fall into ruins. In Dante, though, they also have an allegorical element, as if the greatest punishment of the wicked is not necessarily to receive external chastisement but rather to be left to the desires of their own hearts. Some scholars speculate that the three beasts might represent envy (in the leopard), pride (in the lion), and cupidity (in the wolf). In Virgil's mysterious prophecy, in which he cryptically refers to the "hound" who will bring justice and righteousness to the world (*Inf.* 1.97–102), we do get a clearer sense of what the wolf embodies—that is, the avaricious, lustful, and gluttonous appetite that, even though it gets what it wants, cannot but desire more. In light of this, it is probably best to understand the wolf as corresponding to the sins punished in circles 2 (the lustful), 3 (the gluttonous), 4 (the avaricious), and 5 (the wrathful) of hell; the lion, with its tremendous, violent roar, to circle 7 (that is, the realm of the violent); and the leopard to circles 8 and 9 (the fraudulent and traitorous). But Dante's art is such, as I have suggested, that one interpretation does not have to exclude the other: both of these sinful triads (cupidity, pride, and envy, as well as cupidity, violence, and fraud) could be present in the mysterious beasts simultaneously.

I like how canto 1 concludes on an almost humorous note. After Virgil has just described the alternative path that the pilgrim will have to take, given the fact that the road up the mountain that gives delight is blocked by the beasts, Dante responds: "Poet, I beg you / by that God you did not know, / so that I may escape this evil—or something even worse—, / please, lead me to that place you just described!" (*Inf.* 1.130–33). As if to say, sure, sure, anywhere but here! But this first response, based on fear, will not be enough. The pilgrim will have to commit himself to a more difficult journey, not merely flee the threat of harm, as we shall see now.

The Hero and the Coward in the Dark Wood (*Inferno* 2)

The action of *Inferno* 2 can be divided into four narrative blocks: (1) the pilgrim rethinks his decision to go on the arduous journey, doubting his worthiness to undertake this adventure; (2) Virgil accuses him of *viltade* (cowardice); (3) Virgil, to encourage his charge, tells him the backstory of all those who helped to set up this journey; and (4) Dante is once again infused with the desire to undertake the journey.

It is in this canto, too, that we get hints of why Virgil has been selected to lead Dante through hell. First and foremost, Virgil was the Roman poet of the *Aeneid*—that is, he who described the painful journey of the mythological Aeneas, the hero forced to flee from his native Troy when it was burned to the ground by the Greeks. For ancient man, as historians of religion have pointed out, the destruction of a city was an even greater disaster than it would be for us. Your history, family, and economic well-being would all, of course, be lost, but in the ancient world, at the center of all cities were the sacred shrines where divinities had initiated communication with mortals. These were places where the gods chose to make themselves manifest, where (in the words of Mircea Eliade) the "sacred irrupt[ed] into profane space." All the rest of archaic man's life and society was oriented around these points of revelation.[7] Thus, when Aeneas is forced to flee Troy, he wanders in search of not only a suitable site for a new city but also a place where the presence of the divine, beyond his control, wills once again to make itself manifest. Aeneas is indeed, then, a man of devotion (to family, gods, and followers), but his special strength is his ability to resist any kind of mediocre settlement in which he would capitulate and found a city on a site that could provide mere subsistence. What he seeks is to found a city centered on divine revelation again.

This is at least one aspect of Virgil's importance to Dante. Dante's own pilgrimage has to be understood as a new *Aeneid*, in which he too has to journey to the land appointed him, and he has to resist the temptation of growing content with anything less. Appropriately, canto 2 begins by establishing a high, Virgilian tone from the first verses. In the *Aeneid*, Virgil often describes sleep and rest in a highly poetic way. In a world of war and struggle, the poet says, sleep comes like refreshment from the gods:

> It was night, and through all the land, deep sleep gripped weary
> creatures, bird and beast, when Aeneas, the leader, lay down
> on the river-bank, under the cold arch of the heavens, his heart
> troubled by war's sadness, and at last allowed his body to rest. (*Aen.*
>   8.26–29)[8]

Compare that with the opening of *Inferno* 2:

> Now the day slips away, and the dark air
> frees the souls of the earth
> from their fatiguing tasks. (*Inf.* 2.1–3)

Thus, *Inferno* 2 begins with a Virgilian flavor, which, as we have seen, is appropriate, for Dante is about to begin a kind of double Virgilian journey: the journey of the pilgrim, in which he undertakes a heroic quest analogous to that of the great mythological hero; but also a poetic journey, in which the author of the *Comedy* rewrites the ancient epic, the *Aeneid*, seeking language that can sufficiently arouse and awaken the reader to be moved by what the pilgrim endured. We all know how little good words sometimes do, words about what we ought to do but then don't really put into practice. Dante here announces his intention to write beauties that demand action, that cut like swords and burn like fire. And thus, like a poet from antiquity, he empties himself out and calls for the divine assistance of the Muses:

> O Muses! O lofty genius! May you help me now!
> O you mind! You have recorded what I saw.
> What nobility you have will now appear! (*Inf.* 2.7–9)

The main drama of the canto begins immediately after the first lines of *Inferno* 2. The pilgrim, who in the previous canto was overjoyed to find anyone in the dark wood who was willing to help him, now has second thoughts. He starts to think about this journey, and, in particular, he starts to ask himself who, if any, has accomplished such an enormous task: Who has walked through the land of the dead, still in flesh? Well, according to sacred and classical tradition, both Saint Paul and Aeneas had experiences of the afterlife before their deaths (and it is for this reason that I call canto 2 "The Canto of Saint Paul and Aeneas"). This is what underlies the pilgrim's expression of his doubt:

> "You declare that the father of Silvius,
> still corruptible, nevertheless went
> to the immortal realm, and did it in the flesh!
> . . . .
>
> "And then the Chosen Vessel went there,
> to bring consolation back to the faith. . . .
>
> "But I? Traveling there? Who would grant that?
> I am no Aeneas, nor am I Paul.
> For that, neither I nor any other thinks me worthy." (*Inf.* 2.13–15,
>   28–33)

Look, Virgil, I'm just some guy in modern America with a family, a mortgage, and a job. I respect the old heroes, the old saints, but that's not me. I don't have that kind of superhuman power and strength. Perhaps you should just leave me here in the woods.

It's an extraordinary moment, isn't it? The pilgrim, now that he has been removed from the imminent danger posed by the beasts, announces his contentment with remaining where he is, because of his fear of taking on a great journey. It is at this point that Dante's guide issues some stinging words:

> "If I have well understood your words,"
> replied the shade of that magnanimous spirit,
> "you are plagued by a small-souled cowardice,
>
> "which so encumbers a man
> that it has often turned him back from enterprises of honor,
> just as a false vision among shadows frightens a beast." (*Inf.* 2.42–47)

You are like a beast that shies from its own shadow. Ouch. Virgil is not very gentle here. The Roman poet, significantly called "magnanimous" ("greatsouled," 2.44), accuses Dante of *viltade*—that is, cowardice, lack of nobility, baseness. In courtly culture, this is the greatest insult one knight could give another. *Viltade* is the opposite of that noble self-forgetfulness that the warrior or the lover possessed—that is, the opposite of that noble self-abandon that inspires the one who sees what must be done and charges at the enemy or the monster to do it. In contrast, the cowardly soul waits to see which way the battle turns before he either joins or runs away. He doesn't have that kind of inner strength that nobly casts off fear of harm to self and engages.

But Virgil, like a physician, does not just use his scalpel to expose corruption; he also tries to treat the underlying condition. And so, rather than just accuse the pilgrim of this baseness, or *viltade*, he tells him the story of his commission from Beatrice. Beatrice herself, of course, had been commissioned by Saint Lucy, and before that, in verses 94–96, we find that a "noble lady"—notice here, too, the language of the medieval court—saw Dante's need and set the whole process in action. If you have read the *Aeneid*, you will remember that, at one of the most dramatic moments of the poem, Aeneas goes down to the underworld to find his father, Anchises, who will give him words of counsel to guide him on the final stages of his journey. And so Aeneas seeks out his father among the shadowy souls of the dead, and when he finally sees Anchises, his father shows him a vision of all the heroes who will be Aeneas's offspring. It's a kind of Abrahamic moment, in which Anchises promises Aeneas not just that his descendants will be as numerous as the stars, but also that they will be famous, heroic, and virtuous. Thus, Virgil managed to get Aeneas to move toward Rome by a vision of what was to come; here in the Christian poet, Virgil inspires the pilgrim Dante by a vision of what has already taken place. He says to Dante that long before you even arrived at this juncture, heaven had so ordained things that you would have strength and assistance, provided that you did not reject them through cowardice. Virgil then asks Dante a series of short, impassioned questions:

> "I saved you from the savage beast that stood before you,
> the one that had stolen from you the easy path to the mountain of
>   delight.

> "Well then: What? Why, why do you stay?
> How can you harbor such base cowardice in your heart?
> Where is your boldness and strength?

> "Given that three such blessed ladies
> from the court of heaven take care for you,
> not to mention my words that move you toward the good?" (*Inf.*
>   2.119–26)

We are beginning to see why Virgil was selected. Beatrice told him, "Or movi" (*Inf.* 2.67)—that is, "Go and *move*" Dante with your words. Virgil is the poet who writes about heroism, but he writes with words that prick, stir, and move. He is the poet of magnanimity and eloquence, who uses the *parola ornata* ("the well-adorned word," 2.67). The result is that the pilgrim's heart is filled, once again, with "desire" (2.136). As the simile at the end of the canto points out, the pilgrim's inner virtue and strength, which had been sleeping, is woken up by the words of Virgil. An epic poet is needed to call out an epic hero.

2

The Fear of Hell
and the Fear of God

(*Inferno* 3–9)

Entering Hell

For good or ill, by the end of *Inferno* 2, the journey has been launched. And although the pilgrim will experience doubt on other occasions, he has irreversibly committed himself to Virgil's guidance. The poet describes the pilgrim as following behind Virgil, literally placing his feet in the footsteps left behind by the Roman poet (*Inf.* 1.136; 23.147–48). In this way the two wayfarers walk up to the main portal of hell.

In the Middle Ages, it was common to place an inscription on a gate to a city, to inform travelers who built the arch and for what reason. It was even more common to place an inscription above the grand doors—or portal—of medieval cathedrals, written as if the gate were speaking to the traveler. The inscription would issue some sort of admonition about how to best enter through that portal. One such inscription is above the portal of the Church of St. Lazarus, in Autun, France:

IN THIS WAY, WHOEVER DOES NOT LEAD A DISOBEDIENT LIFE WILL RISE AGAIN, AND ENDLESS DAYLIGHT WILL SHINE FOR HIM. GISLEBERTUS MADE

19

Figure 3. The main portal of the Cathedral of St. Lazarus of Autun, France.

ME. MAY THIS TERROR TERRIFY THOSE WHOM EARTHLY ERROR BINDS,
FOR IN TRUTH THE HORROR OF THESE SIGHTS ANNOUNCES WHAT AWAITS
THEM.[1]

The inscription is certainly as frightening as the image, which shows demons weighing souls in scales, avariciously hoping to add to hell. And yet
the inscription contains a note of hope. It is a call not to despair but to
repentance. The frightening images of demons torturing human beings
promotes an interior sense of awe and reverence.

How different is Dante's portal! The pilgrim pauses to read:

> THROUGH ME ONE COMES INTO THE CITY OF SADNESS,
> THROUGH ME ONE COMES INTO ETERNAL SORROW,
> THROUGH ME ONE COMES AMONG THE LOST PEOPLE.
>
> JUSTICE MOVED MY LOFTY MAKER.
> DIVINE POWER MADE ME,
> HIGHEST WISDOM AND THE FIRST LOVE.
>
> BEFORE ME THERE WERE NO CREATED THINGS
> EXCEPT THE ETERNAL. I AM ONE THAT ETERNALLY ENDURES.
> ABANDON ALL HOPE YE WHO ENTER HERE. (*Inf.* 3.1–9)

Unlike the portal of a church, this portal to the cathedral of hell promises no redemption; rather, it promises the opposite: "Abandon all hope." Thus, hell already is a kind of parody of the church: it is a gate that leads nowhere. It does not open up onto a new condition or a new horizon or offer new hope.

It also comes as a bit of a surprise to hear that the gate—and thus all of hell—was made by Power, Wisdom, and Love. In other words, the Trinity, the God who is love, created this place for the eternal punishment of sinners. The God who asks us to hope in him created a place that declares, "Abandon all hope." This seems to be the difficulty that underlies the pilgrim's statement "Master, for me their sense is hard" (*Inf*. 3.12). Virgil, like an exasperated parent who thinks he needs to explain himself again, starts to wind up: "Now it is fitting that all cowardice [*viltà*] must die" (3.15). In other words, Virgil is giving the same motivational speech he just gave the pilgrim in *Inferno* 2, but we also might have an interesting example of Virgil's first small misunderstanding. The reality is that the words are hard for the pilgrim, not because he is suffering from cowardice, but because it is difficult for him, as a Christian, to imagine how this dreary place of darkness was the work of a loving God. The poet does not answer the question now. He leaves it to rub us, like a rock in the shoe.[2]

Blood, Tears, and Worms

In the second part of *Inferno* 3, Dante describes the pilgrim's first reaction to hell proper. Virgil and Dante now take the plunge into infernal darkness, into the midst of "the secret things" of hell (*Inf*. 3.21). With his sight removed, this is what the pilgrim hears:

> Now sighs, laments, and shrill cries
> resounded throughout that air without stars.
> Yes, I too began to weep as soon as I had entered.
>
> Varied tongues, rough ways of speech,
> words of sorrow, shouts of rage, voices,
> loud and faint, the sound of hands slapping each other—
>
> jumbled together to make a whirlwind of sound
> that spins in a gyre forever in that dark air, devoid of time,
> just like the sand spins when gusty wind blows. (*Inf*. 3.22–30)

The pilgrim breaks down and begins to weep, overwhelmed with fear, confusion, and pity (3.24). He can't see, and what he hears is a crazy jumble of screaming, shrieking, crying, and cursing, all grunted and shouted in a host of languages, a kind of infernal Babel. Dante tries to get all of this chaos, isolation, pain, and regret into the very acoustics of his language. He carefully chooses harsh, grating words, the kind of verbal equivalent of fingernails scratching on a chalkboard:

> Diverse lingue, orribili favelle,
> parole di dolore, accenti d'ira,
> voci alte e fioche . . . (*Inf.* 3.25–27)

The poet gives us these visceral words, momentarily, without reference to the pilgrim's reaction, as if briefly allowing us the opportunity to enter into a first-person experience of the confusion of hell.

Dante soon finds out that the confusing whirlwind of noise is coming from the "pusillanimous," the small-souled human beings, sometimes called "the indifferent," who never committed themselves to a course of action, or as Virgil says:

> "A miserable fate.
> It is endured by those broken souls
> who lived without disgrace but without praise. . . .
>
> "They have no hope of death,
> and their blind life is so base
> that they are envious of every other lot." (*Inf.* 3.34–36, 46–48)

Here they bitterly lament their lives, screaming with rage at themselves and everyone else, because they frittered away their precious gift of life to no end. What a contrast to the Florentine poet who spent his whole life as the servant of love, who, as he will later tell us, stayed up late at night and became thin because he was pouring his heart into the writing of the *Comedy* (see *Par.* 25.3 and chap. 13 below)!

Both C. S. Lewis and Dorothy Sayers were greatly influenced by this passage. C. S. Lewis once wrote that the opposite of love is not hate but indifference. Similarly, Dorothy Sayers, who translated the *Comedy* into English in the middle of the twentieth century, wrote a remarkable essay,

"The Other Six Deadly Sins" (in *Creed or Chaos?*), in which I think she had this passage of Dante in mind:

> The sixth Deadly Sin is named by the Church Acedia or Sloth. In the world it calls itself Tolerance; but in hell it is called Despair. It is the accomplice of the other sins and their worst punishment. It is the sin which believes in nothing, cares for nothing, seeks to know nothing, interferes with nothing, enjoys nothing, loves nothing, hates nothing, finds purpose in nothing, lives for nothing, and only remains alive because there is nothing it would die for.[3]

Ouch. Stinging words worthy to be put into the mouth of Virgil!

But to return to Dante. The punishment of such sinners is repulsive. Because they followed nothing on earth, now, in hell, they chase a swiftly moving banner, which races about without ever stopping. It is an empty sign, a meaningless cause, a flag with nothing printed on it (*Inf.* 3.52). At the same time, the pusillanimous are stung by hornets and wasps, which compel them, against their nature, to keep moving, forcing them into an activity they would not choose on their own, because they had no inner drive and fire to energize them in their lives. Perhaps most tragically, the blood that issues from those welts and the tears that flow from their cheeks mingle and fall to the ground, where the mixture is eaten by nasty worms. In other words, these sinners, who on earth shed no tears and spilled no blood for noble things, here in hell, in a kind of parody of the agony of Christ in the garden, pour forth their vital bodily fluids to be consumed— pointlessly and uselessly—by revolting, slithering insects. This is the first example of that well-known principle of composition Dante followed for creating the vivid landscape of hell: *contrapasso* (a kind of "counterbalance"). To state it simply, the punishment balances the crime; or, perhaps more accurately, the *contrapasso* turns the sin inside out to make the full horror of the sin evident for the first time.

On Castles and Heroes (*Inferno 4*)

In *Inferno* 4 the pilgrim, after waking up confused and disoriented, carefully creeps toward the edge of the highest ring, leans over, and looks down into a deep abyss (*Inf.* 4.7–12). In heaven Dante will be surrounded by song, but in hell Dante is completely enveloped by impenetrable darkness and incomprehensible, chaotic sound. The poet who was so sensitive to the musicality of language, who worried about the sound of his words down to the very syllable (as he describes in an early treatise, *On Vernacular Eloquence*), here uses his poetry to create a murmuring, indistinct roar of darkness. In the following canti, Dante will encounter a series of frightful scenes, one after the other, each of which makes its own dismal addition to this infernal symphony, like a group of instruments in an orchestra each playing its own dreadful song in a different key. But before he moves on, he enjoys one last moment of quiet here in *Inferno* 4.

The pilgrim is led to a little spot tucked away from the noise. Here he sees the souls of limbo. For the medieval tradition, limbo was the part of hell in which unbaptized babies were lodged, but Dante takes this occasion to exercise some real daring. He adds to this realm another group of souls: the souls of the virtuous pagans, who, as Virgil explains to the pilgrim, are sorrowful, even though they experience no special torment (*Inf.* 4.28). These noble pagans are here because they, like the infants, were not baptized, given that they were born either before the Christian era or outside of Christian lands, and thus, as Virgil says, "did not worship God correctly" (4.38).

As Dante draws nearer to the center of the castle, wherein these noble souls dwell, a group of poets come forth to celebrate Virgil's return. This small company is made up of the best poets of all time, whom Dante calls the *bella scola* (the "beautiful school" of poets). It is made up of Virgil, Homer, the Roman poet Lucan (who was widely read in the Middle Ages, though not now), the Roman poet Horace, and Ovid, the poet who wrote about so many of the mythological transformations of the gods (*Metamorphoses*). For the medieval mind, these ancient writers were as authoritative as you could get outside the Christian world. These were the poets who understood the secrets of the world, who had profound insights into how to live well, and whose words could inspire imitation. They were also writers unavailable to many medievals because they wrote in the learned language of Latin.[4] It is at this point that Dante gives himself an extraordinary compliment and, in doing so, makes an important comment on his goals and ambitions as a vernacular writer. This exclusive group of the best poets of all time warmly welcomes Dante and elects him to become a member of the *bella scola*: "And even greater honor still they showed: / they made me one in their company. / I was the sixth amidst such wisdom" (*Inf.* 4.100–102). My students always comment on this line, suggesting that Dante is arrogant. Then Dante follows up that terzina with another:

> Thus we went toward the light,
> speaking of things of which silence is fitting,
> just as in that place speech was due. (*Inf*. 4.103–5)

This is one of many perplexing instances in which Dante tells us he partook of secret conversations with the ancients, most of which seemingly pertain to the craft of poetry. Throughout the *Comedy*, Dante likes to portray himself as an apprentice to the old masters, as when, in *Purgatorio*, the pilgrim will direct his steps to follow the two poets whose talk makes his way easy (*Purg*. 23.7–9). And thus, although it certainly is the case that Dante Alighieri did not lack self-confidence, beneath that bravado we find a deep reverence for antiquity. Dante really thought that sitting quietly with the old masters could result in wisdom. You could pose questions to them, and then, if you read and studied deeply enough, come to possess their wisdom at least in part, perhaps even becoming worthy of the respect of your heroes. A few decades later, Italian humanists would call this walking "in the footsteps of the ancients,"[5] but this knowledge is not easy to win. It's hard and tedious and slow in coming. Only if you long for it with a burning desire, with unquenchable thirst, only if you fast for it (see *Purg*. 29.37–42), will you come to it. I think this is why Dante tells us that he won't tell us, because he is trying to give us that kind of thirst and hunger to look into things deeply—the thirst he himself had.

In the third narrative block of *Inferno* 4, after he is greeted by the poets of the *bella scola*, something amazing happens—at least for a medieval intellectual: Dante is escorted across a moat, and then passes through the seven gates of the seven walls of a castle, to arrive at the smooth lawn that forms the courtyard of the castle. And here all the greats of antiquity are assembled. Here is Aristotle, "the master of those who know" (*Inf*. 4.131), honored by Plato and Socrates; here are the pre-Socratic philosophers (Thales, Heraclitus, and Empedocles). There are Roman thinkers (Cicero and Seneca), as well as the Islamic commentators on Aristotle (Avicenna and Averroës). The great scientists are there, and the great heroes and heroines out of history and old stories: Aeneas, Hector, Julius Caesar, Brutus (the assassin of the tyrant Tarquin who initiated the

Roman Republic and refused to be crowned king), Lucretia (who, violated by Tarquin, ended her own life to guard her honor), as well as Camilla, Latinus, and Lavinia (characters from the *Aeneid*). In other words, the pilgrim has stepped into a library of great books, or rather he's stepped into those books and now dwells amidst the characters he had spent so long reading about. Here Dante is surrounded by all who thought deeply and originally, who stood courageously in battle, who founded cities, or who so steadfastly committed themselves to some virtue that they became its model and exemplar.

Dante truly believed that these noble souls lived without succumbing to their passions: they were not wrathful, lustful, dishonest, or intemperate. They exercised incredible natural powers of self-control and virtue, and they directed their lives to pursuing justice. For this reason, they do not suffer any direct punishment; their only punishment is the "pain of loss" of the vision of God. They are depicted as having "countenances neither sad nor joyful" (*Inf.* 4.84), "people" with "grave, slow-moving eyes / and visages of great authority" who "seldom spoke" (4.112–14, trans. Hollander)—serious, good people who don't waste words and whose inner strength is evident in their commanding visages. And yet, though sober and controlled, they are not happy, let alone joyful, as the saints in paradise will be. In fact, the pilgrim's first impression of this realm is that the air is continuously stirred by sighs (4.26). Furthermore, Virgil, as he reenters this realm, loses all the color in his face because he returns to a land without hope: "We are lost, and afflicted but in this, / that without hope we live in longing" (4.41–42, trans. Hollander). It is because these souls spent their whole lives pursuing goodness and truth that their sorrow is so intense. They are weighed down by the knowledge that they will never be able to know or taste that ultimate Goodness. It is a dream that will never be fulfilled.

The ancient community of nonbelievers stands in sharp contrast with that other ancient community of biblical patriarchs, who, we learn, once upon a time were also residents in limbo. Within *Inferno* 4, Dante hesitantly asks Virgil if any soul has ever made it out of this place. Virgil's response is fascinating: "I was new to this place when I saw / a mighty one come here, crowned in victory. / He dragged out from among us the shade of our first parent, / and the shade of Abel, his son, and that of Noah," and so on (*Inf.* 4.52–56). This is the event that

Figure 4. A depiction of the harrowing of hell from the *Vaux Passional* (fifteenth–sixteenth century; artist unknown).

you find portrayed on Byzantine icons or in medieval illuminations, in which Christ comes into hell and kicks down the doors, which the devils feebly hold against him. Christ, bursting into hell, grabs the wrists of Adam and Eve and the other patriarchs and energetically pulls them out of limbo. This is the so-called harrowing of hell, which, according to

Christian tradition, took place on Holy Saturday, before Christ's own resurrection—the very event that the liturgy is celebrating while Dante walks through this realm.

Thus, the sad, slow, grave souls of the pagans stand in powerful contrast to those biblical souls who also waited, but waited on God with expectancy of deliverance. Virgil's words are telling: for him, that hero who liberated the souls of the patriarchs was just some *possente*, some "mighty one," some generic hero, a Hercules, who from time to time raided hell. But for those who had the eyes to see, who looked to the mountains whence their help came, this was the dawn they had prayed and fasted for; this was the deliverance that they knew they could not provide for themselves.

On the Wings of Doves (*Inferno* 5)

We now come to one of the most celebrated passages in the *Comedy*: Dante's conversation with Francesca da Rimini in *Inferno* 5.[6] From this circle on, all the rest of hell's inmates suffer not only the pain of the loss of God (like the noble souls in limbo) but also some additional physical torment. When the pilgrim comes into the second circle, he first hears the loud moaning of wind (*Inf.* 5.29–33) and then sees that here souls are tossed about in these gusts of wind forever. They have lost, as it were, their freedom to move where they wish. In this kind of infernal hurricane, they see a place to which they wish to move and begin moving in that direction, only to be swept off course to some other place. In fact, three times in this canto, Dante uses lovely similes in which he compares these sinners to birds tossed about by strong gusts of wind. My favorite of these similes is the first one, in part because Dante manages to get into his very language the power of the windswept landscape:

> And just as wings lift up starlings
> in cold weather, in a flock thick and wide,
> so did that windy breath carry forth the evil souls.
>
> Hither and thither, now up, now down, it drives them.
> No hope comforts them that they will ever find
> rest or lesser punishment. (*Inf.* 5.40–45)

The Italian is evocative: "di qua, di là, di giù, di sù li mena" (5.43). The very sound of the language catches the haphazard movement of the souls, tossed about from here to there.

These souls are, of course, the lustful, and all of the famous lovers of antiquity and the Middle Ages are here: Cleopatra, Helen of Troy, Paris, Tristan, and Dido (from the *Aeneid*); they are the equivalent of, for us, Romeo and Juliet, Madame Bovary, Anna Karenina, and, I suppose, some of our celebrities who can't seem to make their marriages work. Thus, the *contrapasso* is appropriate: the sinners now continue to experience something analogous to what they chose in life. They surrendered control of themselves to their passions, and now, as if to unveil and make clear to them what they once embraced, a strong wind drives them about and steals their freedom. They are like very small birds caught in a powerful windstorm.

It is at this time that Dante has a conversation with an extraordinary character, whom an influential Italian critic from the nineteenth century (Francesco de Sanctis) called "the first modern literary character." Dante invites this soul and her companion to come to him, and the wind, seemingly according to providential design, momentarily calms to allow for a brief conversation. And then, like doves,

> who, called on by desire,
> with wings stretched out and held firm,
> come to the sweet nest, carried on through the air by their choosing,
>
> so too did these [Paolo and Francesca] leave the flock where Dido is,
> coming to us through the malignant air,
> so strong was my cry of affection. (*Inf.* 5.82–87)

As you can already see, the remainder of the canto will be expressed in an extremely high and delicate poetry. Woven in and out of these lines, in fact, are quotations from and paraphrases of the authors whom the young Dante had read and imitated during the days of his own love poetry. Dante the love poet is back! And then the woman, yet unnamed, comes forward to speak to the pilgrim:

> "Love, who so quickly takes hold in the gentle heart,
> took hold of this man through the beautiful appearance
> that has been stolen from me; the way it happened afflicts me still.

> "Love, who pardons no beloved from loving in return,
> took hold of me so forcefully, through this one's graceful charm,
> that, as you see, it has not left me yet.
>
> "Love brought us to a single death." (*Inf.* 5.100–106)

Dante's response is immediate:

> "Oh, what loss!
> How many thoughts of sweetness—and what desire!—
> have brought them to this dolorous pass!"
>
> Then I turned to them, and I spoke to them,
> and I began: "Francesca, what you suffered
> brings *me* to weep, with heartache and pity." (*Inf.* 5.112–17)

It's a subtle detail, but note that Dante did not need to be told the speaker's name! Because he was a great master of the courtly love tradition, even just a couple of details sufficed for him to know exactly to whom he was speaking. This is Dante's stuff, the stuff he read and thought about all the time as a young man. And note too the delicate rhetoric of Francesca's speech: she uses a rhetorical device called "anaphora," employing the key word "love" to introduce the three terzine of her speech: *amor* (100), *amor* (103), *amor* (106). Clearly, love was the ruling force of her life, the only reality to which she paid attention, just as *amor* is the fixed point that her rhetoric orbits now. Francesca then makes an argument suspiciously similar to that of one of Dante's poetic heroes (Guido Guinizelli): if you truly have a noble heart, and someone falls in love with you, you cannot help but to return his or her love. Love seized me and wouldn't let me go.

Dante wants to hear the sad end to such a seemingly noble beginning. How could such a great, pure-hearted lover end up here, in hell? Francesca concludes her story:

> "We were reading, one day, for delight,
> of how love once pressed Lancelot;
> we were alone, suspecting nothing.
>
> "On many occasions our eyes were drawn together,
> thanks to the reading! And then it took the color from our faces;
> and yet it was one point in particular that overcame us.

> "When we read about how the long-desired smile
> was kissed by that famous lover,
> this one next to me—and he shall never be divided from me again—
>
> "trembling all over, he kissed my mouth. . . .
> That day we read no further." (*Inf.* 5.127–36, 138)

This is the racy conclusion to her tale of adultery; we can imagine it easily being turned into a trailer for a steamy film. Dante, too, is absolutely smitten. He swoons on account of his compassion:

> Ah, the pity!
> I passed out as if I had died.
> And I fell as a body falls in death. (*Inf.* 5.140–42)

In Italian, the final line is marked by thudding alliteration: "E caddi come corpo morto cade" (5.142).

When you know the background, Francesca's sad story only becomes more moving. Her father, the ruler of Ravenna, was at war against the Malatesta family in Rimini, both cities on the Adriatic coast of northeastern Italy. Now it was common in the Middle Ages to marry off your teenage daughter, the equivalent of a high school sophomore, particularly when you could use that marriage to advance political relations. And so Francesca was married to Gianciotto Malatesta, who was, we may presume, older than she was. The situation is further complicated by the fact that Gianciotto was lame and deformed. Thus, Francesca found herself married to an older man whom she did not choose, whom she did not love, and to whom she was not attracted. And then along came the handsome younger brother, closer to her age and more to her liking—Paolo Malatesta. Francesca concludes her tale by famously describing her afternoon reading with Paolo. They were reading an old French courtly romance, which described, romantically, the adultery of Lancelot and Arthur's wife, Guinevere. Right at the moment Lancelot and Guinevere kiss, Paolo and Francesca closed their book to imitate. One thing led to another. Eventually, they were caught together by Francesca's husband, who murdered them both.

It is indeed a fascinating scene, and it raises a number of questions. Why would Dante portray the sin of Francesca so sympathetically? Is this the *Tragedy of Francesca*? Is her sad tale a story of how unavoidable circumstances in her life left her only one option, to follow her heart to find happiness? Again, Dante refuses to give us an easy answer. He wants us, here too, to be bothered by this passage, to be moved by the story. It's another rock in the shoe.

We will have a chance to return to this scene many times throughout this book, but let me make two quick observations. First, Dante subtly points out that Paolo and Francesca did not finish the tale: "That day we read [the book] no further" (*Inf.* 5.138). They did not read to the end of the story, which is interesting, because if they had, they would have read about the humiliation that Lancelot and Guinevere brought on themselves through their adultery. They would have read about the friendships their liaison shattered. Second, this is another instance in which sinners in Dante's hell get exactly what they think they want. There is no more pesky God or irritating church or outdated guilty conscience to try to deprive you of what you want. And so here Francesca and Paolo, at last, get one another with nothing intervening. They can remain together forever, clinging to that one thing that they chose, and continue to choose, to the exclusion of all else. When you think about it this way, the charm and romance of Francesca's story begin to unravel. And although we might, at a certain level, admire the passion of Francesca's love, in the end we have to admit that it is the only thing she does love. She has a rather idolatrous love. She loves one thing to the exclusion of everything else in the universe. It seems that Dante, in a fascinating way, has set the groundwork for a critique of Francesca's love: it's not that she loved too much and had too great a passion; she loved too little.

Mud, Rocks, and Swamps (*Inferno* 6–9)

In *Inferno* 6, Dante passes through the realm of the gluttonous (which for Dante would have included not just overeating but any kind of abusive use of food or drink, such as drunkenness and epicurean food snobbery). There the pilgrim meets a Florentine, Ciacco, who delivers the first powerful denunciation of Florence found in the poem. His speech is also the first to hint at Dante's unhappy future, which will begin to unfold after the fictional date of the poem (1300). In this third circle, the pilgrim says that the punishment, even if it is not the most painful, is certainly the most disgusting. I know that all my readers have been caught before in one of those blinding rainstorms, from which, as soon as you could, you sought shelter. Well, here the souls in hell are continually buffeted by a kind of mixture of various forms of precipitation: cold rain, thick hail, and snow. The precipitation never lets up, so that the souls, lying on their sides, become tender and bruised. But it gets worse. The ground is mushy, and the rain mixture itself is dirty, tainted water, perhaps closer to vomit than to clean precipitation. The ground absorbs the mixture and reeks, like mud in the spring. This, of course, is Dante's *contrapasso* for those who, in life, buffeted their bodies by eating and drinking too much. They drank and led the party life without moderation, seeking to achieve happiness by filling up their bodies with consumable materials.

Dante and his guide pass on into another circle, the fourth, where they encounter the avaricious and the prodigal, who are continually smashing into one another. As Virgil says, "Evil spending and evil grasping have taken / the lovely world from them and put them to this scuffle" (*Inf.* 7.58–59). Paradoxically, the poet placed into the same circle those who wasted through lavish spending and those who hoarded wealth out of fear of losing it—the person with all the credit card bills and the stingy man who builds himself a bomb shelter, just in case. On the surface, it would seem that these two sins would be the exact opposite and thus might merit different places of punishment, but Dante, along with the classical tradition extending back to Cicero and Seneca, sees a secret connection between them. Both groups, if I may, committed sins against *rest*. The ancients used to say that avarice makes a rich man poor—which is to say that the avaricious man, even as he receives something good, can't fully enjoy it, because he's thinking about the next thing he needs before he can rest from desire, just like the child who leaves the toy store, fists full of good things, talking about what she will buy when she returns. The avaricious man makes himself poor, becomes incapable of enjoying even the wealth he possesses. He cannot think about anything except the wealth he does not yet have or the wealth he could potentially lose. The prodigal man is never at rest because, like Paolo Sorrentino's Jep Gambardella, he is addicted to the roller-coaster ride of pleasures, moving from one sensational experience to the next. At the same time, the miserly man can never rest in the good things he possesses, because he is constantly trying to save up more against some unforeseen disaster.

Thus, both groups become blind to what wealth and beautiful things could potentially bring, because they are incapable of using well what they currently possess.

Dante neatly captures the burden of things by describing the punishment of the sinners: they are made to heave and lift huge boulders and push them forward, assuming at all moments that everyone else is out to take their large rocks. They were idolatrous in life, assuming that their earthly happiness would come from material things, and that narrowness of vision is here sadly embodied in their pathetically intense game of lifting worthless earth.

With this additional sad portrait in mind, Dante and Virgil travel to the next circle below, the fifth circle, where they find a small spring bubbling up with hot, dirty water. The water, though, flows down and collects to form a miry swamp. This is where the wrathful are punished. Again, Dante's brilliant imagination creates this precise infernal landscape, which externalizes the interior condition of the wrathful—a small burning wound slowly leaks out anger, which pools in the recesses of the heart, dirties the mind, and incapacitates us to think about anything else.[7] Ultimately, it breaks out in expressions of violent rage, a rage that does not heal us but just plunges us back into the foul-smelling mud.

After this quick tour of these three groups of sinners (one canto per sin), the pace slows down as Dante and Virgil are ferried toward the eerie city of Dis. They have ample time to survey the city as they approach it on a small skiff. The walls of Dis are made of iron, and tall towers can be seen within those walls; they resemble minarets extending high into the air, and they are all alight with flickering fire. It sounds very much like Hieronymous Bosch's smoky, infernal landscape. More terrifying still for the pilgrim is his discovery that on top of the walls a host of evil guardians is watching over their city, like knights protecting their castle from a siege. Dante says there were "more than a thousand" infernal creatures: demons and unclean monsters of all types, drawn from ancient mythology. And they taunt the pilgrim as he approaches: "Let him—all by *himself*—return along his foolhardy path: / let him attempt it, if he knows how, for you, you will remain here" (*Inf.* 8.91–92). When the pilgrim hears this, his resolve is again shaken, just as in *Inferno* 2. He in essence says to Virgil, "If moving on to that which is beyond has been denied us, / let's just retrace our footsteps together, and right away" (8.100–101).

But Virgil, the magnanimous poet who had written about heroes who are undaunted by such obstacles, steps forward, confident in his own ability to clear the path before him. He met success in doing so several times before this. Earlier, he shouted at Plutus, the guardian of the realm of the avaricious (*Inf.* 7.8–10). When the travelers encountered Cerberus the howling dog at the beginning of canto 6, Virgil gathered up some dirt in his hand and threw it into the dog's mouth. At the beginning of canto 8, Phlegyas thought he had caught them (8.18), to which Virgil replied, "Phlegyas, Phlegyas, this time you shout into a void. . . . / You will hold us / only while we are crossing this bog" (8.19–21), and then he compelled the demonic guardian to ferry them to Dis. And so, here, outside of Dis, the Roman poet has grounds for confidence. He tells the pilgrim, "Be not afraid, since our journey / cannot be taken from us by anyone" (8.104–5). On this occasion, though, the old formula is not efficacious. Virgil's authority and skill utterly fail. By the end of *Inferno* 8, the great Roman poet is both confused and embarrassed:

> I could not hear what he put before them,
> but he did not stand there long,
> before each one rushed back within as if in a race.
>
> They closed the doors, our wicked adversaries,
> in my master's face, and he stood there, outside.
> He then returned to me with slow steps.
>
> Eyes on the ground and brow
> shorn of all confidence, he said in the midst of sighs:
> "Who denies *me* the city of sorrow?"
>
> To me he said: "And you, don't be dismayed
> because I criticize myself. No, I will conquer in this battle,
> whatever it is they are putting together in there for defense.
>
> "This insolence of theirs is not new;
> they displayed it once before at a less interior gate,
> the one that can still be found without lock or bolt." (*Inf.* 8.112–26)

In the final lines of the passage above, Virgil makes reference to the portal of hell, whose inscription we discussed earlier in this chapter. As I mentioned, a lot of medieval artistic images show the gates of hell kicked in by Christ, when, after his death but before his resurrection, he came down to hell as a conqueror and liberated all the souls of the patriarchs. In light of Christ's success against the demons who barred the doors against him, Virgil's failure, and his speech afterward, is revealing. He asks, speaking more to himself than to Dante, "Who denies *me*," soon continuing, "*I* will conquer." At the beginning of canto 9, we hear him arguing quietly with himself: "Yet we must overcome in this fight . . . / or else. . . . It was promised to us. / How long it seems to me till someone joins us!" (*Inf.* 9.7–9). Virgil is not very good at waiting.

It's a fascinating scene, which scholars have compared to a medieval siege (a common thing to describe in medieval literature), but here it's a laughable parody! A proper medieval siege would have been conducted by a vast army, with many soldiers and engines of war. Instead, we have just two dudes, two unarmed travelers standing outside a huge, bolted gate, which is defended by thousands of guardians. And it seems that some of these monsters are such a threat that even one look alone could undo the pilgrim.

Thus, we have a series of images that stack up and issue all kinds of question marks: Why does the divinely appointed journey halt here? Why does Virgil, the poet of magnanimity and eloquence, fail? It is at this moment that the poet appeals to his readers:

> O you who have upright understanding,
> look for the teaching that is hidden
> under the veil of these strange verses. (*Inf.* 9.61–63)

Dante asks his readers to lift the veil, which hides some mystery underneath. And right after this famous address to his readers comes one of the most sublime moments in the *Comedy*.[8] While the pilgrim is waiting for what he hardly knows, worried that his guide has led him, unsuspecting, into a dead end in a remote and dangerous corner of hell, an unexpected rushing wind begins:

> And now there was coming up upon the turbid waves,
> a crash of sound, full of fright,
> on account of which both banks were trembling.
>
> Just like that sound we hear when the impetuous wind,
> moving through the contrary pockets of heat,
> savagely attacks the forest and, without relenting,

smashes against the branches, beats them, and carries them away;
and then the dusty blast moves onward, proud,
and forces beasts and shepherds alike to flee. (*Inf.* 9.64–72)

What appears is an angel of God, who arrives and drives the evil spirits away as if they were just annoying frogs. The evil spirits disappear instantly, terrified. Indeed, Dante's angel is not the saccharine image from those terrible pastel paintings but rather a force of power that would make you tremble. He is disdainful, full of a righteous anger, and irritated that he has to be absent from heaven even for this short time. Again, an earthquake of sorts irrupts in the midst of hell. God invades again (as he had done during the harrowing of hell) and casts aside the evil opponents who oppose him, as if they were leaves in a strong wind.

3

The Graveyard of the Heretics
and the Wasteland of the Violent

(*Inferno* 10–17)

New Beginnings and Infernal Architecture (*Inferno* 9–11)

Inferno 9 ends with Dante and Virgil walking into the conquered fortress. Now they can see what precious thing the devils were so jealously guarding. We are rather surprised to discover what it is: an eerie graveyard in which all the lids of the big stone sarcophagi are off and standing to the side. The pilgrim can see a flame gleaming in each tomb, burning from below. This is the pathetic treasure hoarded by the demons. The souls in heaven will be described as precious gems (see, for example, *Par.* 18.115–17); but the wealth of hell is the dead, gaunt, self-absorbed souls of those punished within.

Passing through the Gate of Dis is a major transition, signaling that Dante and Virgil have entered the antechamber of what we could call "deep hell." Fascinatingly, this is a threshold that Aeneas was not allowed to cross:

> Aeneas suddenly looked back, and, below the left hand cliff,
> he saw wide battlements, surrounded by a triple wall. . . .
> A gate fronts it, vast, with pillars of solid steel,
> that no human force, not the heavenly gods themselves,

can overturn by war: an iron tower rises into the air. . . .
Groans came from there, and the cruel sound of the lash,
then the clank of iron, and dragging chains. . . .
Then the prophetess began to speak as follows: "Famous leader
of the Trojans, it is forbidden for the pure to cross the evil threshold:
. . . all of them dared monstrous sin, and did what they dared.
Not if I had a hundred tongues, a hundred mouths,
a voice of iron, could I tell all the forms of wickedness
or spell out the names of every torment." (*Aen.* 6.535–627)

Clearly, Dante's own Dis has been inspired by Virgil's, but his pilgrim will go where even the great Aeneas was not allowed to explore. Meanwhile, the poet dares to speak about things the classical poets avoided. Seven hundred years before Virgil, the archaic Greek poet Hesiod said that deep hell, Tartarus, is a place that is fearful even to the gods. It was radically off-limits. But Dante the pilgrim will enter. He will see what lies at the bottom of the human heart. For the Christian, real purity cannot be achieved unless the heart is explored down to its base. The monsters, like Medusa, have to be called forth and made to emerge. Thus, in the next twenty-five canti Dante will be exploring new ground, ground that neither Aeneas the hero nor Virgil the poet had previously trod.

Shortly after the travelers pass through the Gate of Dis, the poet (in *Inf.* 11) will take the opportunity to help organize the many bewildering things his pilgrim has experienced and will experience. In the first third of *Inferno*, the pilgrim has had a number of intense face-to-face encounters with sinners, but he doesn't seem to have been aware of how orderly hell actually is. Now his master informs him that hell is divided into two major divisions, separated by the walls of Dis: (1) upper hell, whose circles we have read about, where the incontinent sins are punished (*Inf.* 3–8); and (2) lower hell, which is surrounded by the grimy iron walls of Dis. It is within the walls of Dis, or within lower hell, that the sins of "malice" are punished. Dante, who is loosely cobbling together all kinds of classical theories about vice, thinks that the deep principle that divides the sins of upper hell (the incontinent) from the sins of lower hell (the violent, fraudulent, and traitorous) is malice. In the end, the sinners of deep hell want the same things the sinners of upper hell want, even if they act like they are more sophisticated. The truth is that they too are greedy, wrathful, gluttonous, and lustful. The difference is that they are willing to hurt fellow human beings (or themselves) to get what they want.

Deep hell itself can be divided into three more sections, based on three forms of malice: the first is the circle where the *violent* are punished; then there is a deep pit that leads down to where the *fraudulent* are punished; and finally, at the very base of hell, the pilgrim will encounter the *traitorous*. The architecture of hell is very precise.

Patriotism and Family Values . . . in Hell (*Inferno* 10)

Now we return to the spooky graveyard just within the walls of Dis, which the poet compares to an old medieval graveyard, where Dante and Virgil find the heretics (*Inf.* 9.127–29). It is when walking through this graveyard that the pilgrim is surprised by two souls who hear his Florentine accent and rise up to speak to him. The first soul was a great general, Farinata degli Uberti, who died the year before Dante was born. The second soul is Cavalcante Cavalcanti, the father of Dante's best friend, Guido Cavalcanti (also a love poet, mentioned in the *Vita Nuova*). Guido exerted a great influence on Dante's early poetry, but Guido's poetry, unlike Dante's early love poems about Beatrice, was decidedly *this*-worldly. He has been called "the poet of interiority," and he was especially concerned with the joy and pain of love as experienced in *this* life. Thus, it makes sense that his father is classified among those who followed the sins of Epicurus—that is, those heretics who denied the immortality of the soul and lived only for the goods of this life.

Although there is much to say about Cavalcante, for reasons of space I will focus on the greater figure of this canto: the old general, Farinata. He stands alongside Francesca da Rimini and Ulysses (*Inf.* 26) as one of the most powerful characters of *Inferno*. Dante clearly admires him. In fact, Virgil tells Dante to choose his words with great care (10.37). Later Farinata is called *magnanimo* (10.73)—that is, "magnanimous," the same word that was used for Virgil in *Inferno* 2. And thus, in some ways, Farinata is a modern, Florentine counterbalance to Aeneas himself. Here in *Inferno* 10, he rises up with a stately self-confidence, in perfect self-control—the posture of a dignified soldier who commands the respect of all those around him even when he doesn't explicitly ask for it.

As Dante puts it, he was slowly "rising, chest and brow, / as though he held Hell itself in utter scorn" (10.35–36). In a way, the old campaigner's strength and resolve haven't dissipated in hell. He's a man accustomed to enduring hardship, such that, even here, his dignity is barely broken by the dreadful surroundings.

The question of Farinata's heretical belief, whether he denied the immortality of the soul, ironically doesn't show up at all as an issue in this canto. We have to ask, then, whether his heretical disposition is somehow on display in how he goes about conversing with the pilgrim. And we note, immediately, that Farinata does display the partisan spirit of the heretic, that radically sectarian mentality, in his dedication to his political party. The first question he asks of Dante is "Who were your ancestors?" (*Inf.* 10.42). He does not ask, "Who are you?" or "What are you doing here?" He seems hardly amazed that a man, in flesh, is walking among the shades of the dead. There is only one thing on Farinata's mind: the old strife between the Guelphs and Ghibellines. And when he learns that Dante was a Guelph, he replies, "They were savage enemies / toward me and my people and to my cause / such that two times I had to drive them out" (*Inf.* 10.46–48).

Farinata had led his exiled Ghibellines to a successful victory at the battle of Montaperti in 1260, five years before Dante's birth. And, magnanimously, he exhorted his party to deal with the defeated Guelph party with leniency. But Florence never properly acknowledged him for this generous act and, a few years later, exiled many of his family members.

Thus, he still bears an undying resentment, even in hell. In fact, Farinata, in a Medusa-like way, is frozen: although he barely seems to register his external punishment, he locks his jaws and clenches his fists at the memory of that party strife. His resentment smolders within him, forever. He has, as it were, been given exactly what he wants: he remains committed to his party with a fanatical, sectarian devotion, forever. Farinata holds one truth, maintains one loyalty, even if, ironically, that strife between Guelphs and Ghibellines had become a little out of date. In Dante's day, there were only Guelphs in Florence! And so Farinata is a little like someone who still thinks of the world as divided, let's say, between Democrats and Whigs. Of course, Dante would not have thought that Cavalcante's devotion to family or Farinata's devotion to party were evil in themselves. But because these men love these things and these things alone, they barred from their minds any new vision of reality, of humans, or of ideas; and thus their love is frozen. Their sectarian love has metastasized into an unforgiving sorrow.

The Wasteland of the Violent (*Inferno* 12–16)

After Dante and Virgil leave the circle of the heretics, they must slip and slide down the scree of a mountainside, and when they arrive at the bottom, they are standing in the circle of the violent. From *Inferno* 12 to 16, Dante and Virgil walk through this realm, which Dante imagines as a huge circle. The circle itself is formed by three rings, which wrap around one another, each ring taking the form of a different landscape. The pilgrim and Virgil follow a stream that cuts across these rings, moving toward the center of the circle, where a pit is found that will lead them to the most evil parts of hell. In the outermost of these three rings, Dante and Virgil see those who were violent against others—that is, those who harmed their neighbors' bodies or those who harmed their neighbors' possessions. The second ring is where those who were violent against themselves reside, both those who were violent against their bodies (suicides) and those who radically wasted their own property and health (like celebrities known for their decadence). Finally, in the third, innermost ring, the pilgrim will see those who were violent against God—that is, blasphemers—but also those violent against God by violating his nature, a category that for Dante includes sodomy and, interestingly enough, usury.

The guardians of those violent against others are creatures taken from classical mythology: centaurs. It is a highly appropriate role for them, because these thick-bearded creatures of *thumos* (high-spiritedness) were more rage than reason, more horse than man, a fact that Dante playfully keeps pointing out throughout canto 12 through a series of small details. In any case, one of these centaurs, Nessus, gives Dante a tour of the violent souls who are being boiled in a river of blood (Phlegethon). The pilgrim sees conquerors (like Alexander the Great) and ancient tyrants (like Dionysius of Syracuse), as well as more modern Italian tyrants. In life the violent were often stained by hot blood; in death they get what they freely chose in life—the opportunity to be immersed in rivers of blood. Then Dante sees also those who assassinated out of vengeance, and he hears about souls, on the far side of the circle, who are completely submerged in the depths of the river: those who were outrageously destructive and violent, who loved plunder and war for its own sake, who made no pretense that their deeds were aimed at some final end. Dante mentions Attila the Hun, as well as highwaymen and pirates.

From here the two wayfarers continue to move toward the center of the circle, proceeding into the inner ring, where they walk through a dark wood, full of underbrush made up of ugly, gnarled, thorny plants. This is where Dante and Virgil meet the suicides and those who squandered away their resources, like some modern playboy or celebrity. After this, they walk into yet another landscape, that of the innermost ring, which encircles the pit: this is a desert landscape, completely barren of all life, upon which slow and large snowflakes made of fire drift down and land on the skin of those who were violent against God or violent against his nature.

If you pause to think about the imaginative world we have walked through to this point, from the initial dark wood and the sunbathed mountain in *Inferno* 1, to the allusions the poet made to the sea; from the windswept plains of the circle of the lustful, to the rain and hail and snow of the realm of the gluttonous; from the muddy river that turns into the swampy marshlands of the Styx, to the castles, fortified gates, eerie graveyards, and now these rivers, woods, and desert landscapes, then you can see the extraordinary power of Dante's imagination. He seems to be trying to incorporate not only a full range of characters from ancient history to his present age but also an encyclopedic representation of all possible landscapes. The whole world is meant to fit into this poem.

At this point, having enjoyed this view from above—that is, having zoomed out for a moment—I want to zoom in and consider two memorable scenes in more detail. The first comes from *Inferno* 13: the conversation that Dante has with Pier della Vigna, who was a minor official in the court of Frederick II in Sicily in the early 1200s—a man whom all would have forgotten if he had not been made immortal in the *Comedy*. The second character comes from *Inferno* 15, where Dante meets another Florentine, one who died in 1294 (that is, right around the time Dante was working on his *Vita Nuova*). This is Brunetto Latini, whom Dante describes as his beloved teacher.

Pier della Vigna: The Failed Boethius

In *Inferno* 13, Dante walks into a thick, dark, haunted wood completely barren of clean and healthy vegetation:

> No green leaf . . .
> no branches straight, but twisted and gnarled—
> there were no healthy fruits . . . just thorns with venom in them. (*Inf.*
>   13.4–6)

It is a wood of rough and dense thickets, an abode for wild beasts (see 13.7–8). Here, spooky voices are heard speaking, crying, and lamenting, although Dante cannot see a single embodied soul. The canto recalls a scene from Virgil's *Aeneid* in which Aeneas encounters a landscape that had become spiritually polluted because of an act of betrayal and murder. In Virgil's account, Aeneas goes up to a plant and snaps off a twig. To his horror, human blood flows forth from the broken stem. This act allows the soul imprisoned within the plant to issue his breath through the gurgling blood and to tell his sad story. He was Polydorus, the son of Priam, who, when Troy was nearing its inevitable end, was sent with gold to be protected on foreign shores; but the local king, who was supposed to be his protector and host, slaughtered him instead to steal his riches (*Aen.* 3).

Dante has rewritten this episode and has placed into his thornbush not an innocent victim but one who would wish to appear so: Pier della Vigna. When the pilgrim snaps one of the twigs that make up the house for his soul, Pier asks: "Why do you tear me? / Have you not any spirit of pity?" (*Inf.* 13.35–36). He then proceeds to tell his story:

> "I am he who held both keys
> to the heart of Frederick, and I turned them,
> locking and unlocking, so subtly
>
> "that I kept almost every man from his secrets.
> I carried so much trust in that glorious office
> that first I lost my sleep and then the beating of my heart.
>
> "The slut who never took her greedy eyes
> off Caesar's household,
> the common death and usual vice of courts,

"inflamed everyone's soul against me.
And, once inflamed, they so inflamed Augustus
that my joyous honors became heart-sickening grievances.

"My mind, with a taste of disdain,
believing that I could flee disdain by dying,
made me unjust against myself, though just." (*Inf.* 13.58–72)

Pier, then, was a victim (*Inf.* 13.64–66) of the envy of the other courtiers, and those envious rivals went so far to tarnish his reputation that
the emperor, Frederick II, came to believe that Pier had been embezzling
funds. The destruction of his reputation destroyed his career and, as he says,
"made me unjust against myself, though just" (13.72)—that is, he took his
own life because of his unfairly tarnished reputation. Not surprisingly, the
pilgrim is compassionate—in fact, so compassionate that he cannot ask
him any more questions, because "so much pity fills me, it makes me ache
in my heart" (13.84). Here again we note another sympathetic portrayal
of a damned soul, with much the same effect as the canto with Francesca.
Does that mean that the story of Pier is tragedy?

Returning to the passage from Virgil can help us begin to unravel this
"fearful paradox." In the *Aeneid*, the soul trapped in the branches was innocent, the victim of what Virgil calls that "cursed hunger for gold" (*Aen.*
3.56). It was a story, then, of evil committed out of avarice—the sick and
evil craving that values wealth and personal advancement over human lives.
But, to our surprise, it becomes evident that Pier too, although innocent
of the crimes of which he was accused, was guilty of *avaritia*—not an avarice for money but an excessive fondness for his own reputation. Thomas
Aquinas had said that, just as a man can be greedy for wealth, so too can
he be greedy for honor (see *Summa theologiae* I-II, q. 84, a. 4). He can
love his reputation for being successful, love his own success in climbing
the ranks of the corporate ladder; he can also be greedy to be known as a
man of learning and wisdom. In such a situation, that ambitious man loves
the created good of his own reputation more than he loves Primal Love.
Thus, Pier della Vigna, though indeed unjustly accused, threw away his
own life because he couldn't see anything else worth living for. He forgot
that the one Love, which can never be taken away, would have willingly
remained with him, even in his prison cell.

If we also briefly recall the famous Roman senator Boethius, whose
Consolation of Philosophy so deeply influenced Dante, then we can realize

the sick and sad irony of Pier's decision. Pier, if he had had a longer view of history, could have become the kind of suffering hero who would indeed have gained fame throughout the long ages to come—he could have got, in time, the very reputation he sought in court! But he didn't. When his reputation was stolen, he forgot that he still had his life, his memory, his breath, his Maker. He loved too little.

The Sterility of Fame: Brunetto Latini

We come now to our second close reading from the canti of the violent: *Inferno* 15, where we meet the Florentine Brunetto Latini. This canto has a very different tone from the pitiful, dark, and sighing lamentation of *Inferno* 13. Indeed, Dante's work has a kind of symphonic quality, in which each of the canti, like movements in a symphony, has a different tempo, mood, and key. This Brunetto is not in the wood but in the desert wasteland like the souls in canto 14, but not because he was blasphemous. Rather, he walks about the area where the sin of sodomy is punished. We should note right away that the medieval understanding of sodomy was much broader than we might think today; in fact, it consisted of any use of human sexuality that was not formally open to procreation. Thus, certain private sins would fall into this category: you can commit sodomy by yourself. Sodomy can also take place between male and female couples. Thus, for the medieval mind, the sin, at its base, is a sin against fruitfulness, the transformation of a fruitful act into a sterile one. Remember that this sin is punished in an absolutely barren desert landscape.

But there are some puzzles about this canto. For example, there is no historical evidence whatsoever that Brunetto was guilty of any form of this sin, and Dante remains absolutely silent on the subject. What is more, the pilgrim goes a long way to show great reverence for his former teacher. At *Inferno* 15.45, Dante says the pilgrim reverently kept his head bowed. Later, the pilgrim praises Brunetto, saying, "In my mind is fixed—and even now it causes an ache in my heart!— / that precious and good paternal image / of you, sir, when . . . / you used to teach me how a man can become eternal" (*Inf.* 15.82–87).

It's a very affectionate conversation, like when you go back to your high school and run into your favorite teacher in the hallway. Dante's gratitude is real and palpable. Thus, although the setting is a barren landscape, we have these fatherly images used for Brunetto. It's another one of Dante's literary puzzles. Why is Brunetto here? Dante never directly tells us. And yet, note how insistent Dante is to credit Brunetto with teaching him "how a man can become eternal" (*Inf*. 15.85)—that is, how to achieve literary fame. Brunetto Latini was a politician, a diplomat, and a man of letters in Florence. He wrote a vast encyclopedia in French prose, a long didactic poem in Italian, and a book on rhetoric in Italian. And thus it makes sense to hear him reassure Dante,

> "If you follow your star,
> you cannot fail to arrive at a glorious port,
> if I understood things well in the beautiful life." (*Inf*. 15.55–57)

Even Brunetto's closing words touch on this theme of memory, fame, and literary immortality: "Let my *Tesoro* [Brunetto's encyclopedic treatise] always find favor with you. / In it, I still live on, / —I ask for nothing more" (*Inf*. 15.119–20).

Dante clearly shows that Brunetto taught him the literary craft by which a person can make a lasting contribution to humanity, but surely, within the theological context of eternity, there's something badly mistaken to wish only to be remembered for your literary work. Brunetto rather disturbingly says, "I ask for nothing more" (*Inf*. 15.120). Within the context of hell, Brunetto displays an extraordinary spiritual myopia. Indeed, in light of what the pilgrim will see in *Paradiso*, Brunetto's understanding of "glory" and "eternity" seems sadly limited. The pilgrim will see things so glorious that they will burn his eyes; he will hear music so sweet that he won't even be able to recall its beauty. In light of the unspeakably beautiful and the ineffably true, Brunetto's literary accomplishments and goals seem paltry. Thus, the sad truth is that Brunetto is a kind of failed father, who set up his adopted son, Dante, well, but did not set him up for a life of ultimate fruitfulness. His fatherly love was, we could say, somewhat sterile in that it generated love only for the earthly good of reputation and fame.

4

White-Collar Criminals and Sins against Words

(*Inferno* 18–26)

Exposing the Hidden Things of the Fraudulent Heart (*Inferno* 18–25)

After Dante's wild flight on the monster Geryon (*Inf.* 17), he and Virgil arrive in the first part of "deep hell"—that is, among the rings of Malebolge. As we heard in canto 11, the heart of hell, hidden away in the center of the earth, is a large circle of ice. Around its circumference, the walls of hell begin, sloping upward like the sides of a funnel. Dug into these sloping sides are ten deep pits, and arching over each of these trenches are little bridges—although some of the infrastructure of hell was damaged one thousand years ago, and the local shift managers are still waiting on work orders to be filled. In any case, Dante and Virgil will climb to the apex of these bridges to look down to the bottoms of the pits, or they will make their way down into a ditch to hold conversation with the inmates (*Inf.* 18.1–18).

The ditches of Malebolge, or "evil pockets," make up the eternal abode for those who used their intellects crookedly. To fulfill their lustful, avaricious, gluttonous, envious, or wrathful desires, they devised various crafty, deceptive strategies to get what they wanted. We could think of them as white-collar criminals, but Dante, rather unlike our penal system, doesn't put them in minimum security. Rather, he puts them much farther down, because he sees these sinners as doubly offensive in the eyes of God. Why? Because they were not only fired by the "hot sins" we encountered in the earliest part of hell, but they, like the violent in the circle above them, were also malicious, willing to hurt those human beings who got in their way. The residents of Malebolge, though, exercised their malice not through force but by abusing that most precious gift of humanity: our speech-making, word-crafting, image-producing intellect. The Malebolge, then, make up the realm of "cold sin," and you will notice that the closer we get to the base of hell, the icier the world becomes.[1]

In *Inferno* 18, the pilgrim and his guide cross over two ditches. In the first ditch, they see pimps and seducers, who used crafty stratagems to trick women into violating the marital bond. In the second ditch, they find flatterers—that is, those who crafted their speech to please patrons and gain financial remuneration. Whatever you want to hear can be purchased from the flatterer for the right price. In this disturbing canto, Dante makes reference to contemporary flatterers, those who loitered in medieval courts offering rulers the honeyed words they liked to listen to and, like the political science major working in a modern campaign, dutifully transmitting to subjects those opinions their masters wanted them to possess. But the poet goes further by drawing a shocking association. The banks are slimy and sticky, and the people within are plunged in disgusting excrement (*Inf.* 18.106–8, 113–14). Just as human excrement is that which is left over once useful nourishment has been extracted, so too here we find those speakers whose words had been evacuated of meaning.

Toward the end of this canto, the poet makes a fleeting reference to a minor figure from classical literature: Thais, a flattering prostitute (*Inf.* 18.127–36), who is included among these flattering medieval courtiers to make a striking connection between flattery and prostitution. Just as a prostitute, quite apart from love, is willing to put sacred things up for sale, so too the abuser of words is willing to take something as intimate as language, which binds human beings together, and sell it. We can see how much Dante, the poet, the theoretician of language, thinks of words: for Dante it is a sacred act to speak, and obfuscating the vision of reality through the abuse of language is a serious sin. He felt that these prostitutes and vendors of excrement were the opposite of the poet, who carefully crafts his words to nourish, but who also, when needed, uses his words as a scourge to drive out sinners. Dante's words, according to the divine commission he receives in heaven, are to be "harsh," free of "falsehood": let the reader "scratch" where he itches (*Par.* 17.126–29).

Over the next several canti, Dante and Virgil progress in a spiraling descent toward the center of hell. On several occasions the wayfarers climb down the banks to the bottoms of the ditches for a closer look. In the third ditch (or *bolgia, Inf.* 19), for example, they go down to talk to souls who are being punished for simony—that is, churchmen who offered privileges and offices to those willing to pay money, as opposed to those who were spiritually worthy. Then Dante sees the twisted fortune-tellers (*Inf.* 20), those who longed for the secret knowledge of the future more than tending to what they needed to know for living well in the present. In the fifth ditch (*Inf.* 21–22), Dante and Virgil descend to meet the bar-rators, those who sold public offices or governmental goods for bribes. In the sixth ditch (*Inf.* 23), we meet the hypocrites, who process like monks, except that they wear heavy cloaks of lead gilded in gold. And finally, before we come to the great canto of Ulysses (*Inf.* 26), we meet the thieves (*Inf.* 24–25). At this point, before conducting a reading of the canto of Ulysses, one of the most important canti in the entire *Comedy*, I want to focus on four particular scenes in these canti of the fraudulent: Jason (*Inf.* 18), the barrators (*Inf.* 21–22), the hypocrites (*Inf.* 23), and the thieves (*Inf.* 24–25).

Four Snapshots of Fraudulence

The first figure of note is Jason, the famous Greek hero from mythology, who led a band of hardy sailors (Argonauts) in search of the Golden Fleece. Generally, these kinds of ancient heroes—like Aeneas, Ulysses, Hercules, Theseus, and Perseus—are positive exemplars for Dante. In fact, Jason's voyage—his epic quest to capture something of great value and bring it home—is alluded to three times in *Paradiso* (2.16–18; 25.7; 33.94–96) and used as a model for Dante's own epic literary undertaking. Dante suggests that he too, like a hero, ventures off to a faraway land and brings back its treasure. For this reason, it comes as a surprise to find the hero of epic courage tossed in among the ditches of the Malebolge. The truth, as Virgil points out, is that his greatness seems out of place here:

> "Look at that great man who comes our way,
> and seems to spill no tear over his sorrow.
>
> "What regal bearing he carries still!
> He is Jason, who by heart and head
> deprived the men of Colchis of a ram." (*Inf.* 18.83–87)

Like other magnanimous figures we have encountered in hell, such as Farinata, Jason is too dignified to whimper like the other souls as he is whipped by demons. He maintains something of that heroic fortitude even in the heart of hell, but, as the passage goes on to state, he is in hell because, on his return voyage, he used his smooth words, James Bond–style, to manipulate a few women, such as Hypsipyle, into aiding him. When he had got the assistance he needed through false promises of love, he abandoned her and continued on his journey. Thus, although Jason's quest was admirable in Dante's eyes, he is in hell because he manipulated people to get what he wanted. Threatening the harmony of the human community even in the pursuit of a great and laudable end is a damnable offense in Dante's eyes.

Soon Dante and Virgil climb down to explore the ditch where the barrators are punished. Barrators are those who abused their positions in secular government to dispense public goods to friends or those who offered the appropriate bribes, not to those who needed them. Now these corrupt officials are forced to stay under boiling pitch, under which, of course, they can't breathe. But when they come up for air, the devils are there waiting on the banks, ready to seize them. Of all the canti in the *Comedy*, these (*Inf.* 21–22) are some of the zaniest and most comical, in a lowbrow way. Throughout canti 21 and 22, the pilgrim nervously looks around at the band of demons who have been asked by Virgil to escort them through this ditch. The devils keep eyeing the pilgrim, sarcastically joking about him, and licking their lips. As you read through the canti, including the bizarre gesture of the head of the devils, who farts to signal to his company a forward march (21.136–39), you're supposed to laugh at their slapstick, grade-B movie tone.

At the same time, I think Dante has created this goofy tone of levity for a reason. The sinners in this realm, such as Ciampolo, with whom Dante and Virgil have a brief conversation, find themselves in a situation a little like the poor they chose not to aid when they had the power to do so. Now, like the poor they ignored when they held political office, they live in a condition of desperation. Every time they rise up in order to seek a little relief from their suffocating conditions, there are demons waiting for them. Those who ought to aid them in their plight torture them instead. The strange comic tone of these canti is appropriate. All of this is funny to us, but it is not funny at all to the souls who are actually suffering from the juvenile, careless, and cruel hatred of the demons. It's almost like being trapped in a nightmare, where everyone around you is careless and laughing, completely indifferent to the desperate anxiety you are suffering. This is a good example of what I suggested at the beginning of this chapter: Dante portrays those white-collar crimes in a way that makes us feel their gravity. We perhaps might not get that exercised over a little graft. What's wrong with rewarding some of the folk back home with valuable but useless building projects? Or accepting foreign donations for your foundation? Everyone does it, right? Dante forces us to view these offenses for what they are: threatening to the harmony of a community.

In canto 23 we meet the hypocrites, who are in death (as in life) completely weighed down by their own religious cloaks—lead on the inside and sparkling gold on the outside. They are so weighed down they can barely move, and so they inch along in wearied step after step. For Dante, and for the monastic tradition, hypocrisy is the sin of those who love their reputation for holiness more than they love holy things themselves, the sin more properly called "vainglory." Of course, it is likely that if you seek wisdom and try to live well, you will gain a good reputation. In some ways, this honor is the natural fruit of virtue. And yet there is the danger that, at some point, you will start saying things or doing things *primarily* to support or promote that reputation. It's a subtle distinction that medieval monastic writers dwelled on at length. Imagine that if you were a teacher or a religious leader, you got into the habit of using words to say things not so much because you thought they were true but because you knew they would help enhance your reputation as one who is wise. You would be weaving for yourself a weighty cloak, in which you would eventually be crushed by your own words and false appearances. You would also be suffocated by the fear of being found out for what you really are. One ancient writer, Evagrius, summed it up this way: monks seek "a life lived free of all hypocrisy. For vainglory has a frightful power to cover

over and cast virtues into the shade. Ever searching out praise from men, it banishes faith. . . . The good must be pursued for its own sake, not for some other cause."[2]

Following the canto of the hypocrites is a section that Dante thought was as impressive an artistic tour de force as what he had penned in describing the flight of Geryon (*Inf.* 16–17). In fact, the Florentine poet boasts that he has surpassed those poets he had met in the castle of limbo (*Inf.* 4): "Silence, now, Lucan. . . . / Let Ovid be silent, too" (25.94, 97). Ovid, of course, was the poet of the *Metamorphoses*, the master of describing the transformations of gods and humans (for example, Daphne changing into the laurel tree, or a girl transformed into her own echo). Dante's description, though, he is proud to say, surpasses Ovid's in intensity, because in these canti the Florentine poet imaginatively describes how the souls of thieves are transformed into all sorts of nasty reptiles. Some are attacked by flying snakes that pierce the sinners' necks; they then catch fire and burn down into ash before they are remade again. And so, in this canto, Dante goes all in with his poetry. He takes these inner, abstract truths and lets them figure forth in a poetry of evil incarnation. He gives the thieves the bodies they deserve. To do so, Dante racked his brain for all the passages from classical literature that describe nasty snakes, lizards, or flying serpents. He then poured them all into his hell to create a violent, phantasmagorical poetry that he was very proud of.

Dante also meets a famous "tough guy," a kind of medieval equivalent of the leader of a biker gang. His name is Vanni Fucci, and here he boasts, "The life of a beast pleased me and not that of a man, / just like the bastard I was. I am Vanni Fucci, / an animal! Pistoia was a worthy den" (*Inf.* 24.124–26). But rather to his embarrassment, Vanni Fucci is this far down in hell—he should be up among the violent—because he stole vessels from a sacristy, and he is mortified to have his carefully crafted reputation uncovered. To express his rage, Vanni Fucci uses a medieval gesture of the fig, which is equivalent to flipping someone off, but he directs his obscene gesture, along with all the venom of his heart, at God:

> When he had ended his words, the thief
> raised his hands—both of them made the fig—
> and shouted: "Take this, God!"
> . . . .

> Through all the dark circles of hell
> I did not see a spirit so proud against God. (*Inf*. 25.1–3, 13–14)

We have yet again a sinner who, though he suffers externally, experiences his real punishment within. Vanni Fucci serves as a powerful image of the sinner: eternally flipping off God, cursing God, spitting in his face. His heart remains tempestuous, and he directs his hate at God forever.

The Canto of Ulysses (*Inferno* 26)

By the time Dante arrives at the eighth *bolgia*, he has crossed over bridges and climbed down into ditches; he has seen faces covered with excrement, wept over twisted bodies, stared at men crushed under metal cloaks, and marveled at souls bitten, scratched, clawed, and penetrated by loathsome reptiles. These canti of the fraudulent are intense, and so it is with a start that we leave the serpents behind and come up to a bluff that overlooks a peaceful valley where the souls shine like lightning bugs. *Inferno* 26 opens with a peaceful, pastoral simile, which changes the tone of Dante's poetry from the heavy metal of the canti of the thieves to the string quartet of *Inferno* 26 (26.25–29, 31–32). This pastoral simile is immediately followed by a second one, in which Dante compares these glowing flames to Elijah's fiery chariot (26.34–42). The pilgrim's eyes are clearly attracted to the beauty of these flickering lights. As we shall later hear, the souls here are in fact wrapped in a fiery light that makes them resemble—on the outside at least—the appearance of souls in paradise. This explains Dante's reaction:

> "Master, I sincerely beg you,
> and beg you again, and will beg a thousand times,
>
> "that you not deny me the chance to linger here
> long enough for the horn-shaped flame to come here:
> you can see that my desire makes me lean inward." (*Inf*. 26.65–69)

Imprisoned within this double flame are Diomedes (who never speaks) and Ulysses, who, of course, is the Odysseus of Homer, the hero from Ithaca who designed the deception of the horse to help the Greeks win at Troy. In Homer's account, Odysseus is known above all for his wit, his ability to persuade, and his ability to strategize. After the war, Odysseus began his long trek home, a journey that became even longer because his curiosity and vanity constantly got the best of him. In Homer's tale, for example, Odysseus enters the cave of a one-eyed monster, a cyclops, because he wants to receive a memorable gift from him. He barely gets himself and a few remaining crew members out of the cave alive. Later, Odysseus choreographs his crew so that he can claim to be the only man to hear the song of sirens without being lured to his death. Odysseus, then, is a kind of swaggering, confident, but lovable hero who cleverly twists the truth when he needs to.

Dante did not read Greek, and so what he knew of the Homeric hero had to come indirectly from Latin sources, either Roman philosophers (such as Boethius, who used Odysseus's story to illustrate philosophical ideas) or Latin poets (such as Virgil and Ovid) who added to the collection of stories they inherited from Homer. In medieval academic commentaries, Ulysses became (believe it or not) the *philosophical* hero, the exemplar of the man who was so discontented with the world that he sought out the depths of wisdom. Ulysses's search for his homeland was interpreted as the gradual awakening of the inner power of the soul to know God. This is in part the Ulysses whom the pilgrim meets here—a strong, virtuous, bold explorer looking for something deep.

Dante drew on one more tradition about the ancient hero—that is, that this great and curious traveler didn't end his life in Ithaca but rather continued to journey in order to know more and more of the world. Where he died, no one knew. Dante takes this opportunity to add a tale of his own to this long tradition, one more chapter in the "fan lit," in which Dante presumes to reveal the secret of the ancient hero's death. Ulysses says that he convinced his old shipmates to go on one last adventure with him in search of the unknown:

> "I and my companions were old and slow
> when we came to that narrow straight [the Straight of Gibraltar]
> where Hercules set up his signs of caution
>
> "lest men venture into that which is beyond. . . .
>
> "'O brothers,' I said, 'who have come through a hundred dangers and
>   more
> now to arrive at the West,
> in this our so fleeting vigil

"'of our right minds, while they remain to us!
How could you deny yourself the experience
of that land beyond the sun, of the uninhabited world?

"'Remember your lofty origin:
you were not made to live like brutes,
but to seek after virtue and understanding.'

"I made my companions so ardent for the way,
by this brief speech,
that after it I could have held them back only at great pains." (*Inf.*
    26.106–23)

This is one of those literary passages that sends shivers down your spine. Ulysses continues his narrative, explaining that when he and his men had sailed down into the southern hemisphere, they saw a mountain rising up out of the mist, a mountain he did not know. They were excited because they suspected that this was the mysterious land they had set out for. Dante will later help us understand that this is the mountain of purgatory. They almost made it.

Ulysses's speech and story are so moving that we feel ourselves responding to this narrative as if it were a brief play, the tragedy of the noble Ulysses. In fact, the passage is so powerful that many scholars of Dante over the years have wondered why Dante even put Ulysses in hell. After all, he seems so brave and indomitable, even in old age. He reminds his companions, "You were not made to live like brutes, / but to seek after virtue and understanding" (*Inf.* 26.119–20). Even more importantly, Ulysses seeks experience not just of the world but also of that which is beyond it (*più oltre*, 26.109). Ulysses has a keen sense that there is something more of the depths, something that all things have reference to. Ulysses's ardor, his fervor to know, is so great that he is willing, all over again, to run the risk of all those "dangers" (26.113) he had already been through. Ulysses has a sense of urgency and a strong sense of the brevity of life, what he calls the "so fleeting vigil / of our right minds" (26.114–15).

As his tale comes to an end, the crescendo of hope is dramatically interrupted when the hero is destroyed by a storm. After five months of sailing, the crew sees a mountain that takes their breath away. The men who spent their whole lives fighting giants, killing monsters, and eluding witches are stunned by the mountain's mysterious power. Ulysses and his crew rejoice, convinced that here they have found what they have been looking for, that which was beyond the merely human, *più oltre*. It is at this moment that their hopes and ship are destroyed. By whom? Ulysses does not know. He describes the dramatic moment when they see the mountain in this way:

> "[It was] hazy,
> on account of the distance. It seemed to me taller
> than any I had ever seen before.
>
> "We rejoiced! But immediately that turned to grief,
> since from that strange land there was born a whirlwind
> and it struck us at the head of our ship.
>
> "Three times it made us reel about.
> On the fourth it jerked the stern into the air,
> and the prow went down—as pleased some other—
> until the sea held us within." (*Inf.* 26.133–42)

For what reason? Why such a noble desire would conclude in such a terrible way is beyond his ken. In search of the sublime, Ulysses is overcome by the tragic. You will remember the two similes used at the beginning of the canto: Ulysses, although desiring to ascend to heaven like Elijah in a chariot, actually is more akin to a humble firefly that flutters through the air on a summer evening. So what did he do wrong? And perhaps more importantly, why does Dante work so hard to get us to admire yet another great sinner in hell? In *Paradiso*, in fact, Dante will liken his own spiritual journey to God to Ulysses's journey into the unknown, taking Ulysses's tragic failure as the model for his own poetic undertaking!

At the beginning of his speech Ulysses seems to slip, revealing, just a bit, a bad conscience:

> "[When] I departed from the isle of Circe,
> who, for more than a year, kept me by wiles there near Gaëta,
> before Aeneas named it that,
>
> "neither the sweetness of my son, nor piety
> toward an aged father, nor the due love
> which I owed Penelope, to make her glad,
>
> "could overcome that ardor that burned within me." (*Inf.* 26.91–97)

Ulysses, almost accidentally, contextualizes his own epic journey with reference to that very different journey of Aeneas, and this brings into focus a huge difference between the two epic heroes. Ulysses's journey began with a choice to disembark from the larger human community, a decision that runs—as we hear Ulysses himself say—directly contrary to Aeneas's willful choice to remain united to those human relationships that touched him (his fatherhood, his sonship, his kinship to Trojans, his status as ancestor to future generations of Romans). It is telling that Ulysses, although he first says his passion is to know the ways and customs of men, urges his crew to seek "the experience / of that land beyond the sun, of the uninhabited world" (26.116–17). Ulysses lacks the willingness to found, defend, and cultivate the city. He lacks allegiance to a particularized human community, and he lacks the willingness to remain bound by those human relationships, which, as we shall see, is one of the pillars of the experience of purgatory.[3]

But recall what Virgil had said before the conversation with Ulysses even began: Ulysses and Diomedes mourn "the deception / of the horse that made a gate / whence came the noble seed of the Roman people" (*Inf.* 26.58–60). Long before he launched out on this journey into the unknown, Ulysses developed the crafty trick of the horse to destroy an ancient city. In light of this, Ulysses's end was in some ways the fitting conclusion to his lifelong practice of fraudulence, the end for which he had inadvertently prepared. Ulysses had been guilty of *astutia*, employing false or counterfeit means to pursue a good end, a perversion of *prudentia* according to Thomas Aquinas (*Summa theologiae* II-II, q. 55, a. 5). To state it plainly, Ulysses spent his whole life inventing clever stratagems to win and get what he wanted (most notably, using the deception of the Trojan horse to unjustly destroy his enemies), but that bad formation, that bad practice of cleverly cheating, plays out at the end of his life. Ulysses pursues the highest end, with bravery and heroism, but he forgot the intermediary steps of virtue, which he could only have learned within a human community! For this reason we can admire Ulysses and his boldness to know that which is *più oltre* (that which is beyond), while, at the same time, we can understand why Dante is so cautious: "More than I am accustomed to do, I rein in my intellect / lest it race forward where virtue fails to guide it" (*Inf.* 26.21–22).

$$5$$

Icy Hearts and Frozen Souls: The Lowest Portion of Hell

(*Inferno* 27–34)

Tears and Broken Words at the Center of the Universe

As Dante and Virgil descend to increasingly lower levels of hell, we feel the thermometer dropping, both in terms of the ice that imprisons the souls and the spiritual coldness of the souls they meet. The final canti of *Inferno*—canti 27–34—deal with two groups of sinners: the last of the fraudulent souls, stuffed into the lowest ditches of the Malebolge, and the traitorous souls, who are frozen within the frozen river of Cocytus.

As the two travelers move through the last of the ditches of Malebolge, we notice a number of overarching themes. First, with increasing frequency we hear of souls who refuse to reveal their names. In earlier canti, Vanni Fucci, Farinata, and Francesca were all too happy to share their names, stories, and personal details, but here, in deep hell, the pilgrim begins to encounter souls who have so willingly broken themselves off from the human community that they don't wish to play any part in human society again, either directly or even through being remembered. Second, the final canti are extraordinarily violent. At the beginning of canto 28, for example, the canto of the schismatics, Dante racks his brain to recall all the stories of wounds and cadavers from wars old and new, and says that if you heaped all of those wounded limbs and mangled bodies into a pile, the viewer of that atrocity would not be so horrified as he was in this ditch. The pilgrim will see souls whose bodies are sliced and dismembered, like pieces of meat in a butcher's shop. Later, he will see souls so "spotted with scabs from head to foot" (*Inf.* 29.75) that they feel that their nails are "biting" into them as they scratch (29.79). In canto 33 he will encounter Ugolino, who feverishly bites into the head of his hated enemy, Archbishop Ruggieri, forever. Indeed, it seems that as his pilgrim nears the bottom of hell, the poet pulls out all the stops in his quest to create a poetry of breaking glass and fingernails on the chalkboard, in an attempt to convey the devastating sense of shattered humanity.

Third, in addition to the violence, the wounds, the disease, the hatred, and the intense frigidity of isolation, we have one more motif at play throughout lower hell: tears. Although tears appear throughout the first canticle, they come more often and more copiously as we get closer to the base of hell. In *Inferno* 32 we hear of two sinners who are glued to one another by their tears; in *Inferno* 33 we hear that the sinners are actually unable to cry, because their tears freeze and form visors on their eyes (33.94–99). As much as they would like to give relief to the pent-up pain within, they are unable to do so. Because their eyes are frozen, their souls are almost overwhelmed with the repressed grief they cannot release. Ugolino tells the pilgrim, "You will see me speak and weep together" (33.9). And of course, in the final canto, Satan sheds copious tears as he remembers how beautiful he once was.

Finally, in these last canti, we encounter instances of a language that has become so broken that it leaves the speaker trapped within his own words. For example, when Dante and Virgil meet the old general Guido da Montefeltro, they have to wait because the damned soul's first attempt to speak comes out as an incomprehensible bellowing (*Inf.* 27.7–19); the slick salesman of words and purveyor of selfish advice is here punished by his inability even to get his words out. Similarly, in canto 31, Dante and Virgil meet the legendary king (Nimrod) who was responsible for organizing the building of the Tower of Babel. When he sees the pilgrim, he shouts, "Raphèl maì amècche zabì almi" (31.67), which is not Italian. In fact, it is made-up, nonsense language. Virgil explains:

"He condemns himself.
This is Nimrod. Thanks to his wicked scheming
a single language is no longer used in the world.

"Leave him here. Let's not speak any more empty words,
given that every language is to him as his
to any other: understood by no one." (*Inf.* 31.76–81)

Nimrod, the ambitious and proud king, who had designs to forge his
own path to God, is here reduced to an ultimate isolation. It's a powerful
psychological portrait: he is the completely self-absorbed individual who,
constantly meditating on his own private and secretive plan, slowly loses
touch with reality, like Dostoyevsky's Raskolnikov (in *Crime and Punishment*). Because he is driven by an obsessive, egoistic mania, he severs his
bonds with others, reducing himself to speaking a language understood
by none but himself. With these themes in mind (ice, tears, isolation, and
broken language), let's zoom in and focus on a few passages.

Guido da Montefeltro

When Dante meets Guido da Montefeltro, the old soldier famously
responds:

"If I believed that my answer would be given
to a person who might ever return to the world,
this flame would stand still, without a flicker.

"But since no one ever, from this depth,
has returned alive, if I hear the truth,
without fear of infamy I answer you." (*Inf.* 27.61–66)

Guido, then, does not want to be remembered. In earlier circles of hell,
even if souls pursued a good with immoderation or were snared by an
excessive love, they still could boast at least of having done some good
things, and thus felt they had a right to be recalled among the living. But
as we descend deeper and deeper, we meet souls who spent their whole
lives in self-centered calculation, manipulating the world around them,
setting souls against one another in a radically self-centered existence, and
thus in hell they are embarrassed even to have their names repeated. This
is what I mean by the spiritual coldness of hell: it's a touchiness—that

is, a sad, morose desire to be left alone. As the pilgrim gets closer to the center of the earth, he gets farther away from the stars, away from beauty, away from harmony, away from order, away from love. The landscape gets colder and colder, as a kind of perfect symbol for how the heart freezes the more it chooses its own good and leaves behind participation in loving human communion.

Guido then tells his story. He was a soldier and a famous strategist (we know from other sources that he fought for the Ghibellines against the papal party, the Guelphs). Like Ulysses, he was accomplished at using craft to effect whatever end was desirable to him, but he repented from his life of war and became a Franciscan in 1296. All would have been well for him if he had not failed his final trial. The pope whom Dante hated the most, Boniface VIII, was faced with a rebellion led this time by a Ghibelline faction, and he called on the old soldier for help to suppress the faction he had once fought for. Guido obliged, and died two years later in Assisi. But in Dante's story, Boniface VIII promised the reformed soldier that if he did this one last act for him, his sin would be pardoned. In Guido's own words, the pope told him, "I can lock or unlock heaven / as you know." Guido concludes his speech: "His weighty arguments then pushed me / to the point that silence seemed to me the worse course" (*Inf.* 27.103–4, 106–7).

Thus, the man who spent his life practicing at outwitting others allowed himself to be fooled, but in death Guido could not use his clever tricks to work his way out of eternal damnation. But here Guido, like so many other souls in hell, blames another, Boniface VIII. He is, of course, partly correct. Boniface, as Dante tells the story, certainly collaborated in his damnation. What Guido fails to mention—and this is a theme that will be one of the most prominent in *Purgatory*—is that he still had his own freedom. As quoted above, Guido says that "silence seemed to me the worse course" (*Inf.* 27.107). Pause to consider this a moment. Would it have been worse for Guido to refuse to aid the pope? Guido rightly realized that if he did refuse to give crooked advice, he would be punished by the pope, but we can only truly say this was the worse course within a very limited scope of observation. It might have been worse at that moment, but Guido failed to consider his actions within a larger context, within the context of eternity. He failed to view this choice, as the medieval writers liked to say, *sub specie aeternitatis*—in light of eternity. Thus, we have another personal tragedy, not unlike the suicide Pier della Vigna (*Inf.* 13). With an opportunity to become a hero, Guido balked and chose an evanescent good.

After Dante and Virgil leave Guido behind, they visit the last two ditches of the Malebolge, where the schismatics have their bodies sliced and divided with sharp swords, and then, in the final ditch, where counterfeiters are punished. The counterfeiters include those who practiced alchemy, those who impersonated other people, and those who created false coinage—in other words, those who created worthless, false images and passed them off as true. It is striking for the modern reader that, as I like to say, Dante thinks photocopying a twenty-dollar bill is more evil than getting into a drunken fight in a bar. Or perhaps we could put it this way: a bad and ideologically committed college professor is more evil than a murderer. Such is Dante's commitment to the word and the image: for Dante, falsifying the image of nature—obscuring reality through a false reproduction, producing images that mislead—is more destructive than harming bodies. Dante the poet, the craftsman of language, feels in his gut the sacred responsibility to use language with exactitude and precision and to create images that show forth the actual nature of reality. For this reason, he is also horrified by language that obfuscates our view of what is.

Canto 28, though, is where Dante meets the schismatics (those who were not just heretics but leaders of divisive sectarian groups). The chief example is Muhammad, because the poet thought that Muhammad had been Christian before he broke away to found his own religion in pursuit of power. His description of Muhammad is one of the crudest and most graphically violent of the whole of the *Comedy*. Add up all the wars and wounded, heap up their corpses and lacerated flesh, and you could hardly equal the horror of this pit of hell (*Inf.* 28.7–8, 15–17, 19–21). But then the poet compares Muhammad to a hacked-up barrel split by a crude instrument:

> No cask with a missing side-stave or supporting-stave
> ever splayed open so wide as this man I saw:
> cracked open from the chin down to where men fart.
>
> Between the legs his guts hung down;
> his innards could be seen, and that sick sack
> that makes sh*t out of that which is gulped down.

> While I was frozen, staring at him,
> he, looking at me, tore open his chest with his hands,
> saying: "See how I tear myself to pieces,
>
> "see how deformed is Muhammad!" (*Inf.* 28.22–31)

This is shocking, even for us![1] What happened to the love poet of delicate language and refined sentiment? Here we have rough and crude words, as if the poet were belching or vomiting forth a description. Why so much linguistic violence?

For Dante, Muhammad, as well as the many other sectarian leaders he quickly packs into this canto, was responsible for wounding and dismembering sacred bodies—that is, the body of Christ or the body politic. Because they themselves did not treat those assemblies of people as bound by a mystical love—as a group unified by more than their physical bodies—Dante here allows their own human bodies to be similarly reduced to the crude and broken machinery of bodily functions: the digestive system in poor Muhammad hangs out. Others have their tongues sliced. Bertran de Born, who divided royal son against father, carries his head in his hands. The schismatics failed on earth to pay respect to those sacred bodies of humans gathered into communion, and so they have their own precious bodies vulgarly demystified here in hell. In this way, Dante is a poet of X-ray vision. He aims to turn inside out that which we hide within. The schismatics are made to walk around the circle slowly—twenty-two miles around, Virgil tells us (*Inf.* 29.9)—and as they go round, their bodies begin to heal, only to be reopened and rewounded as soon as they've come back to the starting point of the circle. It's a powerful image of the schismatic—those who don't just disagree on principle but take delight in others being wrong. In their heart of hearts, Dante suggests, they don't wish for true healing; they insist on opening up old wounds.

The Final Canti of Hell

In the final canti of *Inferno*, we meet the traitorous, men who broke the faith of those who had a special reason to trust in them. Some traitors violated the trust of family members, some broke the trust of their countrymen, some betrayed their lords, such as the assassins of Caesar (Brutus and Cassius) and Judas Iscariot. These are extraordinarily fast-moving canti, in which Dante packs a dizzying number of names into just two canti, reserving the final canto for a description of Satan. We have biblical and classical traitors, as well as traitors from medieval history who, apart from Dante, would have been forgotten by most. Appropriately, the traitors of lower hell have their identities, unwillingly, betrayed by the other residents of Cocytus. Traitors still betraying.

It is telling that within these canti the poet interrupts his narrative to express his longing for "rhymes, bitter and harsh" (*rime aspre e chiocce*, *Inf.* 32.1). The opening verses of canto 32 are extraordinary:

> If I but had rhymes, bitter and harsh,
> such as would fit this sick hole,
> upon which all other rocks exert their weight,
>
> I would squeeze the juice from what I perceive
> more fully. But because I don't have them,
> I continue to speak, but with a sense of fear,
>
> since it is not an enterprise for jest
> to describe the center of the universe,
> nor for a language that cries "mommy" and "daddy." (*Inf.* 32.1–9)

In other words, we have it from Dante that he is trying to create a poetry that, by the end of these canti, will leave you dizzy and nauseated upon encountering the human heart in the worst possible state of existence. He wants you to have a deep and abiding repulsion for those actions that, often, even if we know they are harmful, we rarely detest. Dante was also very much aware of how difficult this would be for the ordinary language of Italian; he has to get all the power of the old epics into that language that, as he says, cries *mamma* and *babbo*.

And here the poet, much like the pilgrim, lets all compassion die:

> O race, that should never have been! Worse than all the rest,
> you abide in that place so hard to speak of.
> How much better had you been sheep or goats! (*Inf.* 32.13–15)

Later on, Dante tells the Pisans that he hopes they will drown (33.79–84). You can feel the poet letting go. At the same time, the pilgrim doesn't apologize for kicking the sinner Bocca degli Abati in the face (32.79–84). He then kneels down to start tearing out clumps of his frozen hair in order to force the stubborn soul to reveal his name. In canto 33 the pilgrim fools Fra Alberigo, refusing to help him remove the ice from his eyes. He lets the traitor feel the pain of betrayal: "But now extend your hand and open / for me my eyes." The poet continues: "I did not open them. / But it was courtesy to be a villain to him" (33.148–50). What is going on? Moments like these have led eminent scholars to call Dante hateful and vengeful. Is the poet of love slipping? Is he becoming the poet of hate? Is this his chance to lash out at the world that had betrayed him?

These violent reactions are all the more shocking in light of the pilgrim's *pietate* (pity) for souls in the upper regions of hell. Recall that the pilgrim swooned with *pietate* when he heard Francesca's story (*Inf.* 5.139–42). After hearing Pier's story, he was so moved by *pietà* that he could not ask his follow-up question (13.84). Elsewhere, Dante reverently bows his head before his old teacher, Brunetto (15.44–45), without a word of judgment: "Are you here, Ser Brunetto?" (15.30). In *Inferno* 16.52 Virgil tells the pilgrim to feel sorrow (*doglia*) for the plight of the Florentine heroes he meets. The new Christian pilgrim to the afterlife builds on what the mythological Aeneas had been famous for (*pietas*). Dante, though, stretches the virtue, making it now include a new vulnerability, a feeling of complicity in the fragility of the human condition. Your sin is also mine.

As I said in the introduction, Dante's journey through *Inferno* is the *guerra della pietate* ("war of pity," 2.5–6). It is a struggle of interiority, not just a story of how some brawny Beowulf overcomes monsters in a swamp. To the extent that it is a war, the pilgrim has to develop a whole range of interior responses and then bring peace to those various parties. The pilgrim does have to develop *pietate*, but he *also* has to develop the power to show "disdain" (as he is praised for displaying toward Filippo Argenti in *Inf.* 8.31–60). In addition to feeling the weight of the sin he sees, in addition to feeling compassion for the twisted figure of humanity, he must *also* respond with justice and severity, understanding that what they now suffer was (and still is) freely chosen. The pilgrim must develop the full range of interior responses and then bring them into concert.

And if anyone is worthy of stern judgment, it is the sinners in the bottom of hell, for they do not just err through excessive love of things that are sometimes good (physical love, food, wealth, revenge), but rather they choose things that are always evil, in any circumstance (fraudulence and betrayal). Bocca degli Abati, for instance, was one of the few Ghibellines who was not exiled from Florence in 1258. Although he claimed a new allegiance to the Guelph faction, at the Battle of Montaperti (1260) he cut off the hand of the Florentine standard-bearer, which created panic in the Guelph lines and led to their disastrous defeat by the Ghibellines. He betrayed those who had shown him mercy. Ugolino is the sinner, in canto 33, who is ravenously biting pieces of flesh out of the head of Ruggieri, the archbishop of Pisa. Count Ugolino was the leader of the Guelphs in Pisa, who entered into traitorous negotiations with the Ghibelline party, but he himself was betrayed by Ruggieri. Along with his children, he was imprisoned within a tower and allowed to starve to death. Fra Alberigo is the sinner who asks Dante to remove the ice from his eyes. He was from a small Italian town. In 1284 he discovered that a close relative, Manfred, had been plotting against him. Alberigo publicly said he forgave Manfred, attributing his foolishness to the impetuousness of youth. Years later Alberigo invited Manfred and his son to dinner. After the main course, Alberigo called out to the servants, "Bring out the fruit," at which point assassins, hidden behind tapestries, rushed forward to cut down Manfred and his son. Such sinners existed for themselves alone, and now Dante has to learn the stern justice of letting them be what they chose.

With these sinners fresh in mind, we come to canto 34 and, at last, meet the great king of this realm: Satan. He who was once the fairest of all creatures is now reduced to this: having the wings of a bat, bloody saliva drooling from the mouths of his three repulsive heads, and his engaging in an absolutely futile attempt to escape. Scholars have pointed out that the three heads of different colors help us see Satan as a parody of the Trinity. Even here, in the heart of hell, the image of God cannot be erased.[2] The archtraitor, who betrayed God, here chomps on three traitors who conformed themselves to his image. But what has always interested me is this: the more energetically Satan exerts himself, the more of a prisoner he becomes. If, somehow, Satan could but momentarily stop the beating of his wings, then perhaps the ice that imprisons him would melt and he could go free. But here he is left entirely to his own choosing. He is left free to seek what his heart desires, and thus his furious rebellion ensures he will forever remain in captivity. Satan is the slave of his freedom.

In a similar way, the traitorous souls continue to choose what their hearts long for, a crooked and treacherous love at the expense of all other members of the human community. When harmed by the pilgrim, they cry out, outraged and offended by the pilgrim's seeming lack of justice (e.g., *Inf.* 32.79); but precisely in crying out for justice, they put on display their striking ignorance of the fact that they themselves had committed the same injustice in life. They still have not learned their lesson. None of the souls seem to note the just irony that to be betrayed is the due reward for those who spent their lives traitorously. But even here, even now, they are allowed their freedom. And with that gift of freedom, they continue to choose their life of treachery, to cling to their isolation from the human community.

Conclusion: Fear in *Inferno*

Imagine that you had the opportunity to sit down and listen to *Inferno* recited in a single performance. By the end of such a performance, you would be completely emotionally exhausted. As the poem unfolded, you would listen with tense expectancy; at times you would shed tears of sympathy; sometimes you would even laugh at a sinner's myopic view of the world. Although *Inferno* does call forth this rich range of responses, the master passion invoked is fear. In an earlier chapter, I pointed out that Dante, very intentionally, asks us to compare his *Comedy* to the pilgrim's ride on the back of Geryon.[3] The poet wants your reading of his poem to feel like his wild flight: full of horror, shock, vertigo, and intensity (*Inf.* 16.127–36). And, for Dante, this is a good thing: "The fear of the LORD is the beginning of wisdom: and the knowledge of the holy is understanding" (Prov. 9:10).

Fear is everywhere in the first canticle: the pilgrim experiences fear in the dark wood (*Inf.* 1.19–21); his fear in *Inferno* 2 almost ends the journey before it had begun (2.49–51); Divine Justice is fearfully proclaimed in the inscription on the portal to hell (3.1–9); and then there are the many instances of what Dante calls the *orribil arte* of Justice (the "horror-provoking art" of punishment; e.g., 14.6). References to fear or internal suffering appear in every single canto, and in some passages Dante goes out of his way to create a nightmarish experience of primal fear, such as in the canti of the barrators (*Inf.* 20–21), where words for "fear" appear seven times.

But what is even more remarkable is that those who failed to fear God in this life still do not fear him in the next, despite being immersed in the horror of his wrath. Capaneus and Vanni Fucci, of course, still rage away at God; Farinata ignores his punishment to complain about politics; Pier thinks his life was a tragedy; Francesca is hardly bothered by the wind; Satan flaps his wings with eager hope of escape. Though the souls who arrive in hell are said to be afraid, they do not fear *God*:

> But those souls, naked and listless,
> lost their color and gnashed their teeth,
> as soon as they comprehended [Charon's] brutal words.
>
> They blasphemed God, their parents,
> the human race, the place, the time, the seed
> of their begetting and their birth.
>
> Then, weeping bitterly, they drew together
> to the cursed shore that waits
> for every man who fears not God. (*Inf.* 3.100–108 [lines 103–8: trans. Hollander])

In other words, they still don't fear God, despite the terrors that surround them.

This is perhaps the most frightening part of Dante's poem: the pilgrim has to watch the human community come undone, return to the chaos of formless matter, like some evil act of uncreation. The souls who are plunged into these terrible conditions seem blind to the fearfulness of their surroundings, as if they are at home in the environs they choose to help create! It is as if God, who still respects their freedom, lets them experiment at being creator gods of their own universes. He lets them create the world they wish to become incarnate in, and the evil universes they do create to dwell in do not frighten them as they should. In this way, we can read each of these horrific scenes as doubly fearful: because of the pain sinners suffer, but also because they would rather suffer in the universe they created for themselves than admit their status as creatures.

It is for this reason that the poet felt the need to create *Inferno*, that poem of power, exposure, and fear. It is a poem so intense that, by its end, we are quite overwhelmed by this vision of sin, almost sickened. We feel its weight, almost to the point of being crushed. But remember what the psalm says: "If I make my bed in hell, behold, thou art there" (Ps. 139:8). At the point that is as far away from light and joy and music as possible, God is there; even if in a twisted parody, he is there; even if the damned are blind to his presence, he is still there. The pilgrim had to go down to the depths, though, because as medieval theologians taught, God's power can only really help those who are so broken that they have come to the point that they admit they need assistance. And so Dante had to burn, blow, and break before moving onto his canticle of hope: *Purgatorio*.

Part 2

PURGATORIO

6

Waiting for God:
An Introduction to *Purgatorio*

Joy in the Midst of Sorrow

From a certain perspective, *Purgatorio* is like *Inferno*: souls in purgatory have to endure forms of suffering as extreme as any inflicted on the unrepentant in hell. At the end of *Purgatorio* 10, for example, the pilgrim sees the proud carrying huge rocks on their backs: "Behold, here they are," says Virgil, "though they come with slow steps" (*Purg.* 10.100). They are pitifully weighed down, so much so that they worry their shaking legs will give way any second. But there is one huge difference between this suffering and what might have been imposed on them in hell: here, in purgatory, these repentant souls suffer *voluntarily*. They give their wills to accepting their condition. And thus they possess hope, even joy, that this suffering is dynamic, transformative, and liberating.

In hell, no soul at any time imagines that it can be delivered from the evil it has chosen. More frightening still, the damned souls don't seem to want to be. They find their wills frozen forever, tightly grasping the misery of being separated from God and of being isolated from the human community. They won't let go; they can't. In purgatory, though, souls are animated by the grace of God; they give up, exhale, and let go of all that hatred and attachment to evil. They even do the unthinkable: they begin to desire the cleansing that comes from purgation. Thus, in the same passage alluded to above, the poet says:

> But, reader, I don't want you to lose your nerve,
> and back off your good intentions, just because you heard
> how God wants the debt to be paid.
>
> Do not dwell upon the nature of the suffering:
> think about what will follow. (*Purg.* 10.106–10)

Thus, if hell is a subhuman nightmare, full of darkness and confusion, like living within a Hieronymous Bosch painting, and if paradise is being drowned in a superhuman exaltation of joy, then purgatory is that state in between. It is the most relatable; it is the most human. By this I mean purgatory is the place of transformation and of hope in the midst of bitterness. Or as Dante puts it,

> O proud Christians! You miserable wretches!
> Your minds are sick. . . .
>
> Don't you see that we are worms,
> though born to become the angelic butterfly? (*Purg.* 10.121–22,
>   124–25)

Dante carefully formed *Purgatorio* so that the poetry parallels this spiritual condition of joy emerging in the midst of sorrow. We find, again and again, little oases of pastoral verse tucked away within the stern narrative of suffering. In *Purgatorio* 7, for example, the Valley of Kings is described as alive with an unearthly brightness that would make even the "fresh emerald, the moment it has been split" (7.75) seem pale. In *Purgatorio* 28, Dante walks into the garden of Eden and sees a stream so clean that the purest on earth now seem to him defiled (28.28–30). Even from the very beginning of *Purgatorio*, we hear notes in a sweet and tranquil key. When the pilgrim first stepped into hell, he endured an emotional breakdown on account of the overwhelming tumult of the screams and lamentations of the "pusillanimous" (*Inf.* 3.22–27). In contrast, at the beginning of *Purgatorio*, we have this:

> Sweet color of oriental sapphire . . .
>
> brought delight to my eyes once more
> as soon as I had left behind that dead air. . . .

> The beautiful planet that makes us strong at love
> was making all the east to smile. . . .
>
> I turned to the right and . . .
> I saw four stars
> never seen before except by the first members of the human race.
>
> The sky seemed to take delight in their flaming. (*Purg.* 1.13–26)

Dante seems to want us to note the radical difference between the Schoenberg-like atonality of his first canticle and the sad but majestic Brahms-like music of *Purgatorio*.

In addition to building these lyrical oases into his landscape of wonders, marvels, and suffering, Dante also gives us glimpses of the inner joy and peace that are beginning to take root in the individual souls of this realm, even while they endure spectacularly ascetic exercises. In *Purgatorio*, then, the poet dramatizes a new set of emotions. All of those tears and instances of crying in hell begin to taper off in *Purgatorio*, while smiling and laughter, almost nonexistent in *Inferno* (*sorridere*, "to smile," is used only once!), become a regular feature of the second canticle (e.g., *Purg.* 1.20; 2.83; 3.12; 12.136; 21.127; 25.103; 28.67, 76). This inner joy that bubbles up and works its way out in laughter or smiling is a perfect symbol for the goal of purgatory: transformation from the inside out. Although it is true that souls must pay off the "debt" of their sins to Divine Justice, Dante, rather brilliantly, reinterprets this scholastic understanding: the debt to be paid, what God is owed, is desire, inner fire, love (*fervor amoris*, or what Dante calls *foco d'amor*; see *Purg.* 6.34–42).

Head Knowledge and Heart Knowledge

For Dante and the medieval tradition, the souls of purgatory are, of course, "saved," forgiven their sins, but they are not yet ready to see God.[1] Their ability to participate in the heavenly community is still limited by the vicious habits they did not devote themselves to reforming in life. Their heads are in the right place, but their "hearts" are not there, or, more accurately in terms of medieval terminology, their *affectus* has not yet been kindled.[2] Closing the gap between head knowledge and heart knowledge, though, is a long, slow, and difficult process, one that will take time and repetition, because purgatorial souls still have with them those negative moral dispositions they spent much of their lives rationalizing.

Dante illustrates the survival of this old mind-set, often humorously, throughout *Purgatorio*. In canto 2, for example, we meet Casella, an old friend of Dante's, who dallied before departing for purgatory. Not surprisingly, he now causes the other souls to put off their serious work of purgation and thus becomes the reason for the excoriating lecture from Cato (*Purg.* 2.120–23). Two canti later, Belacqua is explicitly identified as a soul who has taken up his "customary earthly ways" of laziness (4.126). Among the prideful, Omberto Aldobrandesco, who admits to having loved the nobility of his family too much in life, introduces himself as "the son of a great Tuscan," the son of Guglielmo Aldobrandesco (11.58–59). He then cannot suppress his curiosity about whether the pilgrim has heard of his famous family (11.60). Other examples will be discussed. Suffice it to say that, in the language of medieval monastic speculation on purgatory, these souls are *boni* but yet *imperfecti* (good but not fully formed).

In Dante's day, the acknowledged experts for overcoming this gap between head knowledge and heart knowledge were monastic spiritual writers such as Guigo II, Peter of Celles, John of Fecampe, and Hugh and Richard of St. Victor, in addition to more famous writers such as Bernard of Clairvaux. These spiritual masters specialized in constructing personal exercises (*disciplinae*) that could lead to deep transformation—that is, exercises through which souls became capable over time of not just assenting to truth but also loving it, desiring it, and responding with *affectus*. They were rather like personal trainers for the soul. It is not surprising, then, to find throughout *Purgatorio* a monastic flavor: we find souls fasting, engaging in acts of penance, singing hymns, praying, wearing dark-colored habits (*Purg.* 13.48), submitting their identity to the group, and speaking about heaven as the "cloister" (15.57) where Christ is "abbot" (26.129). They have to follow a liturgical schedule and force their voices into the unison of the monophonic chants that season the canticle. The first time we meet them, they are singing "together with one voice" (2.47).[3] In this way Dante's purgatory very much embodies those "spiritual exercises" that Peter of Celle described in his handbook on how to achieve deep transformation:

The true religious voluntarily and freely desires regular discipline in order to be tied back from the appetites of the flesh. . . . The bonds of religion are . . . silence, fasting, and seclusion of the cloister, ways of acting which do not attract attention, compassion and fraternal love, paternal reverence, reading and persistent prayer, recollection of past evils, fear of death, the fire of purgatory, eternal fire.[4]

The souls within *Purgatorio*, then, who were spiritually flabby in life, must submit themselves to such *disciplinae* in death. And yet, for Dante, each one of these monastic *disciplinae* (that is, silence, fasting, fraternal love, paternal reverence, reading, recollection of past evils, the practice of fear) are all aimed at developing an *interior* spirit of prayerfulness. As *Inferno* is to tears, and *Paradiso* is to dance, *Purgatorio* is to prayer. *Purgatorio* is the canticle of prayer: souls argue about it (*Purg.* 6.28–48), practice it (*Purg.* 11), get better at it, beg for it (6.1–27). For the souls in hell, it is an impossibility (see Francesca's comments in *Inf.* 5.91–93); for the souls in *Purgatorio*, their "only prayer . . . was that others pray" (*Purg.* 6.26).

In light of the centrality of prayer, it is fascinating to note how Dante dramatizes his penitent souls as "stepping into" biblical prayer; purgatory becomes a stage where biblical prayers are enacted and performed. The exercises of the souls are choreographed so that the penitent find themselves in a position where the dead text, the dead letter, the boring doctrine they "knew" on earth now becomes their script for heartfelt expression. For instance, in *Purgatorio* 2 the souls being ferried by the angel across the sea sing, "In exitu Israel . . ." ("When Israel went out of Egypt . . . ," Ps. 114)—that is, the psalm that tells how the Israelites were rescued from Egypt by passing through the Red Sea. But now the relevance of the biblical text for their own lives is impossible to miss, as they, guided by a heavenly minister, cross unharmed the violent sea that consumed even the boldest voyagers (we hear echoes of the voyage of Ulysses here; see *Purg.* 1.130–32). Thus, a psalm that must have seemed a bit of outdated history now becomes vital, fresh, and urgent. Purgatorial souls step into, sing, and perform what was before merely a written text.

In the next canto, Virgil ponders, with head meditatively bowed, which way he and Dante should take to get up the mountain. The Christian pilgrim, though, lifts his head and sees a band of souls coming down from the mountains:

> "Lift up," I said, "your eyes, master!
> Look: here are some who will give us guidance
> if you can't, all by yourself, figure it out." (*Purg.* 3.61–63)

In other words, the pilgrim looks up toward the mountains and is excited to see the help they need to move forward—which is to say, he "enacts" or "performs" another biblical text: "I will lift up my eyes unto the hills, from whence cometh my help" (Ps. 121:1).

In this way, the architecture of purgatory and the spiritual disciplines to which the souls submit combine to create the conditions for prayerfulness. For Dante, prayer is the focal point of all these *disciplinae* because it is that precious state of longing in which the soul, convinced of its own lack of resources and frustrated with its cramped condition, opens up, addresses God as if he were close by, and dwells longingly in his presence. In this state of vulnerability and openness, souls establish a connection with God, and as long as they remain connected in this intense way, they undergo the transformative experience of being made into something like him. Prayer is the opposite of the tight grip of the souls in hell; it is the opening of the gates of the heart, an effort to allow God to come, cleanse, and dwell within. But it's a war to keep the gates of the heart open, to keep open the channel for God's love to flow into the heart; thus the exercises the souls must endure are designed to put them in a state of vulnerability so that they will continue to feel the need to open their hearts yet again. Being convinced of your own brokenness creates longing. Longing is what opens the heart, and openness is the requisite condition for God's transformative dwelling within: prayer.

In this introductory chapter, I have discussed the interior journey of the souls in *Purgatorio*. In the next chapter, I will discuss the physical landscape of the mountain—that is, how Dante took a hodgepodge of teachings from his predecessors and used them to construct a concrete, literary place. I will then show how the opening canti of *Purgatorio* illustrate how Dante's mountain is the ideal place for helping souls accomplish their inward journey.

7

The People outside the Gate: Freedom, Responsibility, and Vulnerability

(*Purgatorio* 1–9)

Purgatory before Dante

Dante didn't invent purgatory, of course. Indeed, throughout the Middle Ages, it was held that after death the soul would have to pass through some sort of trial that would test the depth of its love for Christ. That trial was most often likened to the fire of a crucible, which burns off the dross of gold. This trial was called the *ignis purgatories*—that is, "cleansing" or "purging" fire. Perhaps surprisingly for many, the basic principles of the doctrine of purgatory are found in the Bible. Although there are many verses in the Bible that were taken in the Middle Ages as hinting at purgatorial aspects of the afterlife, one passage in particular was used more than any other:

> Now if any man build upon this foundation gold, silver, precious stones, wood, hay, stubble; Every man's work shall be made manifest: for the day shall declare it, because it shall be revealed by fire; and the fire shall try every man's work of what sort it is. If any man's work abide which he hath built thereupon, he

shall receive a reward. If any man's work shall be burned, he shall suffer loss:
but he himself shall be saved; yet so as by fire. (1 Cor. 3:12–15)

This idea of a man being saved through fire, of having worthless works
burned away, was universally read for the first one thousand years of the
church as referring to some sort of after-death cleansing experience. One
early example of this interpretation comes from the *Shepherd of Hermas*,
written as early as AD 70 and almost included among the books of the
Bible. In this enigmatic work, a shepherd is given a vision of a tower that
is being built of many different stones. The stones that fit into the tower,
he is told by an angel, are the just; the stones rejected, the damned. The
shepherd asks the angel "whether all stones that were rejected . . . have
opportunity for repentance and a place in this tower." The angel replies:
"They have . . . but not until they have been tormented and fulfilled the
days of their sins. And then it will happen that they will be transferred
out of their torments, if the evil deeds that they have done come into their
hearts; but if they do not come into their hearts, they will not be saved,
because of their hardheartedness."[1]

Over the next thousand years, it's fair to say that there was a broad
consensus among the fathers and medieval authors—everyone from Origen
to Augustine to Gregory the Great to Bede to Bernard of Clairvaux—that
after death souls yet imperfect in love would undergo some sort of purgatorial, or cleansing, experience. At the same time, no one was sure about
the details: some said purgatory was a real, physical place; others said it
was only a spiritual place. Some even said that the penitent souls were
actually sent to hell to dwell among the damned until the external fires
had sufficiently purified their inner love. At that point, an angel would
come down to hell to get them out.

With so many undetermined questions, medieval descriptions of the
purgatorial experience written before Dante tend to be terrifying. Some
of these medieval authors let their imaginations run wild. For example,
writing in the early 1100s, Honorius of Autun says that the *imperfecti*
were those who, though saved, endured little pain in life and thus missed
out on opportunities for proving their love. After death, they will be sent
to hell for seven days, or nine days, or a year, or longer. These souls are
"like the wicked son who is turned over to a slave to be whipped," because
"with the permission of the angels, [they are] handed over to demons to be

purged." Honorius then describes the souls' temporary abode: "unbearable heat, biting cold, hunger, thirst, and various kinds of pain, some having physical causes, some having spiritual causes, such as the pain caused by fear or shame." There are also "immortal worms, serpents, and dragons, a frightful stench, frightening noises such as hammers striking iron, thick darkness, . . . the depressing din of wails and insults, and finally shackles of fire that bind the limbs of the damned." Only a little reassuringly, he adds: "But the demons cannot torment them more than they deserve or than the angels permit." Honorius further warns that "the least of these trials is greater than the greatest that one can imagine in this life." Likewise, Jacobus de Voragine (1230–98), whom many know as the author of the *Golden Legend*, says that the just are handed over to be punished by evil demons, although they do enjoy visits from heavenly ministers to cheer them in their suffering.[2]

Within a century, a consensus on the basic doctrines of purgatory had begun to emerge. Thomas Aquinas, though with much less drama, confirmed the basic insights of Honorius and Jacobus: the least pain in purgatory is greater than the worst pain in life. Aquinas even allowed for the possibility that angels could be responsible for bringing souls to purgatory and then fetching them out again, although he denied that the souls of the just are punished at the hands of dark angels. Rather, God is directly responsible for the pain they experience; in the heat of God's love they become clean.[3] These basic developments—that purgatory is a place separate from hell and that it is a personal encounter with God—had huge theological implications, which would take the next century of visionaries, mystics, and pastors to think through. Dante Alighieri was one of the first to give a concrete, literary vision to all these ideas. As we began to see in *Inferno*, Dante's genius is often best found, not so much in what he invented, but in how he used his poetry to render abstract ideas concretely.

This, then, was Dante's first gift to the medieval tradition: to give vivid and palpable expression to these ideas, a kind of literary incarnation of doctrine. Purgatory becomes a mountainous island in the middle of the sea (where we now put Antarctica), located at the antipodes to where he imagined Jerusalem to be. It can only be approached by angelically driven boats, which travel at dazzling speeds (see *Purg.* 1). The mountain is extremely steep, and its entry, a gate guarded by an angel, stands halfway up the mountain (see *Purg.* 9). On the slopes of the lower half of the mountain, the so-called antepurgatory, Dante meets those who held the church in scorn, those who repented late in life, those who died violent deaths, and failed kings. Analogous to the pusillanimous in the narthex of hell, these sinners are not yet allowed within the gate. The seven terraces of purgatory proper follow: the terraces of pride, envy, wrath, sloth, avarice, gluttony, and lust.

As I have said, we admire Dante because he creates such concrete literary worlds, in which abstract systems of thought become incarnate. We also appreciate his exceptional ability to synthesize into one vision the divergent medieval traditions he inherited. Dante's literary imagination gives us a place every bit as painful and severe as that of earlier authors and yet, almost paradoxically, every bit as merciful and hopeful as the mystics later hinted at. In fact, it is Dante's juxtaposition of these divergent elements that gives the opening canti of *Purgatorio* (1–8) such energy. In particular, we will see that Dante's purgatory is, at once, a place (1) of stern justice, where human beings must accept the consequences of their freedom; (2) of radical humility, where souls must learn to reimagine themselves as completely feeble unless supported by God; (3) of shockingly generous mercy (4) where a divisive community is healed; and (5) of desire, where complacency is overcome.

Purgatory as a Place of Justice and Freedom: Lessons from Cato

One of the most haunting passages of *Inferno* is that in which the sinners, newly arrived at the banks of Acheron (the first river of hell), curse their parents, their God, their upbringing, everything but themselves:

> But those souls, naked and listless,
> lost their color and gnashed their teeth,
> as soon as they comprehended [Charon's] brutal words.

> They blasphemed God, their parents,
> the human race, the place, the time, the seed
> of their begetting and their birth. (*Inf.* 3.100–105 [lines 103–5: trans. Hollander])

In fact, throughout *Inferno* sinners (e.g., Francesca, Farinata, Pier, and Ugolino) consistently direct blame at other people; they do not accept their freedom. In contrast to hell, responsibility is the first lesson the pilgrim has to learn in *Purgatorio*: this *is* your fault!

As soon as Dante and Virgil crawl out of the narrow fissure that has led them from hell to purgatory, they meet

> an old man, alone,
> whose visage was so worthy of reverence
> that no son is bound to show more to his father. (*Purg.* 1.31–33)

In fact, this severe old man is so deserving of respect that Virgil has Dante kneel down and bow his head (1.49–51), yet another example of Dante's reverence for antiquity. The bearded old man's face shines with "the rays of those four holy lights" (1.37), and he addresses Dante and Virgil severely, making sure they have not violated the rules for how to approach the island properly (1.40–48); this is Cato the Younger, nephew of the more famous Cato the Elder, the Roman moralist who demanded the destruction of Carthage. Cato the Younger, though, was even more esteemed in the Middle Ages because, in addition to being a famous practitioner of Stoicism, he was held to have written a book of wise maxims, the *Disticha Catonis*, which every schoolboy used to learn Latin grammar.

Although Cato the Younger was admired, Dante's choice to make him the guardian of purgatory would have concerned medieval Christian readers because, in addition to being a pagan, he was also the most important republican opponent to Julius Caesar, an offense that landed other souls, like Brutus and Cassius, in the mouths of Satan (*Inf.* 34). Furthermore, in his struggle against Caesar, Cato committed suicide when he realized his cause was lost. And so, although admired as a man of action and discipline, the pagan hero had a triple handicap: he was not a Christian, he was a suicide, and he was an opponent of the empire. So what is he doing here, not just in the Christian afterlife, but elevated to such a prestigious role of governance? Why do we not, at the very best, find him in limbo?

Virgil's speech to Cato might give us a clue:

> "May his advent be a delight to you:
> he seeks freedom, which is so precious,
> as the one who forfeits his own life for it well knows.
>
> "You know this: to you even death in Utica
> did not seem bitter. There you left
> that garment that will be gloriously bright on the great day." (*Purg.*
> 1.70–75)

The passage alludes to Cato's suicide in Utica, in modern-day Tunisia. Before Cato took his life, though, he ensured that his followers were safe; but the way the ancient Roman poet Lucan described Cato's death must have captivated the Christian Dante. Lucan says that Cato hoped his blood would "redeem all the nations, and [his] death pay the whole penalty" incurred by Rome.[4] It seems that Dante was enchanted by this line, and that he borrowed his portrait of Cato from Lucan. Thus, he gave his own readers a portrait of a man so strictly in tune with justice and the good of his community that he had no regrets or reservations about any harm that could result to himself—as if this man, seeking human perfection, arrived at the point where he saw something even beyond human perfection and thus unwittingly participated in a Christlike sacrifice. Cato is then a picture of courage, of justice, of foresight, and of absolute control over his own will, but he brings his human virtues to such a point of perfection that his own life has become a sacrifice for others, a sacrifice he does not regret.

Through his own dedication to what could be known about God's law through the natural revelation of creation, Cato put himself in the position of one of the faithful from the Old Testament, or as medieval theologians had put it, Cato was the recipient of the gift of "implicit faith." Here's how Thomas Aquinas explains the concept: "Many pagans received a revelation concerning Christ. . . . If, however, some were saved without such a revelation, they were not saved without faith in the Savior: for, although they did not have explicit faith, they nevertheless had implicit faith in divine providence, believing God to be the liberator of humankind in ways He would choose according to his pleasure" (*Summa theologiae* II-II, q. 2, a. 7).[5] So, in contrast to the Christian suicide Pier della Vigna, who could only think of his own ruined reputation and gave up when he could see no other way out, Cato had trust that his life meant something within the grander picture and that God would sort out the details if he did his own part. He is, then, a fitting guardian of this most human realm of justice, responsibility, freedom, and trust in providence.

We should also note Cato's command to Virgil:

> "Go and do this: gird him [that is, the pilgrim] round
> with a straight reed. Wash his face for him,
> so you remove all the stain from it.

> "It would not be fitting—with his sight still dimmed
> by any mist—to move forward to meet the first of the
> ministers from paradise.
>
> "This little island, all the way down to its lowest reach,
> there where the waves beat down on it,
> brings up reeds out of the soft mud.
>
> "No other plant that puts out leaves
> or takes on a hard stem is able to retain its life,
> because it cannot sway with the battering waves." (*Purg.* 1.94–105)

Dante then must go and bind himself with the flexible reed—the only plant that can grow in the slimy mud and in the shallow waters around the island, because it is the only plant pliant enough to flow and move with the waters as they roll in and out. Every other plant gets hard and rots. At the same time, the reed is a biblical plant. Isaiah, for example, had said that "a bruised reed shall he not break" (Isa. 42:3), a verse that the Gospel of Matthew interprets as applying to the humble, quiet ministry of Christ (Matt. 12:20).

We also have a classical literary allusion: when Aeneas is preparing to visit the underworld, to receive the last advice from his now deceased father, Anchises, he is told that he must first go into a forest and find a magical tree branch made of gold (the Golden Bough). The Sybil explains this strange ritual:

> Hidden in a dark tree
> is a golden bough, golden in leaves and pliant stem,
> sacred to Persephone . . . all the groves
> shroud it, and shadows enclose the secret valleys.
> But only one who's taken a gold-leaved fruit from the tree
> is allowed to enter earth's hidden places. (*Aen.* 6.36–41)

Aeneas does find the Golden Bough, and the tree, magically and instantaneously, sprouts another golden bough to replace the first as soon as Aeneas cuts it off. Similarly, Virgil, after cleaning Dante's tear-stained cheeks, girds the pilgrim with this reed of humility, using it to bind his cloak about him in the manner of a contemporary Franciscan mendicant. Then the poet notes,

> And O! Miracle! The humble plant, just like the one he chose,
> was reborn, at once,
> in the very spot where he had plucked it. (*Purg.* 1.134–36)

Dante's passage is clearly meant to invoke a comparison with Virgil's Golden Bough. Both the bough and the reed are needed as tokens, keys to gain entry into the mysteries of the afterlife, but the difference between these tokens of entry forces us to reflect on how different the pagan afterlife is from the Christian, and how different the guardians of these realms are: one ruler, Persephone, desires the enchanted branch of gold; the other, Cato, wants a contrite heart and spiritual flexibility. In Dante, it's not enough to be a virtuous, stouthearted, Aeneas-like hero; you have to seek things even higher than the human, and so you must stoop low in search of the divine grace to do so. In *Purgatorio*, Dante begins his own epic quest with a lowly scene of washing, a kind of public confession of interior emptiness, an act of radical humility as preparation for the ultimate gift. And it is *Cato*, that failed hero from antiquity, who teaches the Christian hero how to enter this realm! We must act with justice. We must acknowledge and live under the weight of our freedom, but we also need a radical sense of the fragility of our own projects. Thus, in some ways, Cato's very failure in his struggle for justice was an indispensable lesson that renders him a suitable guardian of purgatory.

Sordello Teaches Virgil a Lesson: Radical Humility in Christian Purgatory

Already in canto 1, the figure of Cato (a self-sacrificing hero, a master of discipline, and a failure) provides a complicated lesson on the virtues needed to be successful in this realm. Paradoxically, purgatory is a place of extreme effort, sweat, responsibility, and self-control and, at the same time, a place of radical humility, radical openness to the gift of being. The laws of purgatory are crafted to provide those hardworking souls with the constant reminder of how they are completely feeble without the assistance of God and without the assistance of their neighbor. With their weakness constantly fresh on their minds, they are put, almost for the first time, in a position where they can appreciate that even their own power of choice, their freedom, is a gift. This is a hard lesson for old, magnanimous Virgil to learn.

In *Inferno* 8–9, the Roman poet, shut out of Dis, is enraged that such base and vile demons would dare to oppose him, the noble guide appointed to oversee this mission of light and justice. But here in purgatory,

Virgil will have many more such encounters with his own limitations. For instance, in *Purgatorio* 6, Virgil and Dante meet a minor medieval poet, Sordello, who is delighted to learn that the man who stands before him is not just a fellow countryman (they were both from Lombardy) but an ancient celebrity: "O glory of the Latins . . . through whom / our language showed what it was capable of, / O eternal honor of the land whence I come," he rhapsodizes (*Purg.* 7.16–18). But interestingly, Sordello, a vastly inferior talent to Virgil, becomes the instructor of the great teacher in a moment that shows how Virgil is increasingly out of place in the midst of this Christian world of humility. Virgil notes that it's getting late, and he expresses a desire to get some more miles in before it gets too dark. At this point Sordello shocks the ancient poet, informing him that here no one can climb at night:

> "How is that? . . . If someone wants
> to ascend at night, would he be impeded
> by someone, or would it be that he was not able?" (*Purg.* 7.49–51)

Virgil, the self-reliant figure of virtue and discipline, can't imagine why you might not want to get a bit of work done in the evening as well. This is the response he gets:

> And the good Sordello rubbed his finger on the ground,
> saying: "You see? This very line
> you would not cross after the sun's parting,
>
> "not because something prevented the ascent;
> no, nothing other than the darkness of the night.
> It binds the will in helplessness." (*Purg.* 7.52–57)

To that, Virgil stands *quasi ammirando*, as if in bewildered amazement (7.61). In purgatory, the very laws of the place are designed to reinforce the experience of your powerlessness. If the light is not shining, if a soul is not filled with that energy that comes from the sun, then it cannot even move; its very legs and arms have to be energized from an outside source. In this extraordinary way, the souls are reminded that what they often took for granted—their health, intelligence, strength, even their power of choice—is something they had very little control over. Their lives are a radical gift from another.

This lesson of humility is reinforced another time, in the Valley of the Kings, the beautiful vale into which Sordello leads Dante and Virgil. Here a group of failed medieval kings, who spent their treasuries fighting one another on earth, are made to dwell for a time in the same valley, in peace. They also are made to pray together, in unison (*Purg.* 8.10–18).

In fact, Dante mentions nine flawed kings and princes, all of whom died between 1274 and 1292—that is, the kings who reigned and fought when Dante was a boy. Keep in mind that the children and grandchildren of these aristocrats and royalty were still alive in Dante's day! But the fiery Florentine, who has now assumed the untiring voice of the prophet, pulls no punches. The pilgrim sees Emperor Rudolph of Austria, who fought a war to secure his throne but entirely neglected Italy and thus lost the opportunity to spare Italy the divisive problems to come, and he sees King Ottocar, who was killed by Emperor Rudolph in battle. Thus, enemies are united in the valley of peace. There is also Pedro III, king of Aragon, and Charles I of Anjou, who in life were also enemies, fighting over succession to the Sicilian throne. Indeed, throughout these canti, Dante convicts these kings as guilty of what I call the "trust-fund phenomenon"—that is, the phenomenon in which the generation that receives everything falls off from the older one. Dante says the children of royalty hang like rotting fruit on the withering branches of the family tree because the heirs do not seek the nobility of the heart of their fathers: "Rarely does human nobility rise up through the branches" (*Purg.* 7.121).

But the primary *disciplina* Dante's kings have to undergo is a peculiarly humility-enforcing exercise: long before they are admitted to purgatory proper, they have to make atonement for misusing their positions of wealth and political office. Toward nightfall every evening, they turn to face the east and chant "Te Lucis" (the liturgical hymn of praise used on solemn occasions). Then they all turn pale in nervous anticipation, because each night a serpent comes silently into this garden from some unexpected direction. Sordello explains that each night two angels are sent from the bosom of Mary to guard the valley from this serpent. This comes as startling news to the pilgrim:

> And so I—unaware of what path—
> turned around, and then I drew near,
> now cold with fear, to the trusted shoulders [that is, Virgil]. (*Purg.*
>   8.40–42)

The serpent, then, slips into this garden, but soon after this, while the kings are praying, the angels chase it off. Every night these failed kings have to endure, even participate in, this performance, like one of those plays in which the actors leave the stage and mingle with the audience. In life the failed kings, spiritual trust-fund babies, took up their inherited duties but without true nobility of heart. They were not alert to the constant and insidious threat of the serpent slinking back into the garden. They ought to have been vigilant for their people, vigilant over their households, vigilant over their hearts, but they took up their office and their wealth as if they were their possessions to dispose of as they wished. Here in purgatory they have to get used to thinking about their vulnerability and fragility—their need to stand in spiritual vigilance.

In Dante's purgatory, souls have to recognize their own powerlessness, and yet, at the same time, this is not a passive place, like some spiritual operating room where you go under and the surgeon repairs you while you sleep. Rather, Dante has made a purgatory that demands absolute activity, tremendous expenditures of sweat and energy, and the realization that the very power to be reformed lies outside your soul. Humility is openness to the radical gift of another.

Surprising Abundance of Mercy

One of the most beautiful aspects of Dante's *Purgatorio* is how easy it is to come by mercy, because he who offers it is so quick to pour it forth. It would be as if a soul suffering from thirst in a desert begged for a tiny bit of water squeezed from a medicine dropper and got a barrelful dumped on it instead. In *Purgatorio*, mercy is "under pressure," waiting to irrupt into the world. This is most clearly portrayed in the pilgrim's encounter with Manfred (*Purg.* 3) and Buonconte da Montefeltro (*Purg.* 5).

Manfred was the illegitimate son of Emperor Frederick II, whom we met among the heretics (*Inf.* 10). In Dante's mind, Frederick II, in his struggle with the medieval papacy, attempted to wrest power from the church and, in doing so, went beyond politics to set himself up as an alternative to the church, thus creating a false dichotomy between the temporal and the spiritual. Manfred continued his father's political campaign, moving ever farther north from Sicily and southern Italy in a slow attempt to conquer the entirety of the Italian peninsula. His advance was stopped by a joint papal and French force at the Battle of Benevento in 1266.

The important point for us is that Manfred's inclusion among the saved would have shocked many of Dante's first readers, especially the papal-supporting, republican, middle-class *nouveau riches* of Guelph Florence. It would be a little bit like if you told Democrats that you had had a vision of the afterlife, and George Bush and Donald Trump were there in bliss; or if you included Barack Obama and Hillary Clinton in a book intended for a Republican readership. "*Manfred*?" Dante's Florentine readers would have asked. The warmongering son of a heretic who tried to divest the church of its property? Dante does, of course, make Manfred admit that "horrible were my sins" (*Purg.* 3.121). It is also true that he is here in ante-purgatory because he spent most of his life holding the church and her sacraments in contempt. In Dante's purgatory, the rule is that for every year a soul held the church in contempt—that is, every year it thought that it did not need the help of "institutionalized religion"—it has to wait for thirty years in antepurgatory even before it is allowed through the gate.

And yet this unlikely soul did get into purgatory, seemingly at the ab-solute last moment. After he was sliced by two deadly blows, he tells us, wounds he still bears in purgatory, he had just enough blood in his body to turn "in tears to Him who freely pardons" (*Purg.* 3.120). But we should note another interesting narrative detail: Manfred, when he introduces himself to Dante, does not describe himself as you would expect a medieval leader to do—that is, according to his father's line, as the son of a powerful emperor, Frederick II—but rather he introduces himself as the grandson of Empress Constance, as if in seeking his true, spiritual inheritance he had to skip a generation and seek out a female relative, a grandmother, for his true lineage. In the light of eternity, Manfred is forced to reenvi-sion his life and find that the inheritance he truly received was not what he would have reckoned important in his earthly life.

Just two canti later, we meet another soul who died a violent death. This time, though, the soul had not held "institutionalized religion" in contempt, like Manfred, but rather he had put off repenting until the ab-solute last second. The soul is that of Buonconte da Montefeltro, the son of Guido da Montefeltro (whom we met in *Inferno* 27), the false counselor turned Franciscan who went back to the game just one last time, thereby sealing his fate in hell. You will remember that although the father, Guido, thought he was in the fold, a demon came to drag him down to hell at his death because he had not actually been repentant for his final evil deed (*Inf.* 27.118–20). His son, Buonconte, continued in the ways of his father: he too was a good general. But in his final battle, fate caught up with him; he was wounded in the throat, and as he wandered across the field, barely able to speak, he had just enough breath to whisper "Maria" (i.e., the Blessed Virgin) before he fell to the ground.

Dante, then, gives us a man of violence and blood who spent his whole life campaigning, delighting in the destruction of his enemies. You would think that for such a bloody life a trip straight to hell would be within the order of justice. But in *Purgatorio*, mercy is surprisingly abundant; you ask for a drop and get a shower. And so Dante depicts this miniscule act of true piety—a whispered "Maria"—as sufficient to win for this soul an eternity in bliss. And thus Buonconte's death plays out just the opposite from how his father's did. Guido, confident that he had covered his bases, goes to hell; Buonconte, even if only in a single instant, makes one sincere expression of his need for help and will ultimately enter into heaven. Buonconte relates that when the demon came to claim his rightful property—that is, Buonconte's soul—the dark angel was surprised and enraged to find that Buonconte would not be his property. Rather, the soul of Buonconte is snatched up by God's angel. The demon, in disbelief and with contempt, asks the angel, "You carry off with you the eternal part of him / because of a tiny tear [*una lagrimetta*]?" (*Purg.* 5.106–7). But the answer, of course, is *yes*. A little tear finds an ocean of mercy in reply.

Healing the Divisive Human Community

Purgatory, then, is the explosive place where a soul's vision of the world is restored, where one comes to see that God's mercy was very near, just under the surface, throughout one's life. But it is also a place where the soul has to be restored to a harmonious position within the human community. Souls in hell, in the pursuit of the goods of the world, were willing to break from communion with the human community to get those things; they wanted their political office so badly that they were willing to cheat on campaign laws, or wanted victory so badly on the battlefield that they were willing to use evil engines of war to destroy the gullible. The souls in purgatory sincerely renounced, even if at the very last minute, their desire to operate within this divisive system. And yet they still have to be brought back into the human community, still have to learn how to work in a nonindividualistic way—a task that is easier said than done! When you've spent your life calculating how to win friends and manipulate people, or strategically planning how to get ahead, or how to start a lucrative business despite the fact that it makes a worthless product, then it's hard to submit your will to a group and truly love their good. The souls in purgatory spent their whole lives doing the opposite. In Dante's purgatory, as we will see, souls have to lean on one another for support, chant prayers in perfect harmony with those who surround them, and rely on one another for the support of prayer.

This reintegration back into the human community is dramatized vividly among the people outside the gate, where they have to wait until those back on earth—the very souls they meant to utilize for their profit in life—pray for them. The souls in *Purgatorio* 5, for example, almost trample one another to get to the pilgrim when they discover he is still alive:

> I have not seen stars shoot
> through a placid sky at nightfall,
> nor bursts of lightning, when the sun is hot, move so quickly
>
> as these [messengers] returned upward—in no time!
> When they got there, they turned back around toward us with all the
>   others,
> like a flock that is dispersed without order. (*Purg.* 5.37–42)

The laws of the place dictate that you either have to wait the allotted time that counterbalances your delayed repentance, or have your time of waiting lessened on account of being the beneficiary of the sincere prayers of those on earth. Thus, in purgatory, the fact that souls can have mercy won for them helps condition them to love the human community again, because they are now dependent on its members.

My favorite example of such reintegration comes from a later passage. In canto 13, a Sienese aristocrat, Sapia, confesses that she spent her whole life envying the success of those around her. And she too would have had to spend a lot of time in the prepurgatorial realm of waiting, given her delayed repentance. But then she found surprising and unsolicited help:

> "Peace: I desired peace with God only at the very end
> of my life; and nor would my debt
> have been reduced through penance
>
> "if it had not been that that man held me in his devout memory:
> Peter the combseller, in his holy prayers!
> He sorrowed for me, in his charity." (*Purg.* 13.124–29)

Extraordinary lines! Peter the combseller, the equivalent of the immigrant street vendor, prayed for *her*! A man whom the moneyed, aristocratic Sapia would have had nothing but contempt for in life becomes a soul with whom she now has a spiritual bond. Through his prayer for her, he has become someone she spiritually leans on. Through such acts of love, the human community, divisive on earth, is slowly knit back together.

Overcoming Complacency

Finally, purgatory is a place of desire, a place where complacency must be overcome. Here in antepurgatory, those lackadaisical souls who stood up God in life now have to wait, to feel the time tick by, to grow impatient and frustrated and almost beside themselves, until there is such an over-whelming desire to just start their purgation that they are, at last, ready to begin. One of Dante's most beloved authors, Richard of St. Victor, said desire—what he even called a "violent desire"—plays a crucial role in the spiritual life. God doesn't give us what we don't want, and thus a holy, burning, passionate desire is a prerequisite for the spiritual life.[6] Similarly, in canto 2 we hear Cato upbraid the souls for standing around. He shouts at them in fury, "Correte al monte!" ("Run you sluggish souls, toward the mountain!" *Purg.* 2.122). Overcoming complacency is also a theme in canto 4, where Dante and Virgil see the lazy soul of Belacqua resting in the shade. Dante points him out to Virgil:

> "O my dear lord," I said, "lay your eyes on that one
> who looks more negligent
> than if laziness were his sister."
>
> He then turned toward us and paid us heed,
> lifting his face just higher than his thighs,
> and said: "You go on up, if you're so strong." (*Purg.* 4.109–14)

It is then that Dante recognizes an old friend from Florence:

> His lazy actions and his curt words
> moved my lips a little into a smile.
> I then began: "Belacqua? I see I don't have to sorrow
>
> "for you any longer; but why are you just
> seated here? Are you waiting for a guide,
> or is it just that you've taken up your old ways?"
>
> And he: "O brother, going up? What's the point,
> since he wouldn't let me enter into suffering—
> the angel of God who is seated up there at the gate.
>
> "No. It is first required that the heavens wheel around me,
> as I sit here outside, as long as I took in life,
> delaying righteous sighs until the very end.
>
> "That is, unless some prayer helps me first,
> that rises up from a heart that lives in grace." (*Purg.* 4.121–34)

It is clear that Belacqua will be here a *long* time. He has not yet been touched by that holy impatience, that keen desire to get his soul ready to see God.

But there is one other note to add on Belacqua. When Dante the pilgrim arrives at the gate of purgatory, the angel tells him that Peter has entrusted the keys of this place to him, with these instructions: "It is from Peter that I have them; and he told me that I should err / in opening rather than in keeping it locked / if people should cast themselves to the ground at my feet" (*Purg.* 9.127–29). It is only in light of the angel's commission that we notice how limited Belacqua's understanding of purgatory is. Belacqua had asked the pilgrim, rather dejectedly, "Going up? What's the point?" But from the vantage of the gate, we realize that if Belacqua's desire were greater, it would find its fulfillment. The only thing regulating his ascent, then, is his own lack of desire. If he but requested a drop of water!

8

In Search of Deep Cleansing: The Middle Canti

(*Purgatorio* 10–24)

At the Center of the Universe: Love and Freedom

As Dante will explain in canto 17, purgatory, just like hell, has its own elaborate moral architecture. In *Inferno* 11, Virgil and Dante came to a halt while they waited for their senses to get adjusted to the stench of hell. There the Roman poet described hell as divided into three major realms: the incontinent, the violent, and the fraudulent. In *Purgatorio* 17, Virgil explains the architecture of purgatory, and every detail of the design is related to love (*Purg.* 17.103–5). We can misdirect our inherent love by loving with too little force; we can love lower goods too much, trying to put them to uses they were not intended for; or our self-love can grow to the point that it is out of control, so that it becomes fear that our neighbor will deprive us of the good we long for (17.94–117). In hell the architecture is indebted to a classical way of thinking about good and evil (explicitly borrowed from Aristotle), but in *Purgatorio* Dante uses the seven terraces to embody the Christian monastic tradition of the seven deadly sins.[1] And yet, at the same time, Dante creatively rethinks the seven deadly sins in order to bring them into harmony with the classical structure: lust, gluttony, and avarice are treated as dispositions that correspond to the incontinent sins of upper hell; sloth and wrath (the misuse of the irascible appetites) are linked to the circle of the violent in hell; while pride and envy are treated as faulty dispositions of the intellect, equivalent to sinful use of the intellect among the fraudulent in hell.[2]

Virgil's speech on how love comes right at the center of the cosmos happens to be at the center of the *Comedy*: the fifty-first canto—that is, the first canto of the second half. Meanwhile, *Purgatorio* 16, Marco Lombardo's speech on freedom, could be considered the last canto of the first half of the *Comedy*. Thus, these canti, which literally lie at the heart of the *Comedy* as a whole, together form a kind of diptych: love and the free response to love are at the heart of the universe. We have a love that irrupts, rushes into, invades, and courses through the world, enticing and persuading human beings to use their freedom to respond to it. This is the drama of human existence.

It is in light of this passionate vision of love—seeking an entry point into the human heart—that we will now turn to the middle canti of *Purgatorio*, which deal with the seven terraces of purgatory, and how the souls here correct their sinful disposition in an attempt to regain the power to respond to love.

The Prideful Learn to Pray (*Purgatorio* 10–12)

When the pilgrim finally gets his first glimpse of souls in purgatory proper, he is horrified and worried that reporting their suffering will actively discourage future readers of the poem:

> And yet, reader, I don't want you to lose your nerve,
> and back off your good intentions, just because you heard
> how God wants the debt to be paid. (*Purg.* 10.106–8)

The pilgrim sees the proud walking around and around the terrace, carrying such enormous rocks on their backs that their faces, bowed down under the extreme weight, are just millimeters above the earth. In this way, the backs of the proud are broken. With each trembling step, they fear their legs are just about to give out under their burden. And so, with each step, they cry out, "Più non posso" ("More I cannot," 10.139). Their words are a painful confession that they are nearly broken. And yet, even in the midst of their pain, there emerges a kind of deep recognition: I myself am not able to do this anymore; nevertheless, somehow I find that I continue moving forward. It is as if the words become not so much a cry of despair ("I can't handle any more of this!") as an acknowledgment that it is not *I* who am mounting the strength to continue ("I, alone, am not able"). Carrying the rocks is a tremendous spiritual exercise for the proud; it leads them to realize that they are fueled by the power of another.

In canto 12 we learn that as they painfully inch along, faces hovering just above the ground, the prideful are made to look at images carved into their path. There they see a dozen famous images of pride—for example, Nimrod, the legendary king responsible for the Tower of Babel; Niobe, the mythological figure who boasted she had more children than the goddess Leto; Saul and Sennacherib—and they see the destruction of the proud city of Troy (*Purg.* 12.34–66). In the Middle Ages, everyone knew these stories. They were used by preachers in sermons, mentioned in scholarly commentaries, reworked by poets in popular verse, or performed in vernacular drama. But the prideful here are forced to read these well-known stories with an attentiveness they had never directed toward these texts before; they read them as if for the first time. The pain of their movements, their own painfully keen consciousness of the littleness of their strength—"Più non posso" (10.139)—sets the context for appreciating their own share in the insolence of man, who forgets that he is supported by another and attempts to rise above the station appointed to him.

These souls do not just undergo this "passive" suffering, though. Rather, through their reading and purgative exercise, they are filled with such a strong desire for transformation, with such a strong desire to be liberated from who they are, that their hearts overflow in prayer:

> "O our Father, you who reside in the heavens,
> not as one limited, but because of the greater love
> you have for those first effects there on high:
>
> "praised be your name and your power
> by every creature, given that it is fitting
> to render thanks for your sweet breath.
>
> "May the peace of your kingdom come to us,
> for if it doesn't come toward us, we are impotent by ourselves,
> even if we try with all of the strength of our intellect.
>
> . . . .

> "Give to us today the daily manna
> without which he who grows weary in going forward
> goes backward through this dry desert.
>
> . . . .
>
> "This, our virtue that is overcome so easily,
> don't put it to the test by the ancient adversary,
> but deliver us from him who goads it [to evil].
>
> "This last prayer, dear Lord,
> is now not offered for ourselves, for whom there is no need,
> but for those who remain behind us." (*Purg.* 11.1–9, 13–15, 19–24)

This is, of course, the Lord's Prayer, but with important variations. For Dante's audience, this passage of the poem would have been astounding, because it was in the vernacular, not in Latin; thus, his audience would have had the strange experience of hearing a familiar text breaking through in the unfamiliar and "homely" language of everyday speech. When we look closer, we realize that Dante has not translated the prayer word for word; rather, his souls perform a kind of spontaneous rewriting of the biblical and liturgical prayer. The forty-nine words of the Latin prayer become the Italian prayer of more than 160 words, as if in the vernacular the Latin prayer releases its potential energy, like the uncoiling of a compressed spring. The "Our Father which art in heaven" becomes three whole verses (*Purg.* 11.1–3), emphasizing God's transcendence; the "hallowed be thy name" is amplified into "praised be your name and your power / by every creature, given that it is fitting / to render thanks for your sweet breath" (11.4–6), lines replete with echoes of Saint Francis's "Canticle of Brother Sun."[3] "Thy kingdom come" becomes "May the peace of your kingdom come to us, / for if it doesn't come toward us, we are impotent by ourselves, / even if we try with all of the strength of our intellect" (11.7–9), which particularly emphasizes the complete impotence of the prideful to get to the kingdom on their own. Finally, the phrase "deliver us from evil" must become a prayer not "for ourselves, for whom there is no need, / but for those who remain behind us" (11.23–24), because the prideful spent too much time on earth using first-person pronouns. In other words, the old, tired prayer now becomes fresh, custom-tailored to their particular measure.

The British scholar Matthew Treherne has commented on this prayer by referencing David Ford's understanding of the "moods of theology," by which he means not emotional moods but grammatical moods. Those who have studied Latin remember learning all those pesky endings for verbs. There are endings for indicative verbs (that is, the mood in which we simply assert and say what is: "The sun is shining brightly"). There are endings for verbs of command and ordering, the so-called imperative mood: "Run to the mountains," as Cato says. There are the moods of the subjunctive—that is, verbs used for tentative and exploratory statements. The subjunctive can also be used as a "hortatory"—that is, a verb of exhortation, the expression of desire that something *be* the case, which is not yet. Ford and Treherne point out that most of the time we conduct theology in the indicative and imperative moods. That is, we say, "God is like this"; "his law is like this"; therefore, "act this way." These are not wrong, of course, but what is fascinating and exciting about the *Comedy* is that, as it progresses, it increasingly adds these layers of complexity. And so here, in canto 11 of *Purgatorio*, we find theology beginning to move into a subjunctive or optative mood, a mood of longing, expressing from the depths of the heart a desire that something be the case. The souls express a desire that they step into that reality that they had believed in their heads but had not gripped with their hearts. Dante's language becomes performative; that is, it does not just describe a reality but tries to speak it into existence through the utterance of a new prayer.[4]

Sapia's Evil Eyes (*Purgatorio* 13)

When the pilgrim climbs up onto the next terrace, he sees the souls of the envious and is struck with pity:

> I do not think there is a man who walks the earth in our day
> who is so hard that he would not be pricked
> by compassion at what I saw then:
> . . . .
>
> [Souls] appeared to me covered in rough sackcloth,
> and each one bore up another with his shoulder,
> and all of them were supported by the bank of rock.
>
> Just as the blind, who lack sustenance,
> stand at pardons to ask for their needs,
> and one lowers his head onto another . . .
> . . . .

an iron wire punctures the eyelids of all
and sews them shut. (*Purg.* 13.52–54, 58–63, 70–71)

Here are the envious: their eyes are sewn shut by metal wire. Blind, they are forced to lean on one another's shoulders. Their neighbors, whose good they envied, have now become the only way they don't fall down. Without their neighbors, they have no support. In this way, the envious are made to feel their radical weakness, and then they are given one another to help them bear it. They are sustained by those human beings they had treated as competitors in life.

In canto 13, the pilgrim will speak to a woman whom we have already mentioned: the Sienese aristocrat Sapia. According to Dante's imaginative version of her life, Sapia is here now because she was envious of her own well-born relations: so much so that one day, looking out of a tower and seeing her family members destroyed on the battlefield, her heart flared up with joy to see her competition—those who had always got the better portion, those who had been written into her uncle's will—brought low.

Envy is an extraordinary passion. In its essence it is, as medieval theologians put it, "the displeasure at another's good." Envy is that secret voice in the heart that, when your friend calls you and tells you about his job promotion, whispers with quiet discontent. Or envy is that voice that murmurs when your old classmate from high school shows up and looks far better than you do. Envy is the first, untamed response of the heart, which would, if allowed to do so, take the good thing it finds out of existence. In your heart of hearts, if asked on your first impulse, you would rather obliterate a good rather than let it shine as something unpossessed by you.

It's somewhat humorous to note, then, that Sapia, even in the afterlife, is still in the process of being cleansed of this vice. We detect a note of envy at the end of her speech to the pilgrim: "But you? Who are you that goes about asking after our conditions / bearing eyes that are not sewn?" (*Purg.* 13.130–31). She's not perfect, but she's on her way. We see an interior joy beginning to well up within. When Dante asks the group of souls if any among them is Italian, Sapia replies:

"O my brother, each is a citizen
of the one true city; but what you mean to say is,
'who lived in Italy as a pilgrim.'" (*Purg.* 13.94–96)

You can imagine meeting people who lived thousands of years ago within boundaries that no longer exist. Those places would seem so puny and insignificant after the centuries. The souls in hell, though, are fixed and frozen in those outdated things. In contrast, we see here that Sapia has begun to view life *sub specie aeternitatis*, in the light of eternity; to look at those things that were so important for an envious person—what precisely belongs to whom and when and how—in a new light. Sapia is beginning to love as a member of the human community.

Marco Lombardo's Wrath and Human Freedom (*Purgatorio* 16)

On the ledge where the wrathful are purified, the souls chant the "Agnus Dei" (the liturgical prayer that begins "Lamb of God . . .") while progressing through thick smoke, like that fatty smoke that comes off the grill. The smoke stings, and so they have to keep their eyes tightly shut against it. Here Dante meets an old courtier who lived in what Dante would have thought of as the "good old days," about a century before he wrote. This courtier, Marco Lombardo, is portrayed as the perfect knight, chivalrous, commanding, brave: "[I] knew the world, and I loved that valor / but men of our day have relaxed the bow" (*Purg.* 16.47–48). Not surprisingly, the pilgrim takes the opportunity to ask Marco his favorite question: why the "world is such a wasteland / of every virtue . . . / and weighed down by malice, covered by it" (16.58–60). To which Marco heaves a heavy sigh and replies:

> "You who live today assign every cause
> to the heavens alone, as though they drew
> everything along with themselves through strict necessity.
>
> "But this would obliterate in you your free will, if it were so,
> and there would be no justice in taking
> delight for good and suffering sorrow for evil.
>
> "The heavens initiate your movements,
> not all of them, but even if I had said that,
> a light has been given you for good and for malice,
>
> "as well as freedom of the will." (*Purg.* 16.67–76)

In other words, Marco Lombardo attacks those who would blame the evil of the world on environmental factors: we might say neuroscience, psychology, or mental illness, while Dante's contemporaries would have said the influence of the heavenly bodies on our dispositions and temperaments—in other words, astrology. While admitting that environmental circumstances do shape our inclinations, Marco insists they cannot account for everything, otherwise human beings would be left guiltless for their faults and undeserving of reward for their virtuous choices. Purgatory is a place of personal responsibility. This *is* your fault. Marco then goes on to explain how it is that the soul abuses its freedom, and to do so he likens the soul to a capricious little girl (*Purg.* 16.85–93). Dante's vision of the soul, then, is delightfully free of any oppressive, puritanical vision of its latent evil. Rather, the soul is pulled toward goods, like a little girl of seven who is delighted by wildflowers along the way and digresses to skip out toward them. But the appetite, if not managed by reason, will keep skipping along after *this* and then *that* and eventually lose itself, having strayed from the path. Sin, then, is getting distracted by a minor good, exalting it, and looking to it for something that it is too shallow to possess fully. Marco concludes his speech by saying that if the law and just rulers do not come to the aid of their communities by holding the reins, then simple souls will keep chasing after their own desires and stray from the path; the world will devolve into the chaotic and broken democracy of pleasure it has become.[5]

We pointed out above that, in the midst of this dark smoke, the souls are singing the "Agnus Dei," the part of the liturgy that repeats, "Lamb of God, you who take away the sins of the world, have *mercy* on us." As they sing, Dante adds, "there was one word for all, and one mode / so that it seemed full harmony dwelt among them" (*Purg.* 16.20–21). Those who were wrathful, who had a tendency to divide the world into neat little categories of "us" and "them," to identify groups of people as their enemies, are now made to rejoin the human community—in harmony. Whereas in life they prayed and longed almost exclusively for justice and vengeance, they now are made to pray for mercy.

It might come as a bit of a surprise, then, that in the midst of these souls singing for mercy, Marco Lombardo delivers an angry rant on how evil the world has grown. He says that there are only three righteous men left in the world, and that even these just men long for death because they are surrounded by a corrupt world (*Purg.* 16.121–26). He says that the Church of Rome has befouled herself and stumbled into the mud, making herself filthy. What's going on? Is Marco still displaying his disposition to wrath?

For Dante and medieval moral theologians, anger is not a sin. To be sure, anger *can* far too easily become sinful, but this happens only when it transgresses its appropriate boundaries. In fact, for Dante and for Aquinas, it is possible to sin by not being angry enough! Fundamentally, anger is the desire for revenge; thus, it is possible to have just anger and to possess the appropriate passion that injustice be corrected. At the same time, the medieval masters knew that it's almost impossible for anger not to slip into sinful anger. In fact, Aquinas, following an earlier monastic tradition, says that anger has "six daughters"; that is, anger can give birth to various sinful offspring, such as quarreling (the propensity to start a fight because you are mad about something else) and contempt (anger that goes beyond an offense at an injustice and leads the angered soul to hate the person absolutely). Aquinas also mentions a cancerous form of anger, what he calls "swelling of the mind," which is an obsessive fixation of anger, an inability to think about anything else. Thus, for Dante as for Aquinas, sinful anger—wrath—is a metastasis of a legitimate desire for justice.[6]

All of this helps us understand the *contrapasso* in canto 16. The souls have to dwell within the smoke and yet remain unharmed by it—that is, keep their vision from being clouded, even while desiring that justice be enacted. They are obligated to remain within very strict boundaries—that is, to dwell within the stinging smoke, without leaving it. Marco Lombardo agrees to walk with the pilgrim, but only "as far as is permitted" (*Purg.* 16.34). In other words, the souls here are instructed in how to hate the evils of the world, while hating within the appropriate boundaries of reason. What a tall order! To be angry, without sinning! It seems almost impossible to be able to do this on your own.

Materialism and Depression: On Sloth and Avarice (*Purgatorio* 18–24)

After leaving the wrathful behind, Dante and Virgil climb up onto the fourth terrace, where they encounter the slothful. The one spokesman for the terrace is a former monk: "I was Abbot of San Zeno at Verona," he tells the pilgrim (*Purg.* 18.118). In this canto, acedia is more than just laziness (although that is a part of it). It's deeper and more dangerous. In fact, in the Christian tradition, acedia, what we now call "sloth," was a vice particularly feared by monks. At its root, it is a deep, spiritual sorrow that paralyzes the will, makes you dull to doing good, and makes you incapable of enjoying the good things of life, even when you are surrounded by them. Acedia leads you to assume that everyone around is better off and that no one actually cares if you are well. Mary Carruthers quotes from John Cassian's *Institutes* (10.2) to illustrate the concern monks had regarding this spiritual cancer:

> When depression attacks the wretched monk it engenders a loathing for his situation, dislike of his cell, and contemptuous disparagement of his brethren. . . . It makes him desultory at any task to be done within the walls of his cell. He makes much of monasteries that are situated afar off, and talks about their advantageous positions and healthier sites. He describes the community of brothers there, how friendly and how deeply spiritual they are: while in contrast everything to hand is disagreeable. . . . He looks anxiously this way and that, unhappy because no brother is coming to see him; he goes in and out of his cell and continuously looks at the sun as if it were slow in setting.[7]

Clearly, the old monks knew something about psychology! Their description of the difficulty of working within the cell could as well apply to the dorm room or office.

Dante inventively imagines an extraordinary spiritual *disciplina* to correct the slothful disposition: the *accidiosi* are made to run with an energy greater than that displayed in any other canto. In fact, the pilgrim is only able to catch part of what the abbot of San Zeno says to him, because the penitent soul is shouting out his story over his shoulder as he races past (*Purg.* 18.127–28). Although canto 18 begins reflectively, it literally ends in this race. The energy of love unexpectedly irrupts in the midst of the abstract conversation of the two learned poets:

> But this drowsiness was ripped away from me,
> all of a sudden, by a group of people. . . .
>
> At one time the Ismenus, and the Asopus too, saw
> along their banks at night a massive herd
> when the Thebans needed Bacchus.
>
> Similarly, a large group sliced through the circle.
> I could see, as they came toward us,
> that they were spurred on by righteous will and just love.

> Soon they were upon us, because they were running,
> and they all moved like one huge mob:
> and two in front, while weeping, were shouting:
> . . . .
>
> "Quickly, quickly, lest time be lost
> for little love." And the rest, behind them:
> "So that our zeal for doing good make grace green again." (*Purg.*
>   18.88–89, 91–99, 103–5)

They run, then, as a frenzied mob, shouting to one another to add even more speed to their race. In fact, they are compared to the Bacchic revelers of ancient Thebes, who employed wine, wild music, and crazy dancing in their religious ritual. In opposition to the indifferent, who are stung by wasps to keep them moving after a meaningless banner, each of these runners submits to this *disciplina* in order that he may develop the ability to exert himself voluntarily in a frenzied outpouring of joy. This, then, is the *contrapasso* for those who reform slack love.

In the next terrace, we find an equally dramatic scene: the penitents on the fifth terrace of Mount Purgatory are bolted, as it were, face down onto the ground, with arms and legs stretched out, with noses squashed and foreheads flattened. They are forced to stare directly at the floor of the terrace. Dante has the spokesman of canto 19, the pope Adrian V, explain the fitting nature of this *contrapasso* for those who spent too much time in life fixated on earthly wealth:

> "Just as our eye was not raised
> on high, fixed rather on earthly things,
> so does justice make our vision plunge toward the earth.
>
> "Because avarice quenched our love for each good,
> and thus spoiled our good works,
> so justice here holds us fast." (*Purg.* 19.118–23)

The vice of avarice, or covetousness, was also a vice feared by Christian monks. Many theological writers repeated the biblical warning that "the love of money is the root of all evil" (1 Tim. 6:10). Monks such as Evagrius feared avarice because it was an appetite that could never reach satiety. As Evagrius puts it in his *Eight Thoughts*, "The sea is never filled up even though it takes in a multitude of rivers; the desire of the avaricious person cannot get its fill of riches."[8] Avarice makes you feverish in your labor and work, to get to the next stage, to meet the next goal. Unlike the slothful, the avaricious are self-motivated, but the problem is that they forget why they started climbing the ladder in the first place. Avarice is a kind of materialistic warping of the theological virtue of hope. In this way Dante's *contrapasso* is perfect: the law of the terrace is that the souls are rigidly fixed and bolted down, unable to move. Enslaved in this position, they begin to crave the freedom of mobility that the man who is not weighed down has. Or, again, as Evagrius puts it: "The monk free of possessions is like an athlete who cannot be thrown and a light runner who speedily attains 'the prize.'"[9]

Dante's French Bakery: The Gluttonous (*Purgatorio* 22–24)

In the sixth terrace, the pilgrim and his guide meet the gluttonous, who have to endure what I call the purgation of the French bakery. You can imagine arriving early in the morning on a cold day at a French bakery: the smell of butter and chocolate and freshly baked bread is in the air, as well as strong coffee. But you have to sit there at the table, smelling the scents and watching others eat, all morning long. In a similar way, Dante's gluttonous souls are forced to smell the delicious fragrances that come from a talking tree, as well as listen to examples of temperate eating (such as Daniel and John the Baptist; *Purg.* 22.131–52). If avarice takes place when desire for material things eclipses desire for all intangible goods (e.g., friendships, relationships, virtues, and wisdom), then gluttony is living as if only festive moments of sensual enjoyment are invigorating. The medieval concept of gluttony was more than overeating: it was dainty eating, food snobbery, and the party life. This is the disposition of both the young thirtysomething who lives for the metropolitan culinary scene and the American college student living the party life. The glutton feels that every activity he must do is dull and tiring, except that which happens on the weekend. It should not surprise us, then, that in canto 23 Dante runs into his old drinking buddy, Forese Donati. Dante is overjoyed to see him and actually a bit shocked that he made it:

> "If you call to mind
> what you were with me, and I was with you,
> remembering that now would still be painful." (*Purg.* 23.115–17)

Keep in mind that the souls throughout this region are chanting verses from the penitential Psalm 51—for example, verse 15: "O Lord, open thou my lips, and my mouth shall show forth thy praise." This narrative detail helps us appreciate Dante's critique of gluttony: the problem with the party life is that it effectively eclipses concerns for all else; or, to put it otherwise, if the lips and mouth are overemployed in consumption of physical things, then they are not available for the use of the higher end of praise.

Reading into Prayer: Summing Up the Middle Canti of *Purgatorio*

As I said in the previous chapter, although the souls in *Purgatorio* are "saved," they are not yet ready to see God, and thus they are assigned the various spiritual exercises in these middle canti (such as those mentioned by Peter of Celles: fasting, fraternal love, recollection of past evils, and so forth). While all of these exercises are useful, medieval spiritual masters of Dante's day recommended a spiritual exercise that was held as more valuable than any other for creating the conditions of prayerfulness: *lectio* (what we could call "deep reading"). On closer inspection, *lectio* is everywhere in the middle canti of *Purgatorio*.

In his *Scala claustralium* (*The Ladder of Monks*), one of the great medieval authorities on *lectio*, the Carthusian monk Guigo II, describes this deep reading as a ladder with four steps, which, like Jacob's ladder, stands on the ground but "penetrates the clouds of heaven and explores the secrets of heaven."[10] The first step of the ladder consists in an attentive and quiet reading of the plain text of Scripture, in which each of the words is pronounced slowly, letter by letter, while the reader has an intense expectation that the scriptural passage under consideration is, as Guigo says, "sweet and full of meaning." The second step is what Guigo calls *meditatio*, in which the reader seeks a fuller explanation for the text he has read. For example, when meditating on a verse such as "Blessed are the pure in heart: for they shall see God" (Matt. 5:8), the reader takes each phrase in turn, asking why Scripture says this and not something else, such as "Blessed are those who are pure in *body*." The mind also plays freely over all of Scripture, in search of other scriptural passages connected to the subject. The mind recalls, for instance, how Psalm 24 says that those who have "clean hands, and a pure heart" will ascend to God; or how the psalmist prayed, "Create in me a clean heart, O Lord" (Ps. 51:10); or how Job "made a covenant with [his] eyes" (Job 31:1). *Meditatio* then builds up this network of connections, of parallels and contrasts. It then continues on to ask what it means to "see God," meditating on what that experience would be like and how it must supremely satisfy all desires. And finally *meditatio* asks how one might go about acquiring such "cleanness of heart."

This chain of thoughts leads the soul to see—indeed, *feel*—the greatness of the promise of the vision of God, but in light of the vision of God's greatness, the soul begins to feel how weak it is, how little able it is to attain that vision. The soul is thus led to the third rung of the ladder, the impassioned state of *oratio* (or prayer), in which the soul is pained by its inability to conform itself to truth. It pants, thirsts, and longs for heavenly things. In *oratio*, the soul no longer longs to hear *about* God but wants to taste an experience *of* him. In this state of prayer, according to Guigo, "increased desire" comes and "fire is ignited." In short, this process of meditating on words leads to a point where speech ends: "By words such as these and similar ones the desire is inflamed: in this way the soul's *affectus* is stretched out broad." Guigo says that tears are the certain sign that one will have such an affective experience, for they effect the inner washing, the inner purgation (tellingly called *purgatio*): "O blessed tears, through which interior blemishes are purged." *Oratio* leads directly into this fourth stage, what Guigo calls *contemplatio*—that is, the precious moment in which the desire for healing becomes a fleeting moment of unity with God.

Such an affective end was the goal for all monastic *deep reading*, and it was for this reason that it was woven into the fabric of a medieval monk's day:

> *Lectio divina* was one of the lengthiest and most important exercises of the medieval cloister. With manual labor and the office, it was a primary enterprise. This sacred reading took place each day, lasting several hours—about six in the winter and three in the summer because of that season's more important agricultural work. On Sundays and major feast days *lectio* filled all the canon's free time. Each remained in the cloister or scriptorium, covering his head with his hood for the sake of easier recollection, to read the scriptures or the Fathers of the Church in order to find God.[11]

It is also this kind of *lectio* that is woven into the fabric of *Purgatorio*. It helps us understand what all of those voices and examples and carvings are doing in each terrace in each of the middle canti of *Purgatorio*. For example, in 19.73, the avaricious pray Psalm 119:25: "My soul cleaveth unto the dust: quicken thou me according to thy word"; that is, they repeat the psalmist's despairing cry to God for help. But now the souls of the avaricious, who are bolted to the ground, "see" up close how their own fixation on earthly things prevented them from making such heartfelt prayers in life. Through their posture they literally reenact the biblical prayer, and thus in their hearts they pray a biblical verse, now in a heartfelt way. Adrian V, in fact, politely asks the pilgrim to leave him alone to his tears (*Purg.* 19.139–41). If we remember Guigo's words about tears presaging *affectus*, then we realize he has already reached the level of *oratio*, a painful conviction regarding his own powerlessness and a longing for God to come and cleanse within.

Indeed, in every one of the middle canti, we see souls meditating on classical and biblical examples of vice and virtue, but *Purgatorio* 20 and 24 give us the best insight into the practice of *lectio* in purgatory. In canto 20, the pilgrim speaks with Hugh Capet, the founder of the French dynastic line that was still ruling in Dante's day, the Capetians. Here Hugh makes yet another of those savage political denunciations of the evil shepherds of Dante's day,[12] but what is more important for us are the details surrounding Hugh's speech. Dante at first doesn't know who he is. As he is passing through the ranks of prostrate souls, he hears one soul shout out, "Dolce Maria!" (O sweet Mary!), "in tearful lamentation, / just like a woman does when she is giving birth" (*Purg.* 20.20–21). This soul is clearly deep in some personal meditation and is so moved by what he meditatively sees in his imagination that he shouts out with compassion as if Mary were standing before him. But then the voice goes on: "How poor you were / can been seen by that inn / where you set down your holy burden" (20.22–24). While meditating on how Mary gave birth in the stable, Hugh is so moved that he himself shouts out, as if *he* were a woman in labor (20.20–21)! Thus, we have a great example of a soul entering imaginatively into the scene and dwelling in it with such a vivid imagination that his *affectus* has been warmed; the text has come alive within him. His *lectio* is turning into prayer.

Later, Hugh explains to the pilgrim that souls in purgatory do not just "go over [these stories] again and again" (*Purg.* 20.103), but they also "celebrate" (20.113) the destruction of Heliodorus and shout out loud with righteous anger, apostrophizing Crassus and mocking him for his taste for gold (20.116–17).[13] Some souls are loud and some are quiet in the vocalizations of their condemnations. The more passion they feel over evil, the more their hearts are pricked and goaded to express that righteous anger or joy in the good (20.118–21). They cry out "according to the zeal that spurs our speech" (the key word is *l'affezion* [= *affectus*], 20.119).

With this in mind, when we come back to Hugh's speech, in which he decries the political evil of his day, we note another detail: Hugh offers a prophecy in which he likens the besieged pope to Christ and the reckless French king to Pilate (*Purg.* 20.87–93). His righteous anger is clearly shaped by biblical passages of longing:

> "O my Lord, when shall I be made happy
> by seeing your vengeance! Concealed for now, it
> makes your wrath sweet in your secret thoughts." (*Purg.* 20.94–96)

Hugh's biblically molded outcry is a sign that the sin to which he was once prone—the avaricious acquisition of land—is now becoming repulsive to him. His heart is being rewritten through his deep, affective *lectio*.

But it is in canto 23 that we find these things even more evocatively portrayed. As we have said, this is where Dante meets Forese Donati, his old drinking buddy. Donati and the other penitent gluttonous souls are "dark and sunken in the eyes, / pallid in the face, and so gaunt / that the skin took all its form from the bones" (*Purg.* 23.22–24). Then the poet says something amazing:

> Their eye sockets looked like rings with gems;
> and he who sees "omo" written into the visage of men
> would have recognized the "m." (*Purg.* 23.31–33)

In other words, their faces have become so thin, their eyes so sunken, that the nose and cheek bones form the letter *m*, with the eyes forming two *o*'s in the middle—that is, spelling out the word *omo*, Latin and Italian for "man." This is an extraordinary moment. We know that Forese, like the others, is reading in a meditative way, contemplating the examples of temperance, while performing these exercises of fasting. And thus, while he is *reading*, his very face, his very visage, is being *rewritten*, so that his humanity is now becoming apparent once again. Forese, then, was like a text poorly written, but now it is being scratched out, and through his cooperation with God he is being rewritten to become the text he was meant to be. His humanity, as represented by the word *omo*, is being restored. His deep reading is the vehicle by which he is being rewritten in prayer.

9

Returning to Humanity's First Home: Epic and Lyric in the Garden of Eden

(*Purgatorio* 25–28)

Dante the Apprentice

In the previous chapter, I discussed how the spiritual exercises of purgatory, especially *lectio*, lead to that state of prayerfulness that is the precondition for the "deep cleansing" of the purgatorial souls. But what is interesting is that at exactly the same time that Dante dramatizes souls engaged in this transformative *reading*, he also weaves in and out of these middle canti the theme of *writing*. In other words, Dante doesn't just portray souls becoming affectively vulnerable through their *lectio*; he also stages a number of encounters between the pilgrim and various poets, both ancient and medieval, so that through these meetings and conversations he can work out his own poetic identity.[1]

The full consequences of this self-portrait can only be fully seen in light of *Paradiso*, but for now we can note, quite simply, that these middle canti are full of conversations with poets about poetry. In particular, Dante orients these conversations around two poles: the conversations and events that unfold around classical poets (Virgil and Statius in *Purg.* 21–22), and the conversations and events that Dante holds with contemporary medieval poets (Bonagiunta da Lucca, Arnaut Daniel, and Guido Guinizelli in *Purg.* 24–26). As we shall see, these conversations culminate in *Purgatorio* 27 and 28, precisely as the pilgrim reenters humanity's first home, the garden of Eden, where language was originally born and fitted to reality.

The Poetry of Light

In the midst of the pilgrim's journey through the terrace of the avaricious, Dante complicates the narrative by introducing a third traveler into the group. He is Statius, the ancient Roman poet, who was born in France, wrote in Latin, and lived a half century after Virgil. He wrote an epic poem about the mythological war over Thebes (*Thebaid*). In the age of Statius, it was not possible to write an epic without paying homage to the greatest Roman epic (*Aeneid*), and thus we hear Statius praise Virgil as the one who taught him to be a writer (*Purg.* 21.94–99). As the conversation between Statius and Virgil continues to unfold in the next canto (*Purg.* 22), Dante has Statius confess even more: Virgil was not only responsible for helping him become a craftsman of the Latin language, but Virgil—*pagan* Virgil—also made him a Christian! In their exchange, Virgil gives voice to a doubt: there is no indication in Statius's poetry that he was a Christian (indeed, as far as modern scholars know, there shouldn't be any—he never was a Christian). But Dante takes advantage of the silence of history to fill in a backstory of his own devising (like he did with Ulysses). Dante has Statius say that he had indeed become Christian but hid it; he was a closet Christian:

> "You first set me on the way
> toward Parnassus to drink in its grottoes,
> and you first illumined me for God.

> "You acted as one who goes through the night
> and bears a light behind him. It does no good for him,
> but those behind are instructed.

> "When you said: 'The *saeculum* is renewed;
> justice returns and the first age of man,
> and new offspring descends from heaven.'

> "Through you I was a poet, through you a Christian." (*Purg.* 22.64–73)

Virgil, then, was a man who carried a lantern behind his back: it lighted the path for those behind him, although it was of no use to him. The poem that Statius quotes is Virgil's "Fourth Eclogue," a lyrical, pastoral poem written as an impassioned expression of hope that peace would soon return to war-torn Italy during the Roman Republic. The imagery the ancient poet used to express his desire, though, was so close to Scripture that later medieval readers accepted it as a prophetic announcement of the imminent advent of Christ:

> Now the last age by Cumae's Sibyl sung
> Has come and gone, and the majestic roll
> Of circling centuries begins anew:
> Justice returns, returns old Saturn's reign. . . .
> The iron shall cease, the golden race arise. . . .
> Whatso tracks remain
> Of our old wickedness, once done away,
> Shall free the earth from never-ceasing fear. . . .
> For thee, O boy,
> First shall the earth, untilled, pour freely forth
> Her childish gifts. . . .
> The serpent too shall die,
> Die shall the treacherous poison-plant. (*Eclogue* 4)[2]

This pagan poem, written several decades *before* Christ, almost sounds like a Christmas hymn or a passage from Isaiah! There will be no more tilling of the soil, because all plants will spring up in every land; there will be no more avaricious merchants, because all will have what they need; all our crimes will be wiped away, and the peaceful Golden Age will return when a mysterious boy comes to rule the world. Later in the *Comedy* Dante has the young woman in the garden of Eden, Matelda, tell the three travelers that such pagan, poetic dreaming of the Golden Age wasn't mere fancy but rather was a groping attempt to recollect the bliss that humanity enjoyed in its infancy (*Purg.* 28.139–47).

This, then, is the extraordinary compliment that Dante pays classical poetry through Statius's praise of Virgil. Poetry is not an escape from reality; it is its intensification. It is the attempt to recollect humanity's origin. As J. R. R. Tolkien put it, good poetry brings with it a "curious thrill," as if something stirs in you, half wakened from sleep. "There is something remote and strange and beautiful behind the words . . .

something which derives its curiously moving quality from some older world."[3]

Dante wants us to see, then, that he is the diligent student of these ancient poets, even if separated by more than ten centuries:

> [Virgil and Statius] were moving along in front, and solitary I
> behind. I was listening to their discourse,
> which gave me rich understanding of the poet's craft. (*Purg.*
>   22.127–29)

For Dante, ancient epic poetry represents the attempt to put in words the highest ambitions of human beings. It is the pursuit of the best possible language to frame the subtlest and most elusive dreams of the heart, and thus it involves a lifetime of slow and quiet study of the greatest books by the greatest masters to develop the craft. For Dante, this meant copying them, word by word, with quiet patience, attentively searching out the secrets that undergird their art. And it is this habit of study that Dante represents himself as following when he had his pilgrim listening, with carefully attuned ears, to the private conversations of the two Roman masters about the secrets of their poetry.

Love and Language (*Purgatorio* 26)

For Dante, Statius and Virgil were the masters of *epic* poetry, the long poems that describe the great tasks and undertakings of magnanimous heroes in language that is highly elevated above ordinary speech. Dante styles himself as the student of these morally serious epic poets, but, fascinatingly, he also has his pilgrim meet and talk with and even declare himself the faithful disciple of contemporary lyric poets. These poets are not the Latin-using, venerable poets of antiquity but the passionate, fashionable love poets who wrote in the vernacular close to Dante's own time: the troubadour Arnaut Daniel (who wrote in Provençal) and Guido Guinizelli (from Bologna, who wrote in Italian in the century before Dante).

In canto 24, Guido Guinizelli is referred to as the great poet who wrote in the "sweet new style," because he aimed to praise love and provide philosophical reflections on beauty. In his most famous poem, Guinizelli

meditates on the relationship between love and beauty, saying that love is
to the noble heart as heat is to the flame: the two naturally accompany
one another. Guinizelli finishes that poem in a bold way:

> My lady, God will say to me, "How could you presume?"
> when my soul is before him:
> "You passed beyond the heavens and came all the way to me
> And you used me as a likeness to vain love;
> All praise is due to me
> And the queen of this worthy realm. . . ."
> But I will be able to say to Him: "[My lady] had the likeness of an
>   angel
> who was of your kingdom.
> The failure is not mine, if I set my love on her."[4]

It is an audacious claim by the poet: he prefers earthly and tangible
beauty to abstract ideas in a far-off place—earthly experience of love
more than theological reflection. Not surprisingly, now, in this terrace,
poets such as Guinizelli and Arnaut Daniel have to be purged of that
preference for earthly love over heavenly love, as Arnaut says at the end of
canto 26:

> "I am Arnaut, who weep and make my way in song.
> I see with grief at the folly behind me,
> and I see, with delight, the joy for which I hope before me." (*Purg.*
>   26.142–44)

But Dante doesn't dismiss this lyric poetry and earthly love; rather, he
suggests that their interior fire was the secret of their success! Perhaps to
our surprise, Dante now reenacts the same reverence for his father figure,
Guinizelli, that Statius had shown for Virgil (in canto 22). Like Statius,
who was overwhelmed by the revelation that it was the great Virgil who
stood before him (*Purg.* 21.121–36), Dante is astounded to learn that he
stands before Guido Guinizelli, who had been the father

> of me and many others—my betters—who always
> used the rhymes of love that are sweet and graceful.

> And without hearing or saying a thing, lost in thought, I went on
> for a long time, staring at him . . .
> . . . .

And he to me . . .

"Tell me what is the reason you hold me
so dear in your speaking and in your looks."

And I to him: "Your sweet lines,
which, as long as modern custom will endure,
will make precious even the ink used to write them." (*Purg.* 26.97–101,
    106, 110–14)

Guinizelli, unlike Virgil, deflects this praise, pointing out that vernacular writers will always be coming in and out of fashion because the language changes so fast.

Dante's Epic and Lyric Pilgrimage

This, then, is how Dante explored the roots of his own poetry. On the one hand, he, the modern poet, has a reverence for the past; he eavesdrops on the conversation of Statius and Virgil and learns the secrets of the classic craft that aims to return to the garden. On the other hand, the Italian poet hints that the classic craft is not enough; rather, he needs to draw on the resources of the love poet, who spent his life trying to give external form to his interior experience. Within his epic journey, Dante needs a lyric reality.

Dante is trying to do the impossible: to have the power, depth, gravity, magnanimity, and thoughtfulness of classical verse, while injecting into it the inspiration, timeliness, urgency, and vitality of the contemporary. Dante is writing a new epic: the epic of love. Like two sides of an arch, both traditions are needed to support Dante's project. Dante, though he praises Guinizelli, admits how quickly the modern fad fades. Nothing looks so dated so quickly as fashion and popular customs. But in the narrative part of *Purgatorio* 26, Dante hints at the limitations of the epic tradition.

Virgil fails to motivate the pilgrim, who is faced with one last ordeal: walking through a wall of fire. Virgil and Statius won't feel any pain at all when they pass through these flames, but, as we might expect, this is the moment that Dante, the man who spent most of his life writing hot love poems, has been dreading. The angel calls to Dante, "Blessed are they who are clean in heart," and then says, "There is no going on unless you taste the bite, / of fire, you holy souls" (*Purg.* 27.10–11). When the pilgrim hears

this, he freezes: "For this reason, when I understood his words, I became /
like a man who has been put into his grave" (27.14–15). Dante won't budge.
Virgil tries to comfort him with all of those unconvincing arguments that
a parent or teacher uses: he tells him that this bitter medicine will be good;
it might be painful, but it won't last *too* long. All these words are without
any motivational power. And so Virgil tries one last argument:

> When he saw me stay where I was, yet still and unmoving,
> disturbed, he said: "Now look, son,
> this wall is between you and Beatrice." (*Purg.* 27.34–36)

That's what was needed. At the name of Beatrice, Dante plunges into the
fire, which is hot beyond imagination:

> As soon as I was within, I would have cast myself
> into a boiling caldron of molten glass to cool myself,
> so intense was that burning heat, beyond all measure.
>
> My sweet father, to comfort me,
> kept moving along, all the while reminding me of Beatrice,
> saying: "Her eyes! Already, I seem to see them." (*Purg.* 27.49–54)

What the poet of magnanimity failed to accomplish through lofty epic
words, he was able to accomplish through the magnetic power of love. The
lyric of love and the magnanimity of epic are needed together. Dante's
epic journey has a lyrical interiority.

In Humanity's First Home (*Purgatorio* 27–28)

When the pilgrim arrives at the other side of the fiery wall, he participates
in a ritualistic ceremony. On the borders of Eden, Virgil declares the pilgrim
whole, healthy, and morally restored.

> "I have brought you here by learning and by art.
> Now, take the inclination of your heart as your guide.
> . . . .
>
> "Look at the sun that shines there before you;
> look at the grasses, flowers, and trees,
> which here the soil produces of itself.

> "Until those happy, beautiful eyes come,
> that, once with tears, made me come to you,
> you can seat yourself or you can go among these things.
>
> "No longer wait for a word or nod from me.
> Your will is free, upright, and healthy.
> It would be folly not to do what your heart suggests:
> for this, I crown you and miter you sovereign of yourself." (*Purg.*
>   27.130–31, 133–42)

Dante is now his own bishop and his own king. He doesn't need law, judge, or pope now to regulate his behavior. He doesn't even need rules. He is now free. Ordinarily, the advice to follow the desire of your heart is terrible, isn't it? But here, with his passions under control, all that Dante has to do is consult his desire. What he wants is good, and that which is good is inherently desirable. He has once again returned to the original state of justice.

With this moral constitution, the pilgrim walks back into the original home of humanity. Thus, the twenty-eighth canto of *Purgatorio* is a momentous one, whose dramatic action has been long anticipated. It is the apex of the mountain of purgatory and has been the goal of the pilgrim's journey throughout this canticle. The moment is psychologically charged with those emotions of relief, joy, and surprise that usually attend a homecoming, but it is intensified, because the pilgrim represents all of humanity. Dante the poet needs a special poetic power to capture the joyful and long-awaited event.

Purgatorio 28, then, is a kind of poetic manifesto, an instantiation of what the Christian disciple of Virgil and son of Guinizelli can accomplish. And if that were not enough pressure, there is also the fact that according to medieval theory, Eden was the place wherein language was born and fitted perfectly to the reality it was meant to signify, before the rift emerged between words and things. Eden is where Adam, the so-called name giver (*nomothetēs*), was inspired to use words to name creation around him (see Gen. 2:19–20). In a certain sense, Adam was the father of poetry, given that he was the ultimate, God-inspired practitioner of language.

With so much anticipation, it is exciting to see how Dante actually does represent his brief sojourn into this linguistically charged locale. From the opening lines of canto 28, the poet describes not so much the details of the garden as the pilgrim's experience:

> Keenly eager now to search within and about
> the sacred wood, so dense and alive
> that it tempered for my eyes the brilliance of the new day,
>
> without waiting any longer, I left the bank
> taking to the open, with slow and stately steps. (*Purg.* 28.1–5)

Whatever we know of the garden is filtered through the pilgrim's subjective response to it. We learn of the sweet breeze, but only as it strikes his brow. We hear of the river because it bars his progress. The whole scene has almost a cinematic quality, filmed, as it were, from a first-person angle, so that what is described always has the feel of being viewed through the pilgrim's eyes.

It is this extraordinary use of the lyrical, then, that marks Dante's entry into the garden. The pilgrim, who has now returned to the original state of justice, has also returned to an original state of language. To get at this original, divinely inspired language used at the dawn of creation, the poet has to develop a poetry that traces its genealogy through two lines of descent. The first part of his inheritance is from those poets who cultivated an exalted, epic language, needed to describe humanity's epic struggle to return to the spiritual landscape of its origin. It is the poetry of learning, but also of virtue, piety, discipline, and study. The second part is from the vernacular love poetry, which cultivated the intense, the personal, the immediate, and the present, in direct contrast to the long view of history. Its power lay in its ability to bracket off all else but the immediate, first-person experience of overwhelming love. The genius of Dante's poetry, then, is that it maps these two traditions on top of one another, uncovering the radical joy of the garden, what Augustine and Aquinas called *magnitudo delectationis* (intense delight), which man now recalls only as a half-remembered dream. Dante uses the intensity of the first-person view of lyrical poetry so that goodness, justice, and joy come across not as the dull virtues they often strike us as, but as spiritually radioactive, even erotically desirable. Dante rewrites Virgil through Guinizelli. And in doing so, he makes us nostalgic for the original state of purity and justice.[5]

10

As the Heavens Are Higher Than the Earth: Dante's Apocalyptic Vision

(*Purgatorio* 29–33)

The End of the Story?

By the end of *Purgatorio* 27, it seems that our story is coming to its close. Virgil has accomplished his task. He saved the pilgrim from the dark wood and restored his ability to choose the good. He leads the pilgrim to believe that all that remains is for him to enjoy this fresh and verdant place and await the time at which he may look into the beautiful eyes of his beloved Beatrice (*Purg.* 27.136–37). At any moment, then, the reunion between lover and beloved will take place. Zygmunt Baranski summarizes it in this way:

> After several dramatic days of testing travel through Hell and Purgatory, which have taxed him intellectually, emotionally, and spiritually, Dante-character, re-assured by an enchanting dream, wakes—for the first time on his journey—in a peaceful and relaxed manner. . . . He soon finds himself on the edges of a *locus amoenus* [perfect garden]. . . . The pilgrim is nearly home. . . . The *viator* [pilgrim] seems, at last, to have reached a deserved haven of calm and repose;

he is about to be rewarded for his efforts. . . . [But the canti that follow] most
certainly do not depict a moment of calm and harmony; nor do they describe
a charming reunion between long-separated lovers. . . . Beatrice is angry, unre-
lentingly reproachful, and vigorously incisive. . . . The pilgrim, in his turn, is
ashamed, confused, and almost at a loss for words.[1]

As we will see, something is about to spin terribly out of control.

As it turns out, this is not the end the pilgrim thought he was in for.
Rather, Dante the pilgrim witnesses not the serene advent of the lady he
had once loved so much, a kind of romantic reunion in this ideal garden,
but a supernatural apocalyptic procession. Just as he begins to look about
the woods expectantly for Beatrice, the pilgrim sees this instead:

> And behold: a burst of light all of sudden passed through
> every part of the great forest,
> such that it struck me: this is lightning, perhaps.
>
> But since lightning, as soon as it comes, then settles down,
> and this brilliance, shining on, became more and more resplendent,
> I said to myself in my thoughts: "What thing is this?" (*Purg.* 29.16–21)

The pilgrim has difficulty even identifying the nature of the eerie event. The
images he uses to describe it become more unnatural as the canto proceeds.
A sweet melody courses through the luminous air, as if the sound and the
color were the same (29.34–36). The company flames more brightly than the
moon at midnight (29.52–53), and as they advance, the air is transformed
into a colored substance (29.73–74), as if they are so steeped in heavenly
light that they burn color into the air as they pass through it. The poet
turns to a synesthetic blending of images to gesture at what he saw, as if
wildly gesticulating at something well beyond language (he sees sounds
and hears sights). The world of nature begins to melt down in the heat of
this extraordinary event.

In the previous chapter, I talked about the beautiful, moving poetry
that Dante used to craft a description of the pilgrim's experience of the
earthly paradise in canto 28. In contrast to that tranquil melodic flow, we
have now a violent, experimental poetry in canto 29. In earlier canti, you
can find poetic traces of the "sweet new style": echoes of the poems of
Cavalcanti and Guinizelli. But now, that mellifluous lyricism is replaced
by bizarre imagery, opaque symbolism, strangely symbolic pageants, and

intentionally dark and difficult "explanations" that make things *less* intelligible rather than clearer. In a word, love poetry has yielded to that frightening landscape of the biblical apocalypse.

Dante, the Numinous, and the Apocalypse

At the beginning of the twentieth century, the German Lutheran theologian Rudolf Otto wrote the now-famous *Idea of the Holy*. In this book, which influenced, among others, C. S. Lewis and J. R. R. Tolkien, Otto pointed out that modern people have rather lost a sense of what the holy is. We tend to think of "holiness" as good brought to the highest level. In reality, Otto claims, all ancient religions treat the holy as an "irrational over-plus of meaning" that extends beyond goodness, what he termed the "numinous": "There is no religion in which [the numinous] does not live as the real innermost core, and without it no religion would be worthy of the name."[2] For Otto the numinous is that reality whose majesty is so far beyond our ordinary experience that it is difficult for us to classify it simply as good or bad; it is at once both alluring and dangerous, beautiful and terrifying. The numinous is what Tolkien had in mind when he describes Lothlorien, the land of the elves in *The Lord of the Rings*, and what Lewis had in mind when he describes those moments in which Aslan appears in *The Chronicles of Narnia* in the fullness of his power. Visionaries describe an encounter with the sacred as a sense that it is rushing forth while at the same time drawing them in. For this reason, it inspires a *dread* in the creature who comes into contact with it. It inspires a feeling of terror and vulnerable creaturehood.

In any case, it is this perception of the awful majesty of God that Otto thought the modern world needed to recover. In contrast, this sense of the awful, sacred presence of God was palpable in the medieval world, particularly within the visionaries and commentators who took as their inspiration John's Apocalypse, the book that uses famously difficult and symbolic language about the lady, beast, righteous martyrs, seals, and bowls of judgment. In addition to providing the secret history of the world, medieval readers believed that the Apocalypse, in all its strange and enigmatic language, briefly pulled back the veil of reality and let us see the awful truth of the majesty of God enthroned.

This is also what our poet was aiming for in these canti: to conclude *Purgatorio* in a way as phantasmagorical and brilliant as any vision or

Figure 5. Imagery from John's Apocalypse in the Morgan Beatus, a tenth-century illuminated manuscript.

illuminated manuscript inspired by the Apocalypse. It shouldn't surprise us, then, that what Dante sees, and indeed feels, in these last canti is steeped in the imagery of the books of Revelation and Isaiah and Ezekiel. He sees a bizarre procession that comes from heaven and dreamily alights within the garden in order to present Dante with a silent play. He is ordered, like John, to write down what he sees, although he barely understands what it means (*Purg.* 32.103–5). Thus, he dutifully records that the long parade is led first by twenty-four elders carrying lilies, four beasts with brightly colored wings, and a chariot pulled by the griffin carrying Beatrice. On one side of the chariot is a group of three female figures, dressed in red, green, and white (they represent faith, hope, and charity); on the other side a group of four ladies are dancing in purple (the cardinal virtues); then come two old men, a doctor and one carrying a sword. The old men are followed by four humbly dressed men, who are in turn followed by a sleepwalker. Canto 30 tells us that one hundred angels will join the procession, for a total of precisely one hundred forty-four members in this sacred parade.[3]

Dante doesn't tell us explicitly, but the twenty-four elders seem to be the twenty-four books of the medieval Old Testament; the four living creatures symbolize the four Gospels; the two old men, Luke and Paul, are followed by four humbly dressed individuals—Jude, John, Peter, and James—who are in turn followed by the sleepwalker, the author of the Apocalypse. So the Bible and the virtues, as it were, are processing into Dante's world to meet him.

Note how painstakingly the poet points out the color of everything throughout these verses, as if he wants us to read this scene and feel it as a painted illumination. The procession strikes like a bolt of lightning that doesn't flicker out; it paints the air it passes through; ladies wear bright dresses; the griffin has golden wings; Beatrice wears an olive crown, white veil, red robe, and green mantle. But the pilgrim barely registers any of this. He's too stunned by the glory of the event. At two points he turns to Virgil for help in understanding:

> I turned, full of wonder and marvel,
> to my good Virgil, but he answered
> with a look no less full of stupor. (*Purg.* 29.55–57)

Garrulous and avuncular Virgil, always full of calm and beneficial advice, just shakes his head; he too is completely at a loss to explain this event.

Then it gets worse. When Beatrice does arrive, she is brutally personal, even sarcastic. When the disoriented pilgrim turns for the last time to Virgil, to discover that his faithful guide and friend is not there, Beatrice says, "Do not weep yet, do not weep yet— / it is better that you weep by another sword" (*Purg.* 30.56–57). She later asks him, "How did you dare come to the mountain? / Maybe you didn't know that here man is happy?" (30.74–75). Beatrice shames Dante in front of a huge crowd, which makes the experience all the more painful. In fact, she's so harsh that the pilgrim passes out, overwhelmed by the surprise of this verbally abusive encounter. How great a contrast to what was expected! What is the point of these final canti, this shocking reunion?

At exactly the same time, Dante portrays his encounter with Beatrice as intimately personal as well as representative of all humanity. When the pilgrim first comes into the presence of Beatrice, he experiences again that trembling that he felt as a young man, described so vividly in *Vita Nuova* (*Purg.* 30.34–39). Dante is, once again, the overwhelmed lover, shaken by the glory of Beatrice's beauty. In fact, Beatrice can unabashedly say to Dante, "Never, never did art or nature present to you / delight like my beautiful members did / in which I was enclosed" (31.49–51). For this reason, Beatrice can accuse Dante of being unfaithful—that is, unfaithful to her beauty:

> "And if the highest delight failed you
> upon my death, how is it that a mortal thing
> could draw you after it in desire?
>
> "You ought to have, at the very first wound
> inflicted by deceitful things, risen upward
> after me who was no longer merely mortal." (*Purg.* 31.52–57)

In other words, how is it possible that you could have settled for anything less? Surely, any other attractive thing ought to have struck you as a pale shadow after you had a real experience of beauty. Beatrice exposes, as it were, the pilgrim's primal act of infidelity: sinning against the memory of her. Dante falsified his own experience, feigning to himself that any beauty could remotely compare.

It is at this point that Beatrice forcefully elicits a confession from the confused pilgrim; she demands that he admit that he had been unfaithful to her, unfaithful to love, unfaithful to beauty. In the midst of this overwhelming experience, the pilgrim can barely whisper an answer:

> After drawing forth a bitter sigh,
> I found my voice to reply, but only with great pain,
> and my lips gave shape to my voice, but with labor.
>
> In tears, I said: "Things put in front of me,
> with their false delight, turned around my steps,
> the moment that your face was hidden from me." (*Purg.* 31.31–36)

In a moment of complete vulnerability and spiritual nudity, Dante has to let his soul be *radically* known, to let all of its secrets be viewed by all. From this vantage point, all the "false images of good" don't just seem misdirected; they seem paltry, pathetic, reprehensible, detestable, sick, and small. By confessing his primal act of infidelity against Beatrice, the pilgrim is forced to return to the "root" of his soul, an idea that Dante hints at in one of the most powerful passages of this scene:

> With less resistance you can rip out, by the roots,
> a massive oak . . .
> . . . .

than I lifted my chin at her command.

. . . .

Then the nettle of repentance so stung me
that whatsoever had once drawn me,
the more I loved it, the more it now became hateful. (*Purg.* 31.70–71,
    73, 85–87)

And yet, while Dante endures this excruciatingly personal confession, being made to uproot sin from the core of his being, he also has returned to the root of humankind in the garden. Having returned to the garden on behalf of humanity (and reentered the state of original justice), Dante has become a kind of new Adam, and thus he must also confess and unchoose, as it were, humanity's original act of infidelity, the act in which humans presumed that all things lay within their reach. Human perfection is a beautiful thing, but even such perfection has to be understood as a limited power within the larger context of God and the cosmos.

Thus, throughout these canti, the poor pilgrim, laboring to keep up, can barely understand what's happening around him. And when he asks for explanations, Beatrice's words only make things more difficult to understand. For example, Beatrice's explanation of the mysterious pageant just adds to the riddle: "Know that the vessel which the serpent broke / was and is not," she says (*Purg.* 33.34–35). She refuses to explain what the eagle stands for. Nor does she explain the fox, the harlot, or the giant, but rather says that those figures have to be understood as referring to "the 500, 10, and 5." Here her speech becomes "dark narration" (33.46), a "hard enigma" (33.50). And so the pilgrim quite understandably asks:

"But why do your words, so long desired,
soar so high above my sight,
so that the more they help me, the more I am lost?"

Beatrice responds:

"So that you know," she said, "that school
you followed, and see how well its doctrine
can follow my words;

"and so that you may see that your way is as distant from
the divine as the highest heaven, which moves so swiftly,
is out of tune with the earth." (*Purg.* 33.82–90)

Dante never mentions what specific "school of thought" it is that Beatrice criticizes, but scholars have suggested that Beatrice here rebukes, not so much particular false doctrines, but rather a presumptuous mind-set that could believe that any set of human, rational explanations could effectively communicate all that needs to be known. Indeed, Beatrice suggests that the very darkness of her words was intentionally planned in order that the pilgrim recognize *by how much* heavenly realities exceed earthly ones, that he recognize how poorly equipped he is to understand opaque celestial truths with earthly rational instruments. The poet then creates a dreamlike sequence of canti, full of obscurity and mystery, in order to help the pilgrim, standing in for humanity, "unchoose" man's original act of presumption. Dante has returned to the garden, as a second Adam, to undo the original father's mistake.

In a way, then, this is Dante's ultimate justification for using poetry. Here in the garden, the dreamlike, apocalyptic images, which resist rational categorization, invade, as it were, the supreme seat of human reason. We have a de facto announcement that the poetry that is to follow will be something that has never been seen before, because it will attempt to treat what is beyond nature. From here on out, the Virgilian tradition will be able to offer little assistance, just as the Roman poet is of no help here in the garden. From here on out, the poet will have to strike out on his own; he will have to be radically innovative as he treats something never attempted before—and this is exactly what he says at the beginning of the next canticle: "The waters that I enter have never before been crossed" (*Par.* 2.7).

Part 3

PARADISO

11

Great Fires Come from Tiny Sparks: An Introduction to *Paradiso*

(*Paradiso* 1–2)

Turn Back, Reader!

Although modern readers are often left cold by *Paradiso*, Dante himself thought it was the greatest thing he had ever written. This does not mean that he was unaware of the difficulty of his final canticle. In fact, it is so difficult that he urges his readers to quit and turn back:

> O you, within your little boat,
> desirous of hearing more, having followed
> behind my ship that makes its way by singing,
>
> turn back if you would see your shores again!
> Do not set forth upon the deep, since should it happen
> that you lose sight of me, you would be lost forever.
>
> The water I venture out upon has never been crossed before.
> . . . .
>
> But you few who have lifted up your heads, longingly,
> and for a long time, for the bread of angels . . .

you may indeed set forth a proper ship
upon the salty deep, taking advantage of that furrow
in the water that so quickly returns to being level.

The glorious men who crossed the sea for Colchis
did not gaze in wonder as much as you will,
even when they saw Jason become a plowman. (*Par.* 2.1–7, 10–11,
    13–18)

It's not a very good marketing scheme for reaching a large public, but the poet says that he only needs a few dedicated readers. In words that echo Ulysses's speech to raise a crew (*Inf.* 26), the poet calls for those who thirst for adventure and are willing to endure extreme intellectual hardship, analogous to the hardships endured by the legendary heroes who accompanied Jason in pursuit of the Golden Fleece. And if it just so happens that you are bold enough, then "the glorious men who crossed the sea for Colchis / did not gaze in wonder as much as you will" (*Par.* 2.16–17). Dante alludes to the Argonauts, who watched their captain crush the teeth of a magical serpent and plow them into the ground. From this unusual sowing, a group of warriors sprang up and cut one another down. You will be more amazed than they. Thus, although Dante knew his final canticle was extremely difficult, he also thought that if we could stay in his wake, then we would come to see his vision as breathtakingly beautiful. This insight will guide the concluding chapters of this book.

Although difficulties are inevitable, my goal is to help my readers come to see why Dante loved his *Paradiso* so much. To do so, I will use the remainder of this chapter to clear away two obstacles to appreciating *Paradiso*. The first is Dante's strange conception of "the heavens."[1] Just as in our day, so in Dante's, readers felt there was something inherently exciting about space travel. If we don't appreciate Dante's sci-fi journey through the heavens now, this is simply because of a historical accident; that is, because so much has changed in our cosmic imagination, we first have to reconstruct Dante's understanding of the heavens before we can appreciate the adventure of the story on the most literal level. The second obstacle to our appreciation of the canticle is an "inherent difficulty"; that is, the poet hopes to talk about the joy of the saints, the bright fire of God, but these things are higher and lighter than ordinary human language.

For Dante, God simply cannot be "known," because any word we might use to describe him fails to do him justice. This is what theologians call the problem of "ineffability" or "unspeakability."

Perhaps it also strikes you as strange that we are only now taking up a discussion of the failure and limitation of language, two-thirds of the way through Dante's wordy, thousand-page book! Thus, in this introductory chapter, we will also have to deal with this complementary feature of Dante's poem: at the very same time that Dante believes that his subject is ultimately "unsayable," he remains a *poet*, a craftsman of words, who tries to use his language to point at that which is beyond it. Thus, throughout the final canticle, there is a kind of war of language, a tension between Dante's desire to write the most penetrating poem in the history of human thought and his unshakable conviction that even *that* will be a failure.

Dante dramatically illustrates the tension between ineffability and eloquence in the opening lines of *Paradiso*. Invoking the classical god of poetic inspiration, he implores:

> O good Apollo . . .
> . . . .
>
> Enter into my breast! May you breath in me,
> as when you drew Marsyas
> out from the scabbard of his limbs. (*Par.* 1.13, 19–21)

The image is the brutal death of the mythological Marsyas, the musician who so recklessly challenged Apollo to a competition. When the mortal inevitably lost, Apollo punished Marsyas by flaying him alive, a gruesome death famously portrayed by the Venetian painter Titian. This is the story Dante uses, in the very first lines, to describe the kind of inspiration he needs! He calls for an inspiration so profound that he is stripped and drawn out of himself, an inspiration by which he radically leaves the limitations of his mortal humanity behind.

Dante and Medieval Space Travel

These days we moderns all possess a kind of built-in arrogance about our superiority to earlier cultures, what C. S. Lewis once called "chronological snobbery." In contrast to medievals, who tended to believe that the ancients were greater, we moderns are inclined to think that, because of our technological and scientific progress, we know more and live better than anyone who came before. In particular, we like to think of ourselves as vastly superior when it comes to knowledge of space. Watch Christopher Nolan's *Interstellar* (2014) and you'll hear terms like "black holes," "neutron stars," "gravitational fields," "relativity," and "worm holes" batted around. Dante's cosmos, then, with the earth at the center and all the planets neatly revolving around it, seems, at first glance, positively primitive.

Before we can appreciate how exciting Dante's readers would have felt his journey in *Paradiso* to be, we have to know something about what medieval men and women thought about the heavens in the first place. In this section, though, I don't just want to relate some medieval ideas about the cosmos. Rather, I want to try to re-create the medieval experience of looking at the nighttime sky; that is, I want to conduct a kind of phenomenology of the medieval cosmos, relating not just what it looked like to them and how it worked, but also how it felt.

We have to recognize that even if we might have more knowledge about *some* things far away, Dante and his contemporaries had a better understanding about the practical appearance of the nighttime sky on any given evening. Unless you have an annual subscription to *Astronomer's Monthly*, you will not have a clue what Dante is talking about in *Paradiso* 1 when he begins to describe his ascent into the heavens:

> The lamp of the world rises on us mortals
> at different points. But, by the one that joins
> four circles with three crossings, it comes forth
>
> on a better course and in conjunction
> with a better sign. (*Par.* 1.37–41; trans. Hollander)

In other words, it's late March, and the sun is in the constellation of Aries. This and many other bits of astronomical information lead us to see that Dante had a sky chart entirely within his mind, and he seems to have expected his readers to possess the same internal map. He knows the constellations, how the planets move through them, the phases of the moon, the appearance of the sun throughout the zodiac, and so forth. It is as if he could close his eyes and, not just visualize a model of the earth at the center and the planets around it, but spin it in his mind and watch it revolve.

In addition to being more familiar with the nighttime sky's ordinary appearance, medieval people took delight and even comfort in looking up at it. This was in part because the medieval model of the cosmos was of a universe that was orderly and close in. At the center of the cosmos, of course, was the earth, and then came the moon, which divided the atmosphere from the heavenly ether. Next was Mercury, Venus, the sun, Mars, Jupiter, Saturn, then the sphere in which the stars were thought to be lodged, like gems set into a transparent band of crystal. The pilgrim will travel through each one of these spheres and meet souls within, and on several important occasions he will step back, turn around, look down, and take in a view of the whole cosmic system. This is important because medievals thought the distance between these planets was spaced out in harmonic intervals. In a way similar to how the frequency of one note in a chord resonates harmoniously with a second note in the chord, to make, for example, a fifth, medieval men and women thought the interval between one planet and the next was spaced out in harmonic chords. The world, then, in its ordinary existence, constituted a visual symphony, notes written into the heavens to be plucked by the daily movements of the planetary bodies. And Dante the pilgrim ascended high enough to "read" the score!

In this way, Dante recycles a bit of classical literature, Cicero's "Dream of Scipio," an ancient text famous throughout the Middle Ages. Cicero describes the visionary dream of a Roman general, Scipio, during which the soul of the general flies through the spheres of the heavens to reach the apex of the universe. Scipio then turns around and sees the universe, stretched out at his feet: "What is this sound, so loud and yet so sweet, that fills my ears?" he asks. His guide answers:

> That is the sound produced by the impetus and momentum of the spheres themselves. It is made up of intervals which, though unequal, are determined systematically by fixed proportions. The blend of high and low notes produces an even flow of various harmonies. . . . By imitating this system with strings and voices experts have succeeded in opening a way back to this place. . . . Filled with this sound, people's ears have become deaf to it.[2]

In other words, the music created by the spheres, to which we have become deaf, can be regained through study or through beautiful music that imitates the same harmonic proportions that space out the heavenly bodies. And so, if Dante wrote a poem that had the same order that the cosmos has, then he could provide his readers with a kind of harmonic template that could help them see the deeper harmonies underneath.

Thus, we can see that whereas we moderns tend to think of space as being a cavernous depth in which there are things billions of miles away, hidden away in the utter darkness of their chaotic landscape, medievals saw the universe as harmonious and comforting. As C. S. Lewis famously put it,

> Nothing is more deeply impressed on the cosmic imaginings of a modern than the idea that the heavenly bodies move in a pitch-black and dead-cold vacuity. It was not so in the Medieval Model. You must conceive yourself looking up at a world lighted, warmed, and resonant with music. . . . Pascal's terror at the eternal silence of that infinite emptiness never entered his [i.e., the medieval's] mind. He is like a man being conducted through an immense cathedral, not like one lost in a shoreless sea.[3]

Similarly, Dante describes his first entry into heaven as entering into a world of warmth, light, and harmony:

> When the great wheel that you, through being desired, make eternal
> attuned me, too,
> with the harmony you moderate and discern,
>
> it struck me, all of a sudden, that the heavens were lit on fire
> by the flame of the sun. . . .
>
> The extraordinary newness of sound and the brilliance of the light
> enkindled in me such a desire to know their cause
> I had never felt something so sharp. (*Par.* 1.76–80, 82–84)

Dante, then, sees the heavenly sky and, rapturously, feels it saturated with peace and with love.

At the same time that the pilgrim feels the order of the heavens, he is also struck by its dazzling brightness. In the medieval world, the spectator delighted in the mere quality of color or light in a way that is hard for us to conceive—we who live in a world flooded by artificial lights. He could almost taste its radiance. Umberto Eco describes how beautiful gems, flowers, colorful works of art, or sparkling objects were "sensuously present" to medieval men and women: "The passage from aesthetic pleasure to mystical joy is virtually instantaneous," he writes. "Their love of colour and light . . . was a spontaneous reaction. . . . The beauty of color was everywhere felt to be beauty pure and simple, something immediately perceptible and indivisible. . . . Feelings of artistic beauty were converted at the moment of their occurrence into a sense of communion with God and a kind of joie de vivre."[4]

What is more, just as we all know that the orbit of the moon affects the tides of large bodies of water, so too did medieval people think *all* heavenly bodies exerted their influence on earth. Looking at the stars wasn't just pretty: it was opening yourself to spiritual powers that penetrated your body. Their beauty was spiritually radioactive. For Dante's contemporaries, then, even the basic idea of flying through this place of peace and radiance would have been a wildly exciting sci-fi journey. The pilgrim visits that region bathed in happiness and light, which flows into his body. It is this visceral feeling for the physical effects of light and music that appears everywhere throughout Dante's final canticle.

And so medieval men and women looked up at the sky and saw it as beautiful, radiant, dazzling, and ordered—or rather, felt it as perfection. It always moved in order, always obeyed, always sang. But although this ordered motion was most perfectly embodied in the starry sky, this order, this love, if you will, also flowed throughout the world and, in fact, was thought to keep everything in motion. It was love that regulated the seasons as they yielded to each other; it was love that ensured that the sea harmoniously lapped the land without overflowing its boundaries; it was even love that bound the soul to the body. In a famous poem that monks memorized and schoolboys chanted, the Late Antique philosopher Boethius praises the order of the world, ruled by what he called "cosmic music" or "cosmic love":

> O Lord, you govern the universe with your eternal order:
> You brought time itself into being, and all that marks
> Its changes in the heavens and here on the earth,
> [you who are] Both moving,
> And also in stillness. . . .
> The world's beauty is your beauty: your mind is the source of its
>   grandeur
> As you shaped it to your liking, imposing upon it your order,

> Which harmonizes the many elements that compose it,
> The cold with the fiery hot, the dry with the wet, lest any
> Fly off on its own and unbalance the equipoise of creation.[5]

In other words, there's no good reason why the elements don't just repel one another and fly off in their own directions. Somehow, someway, they remain united, in a body. For Boethius, then, this harmony or glue that holds them together is divine love, which has its source in the heart of God, who generously pours forth his love to keep the world together.[6]

There is one final point to make about Dante's cosmos: although love flows through the universe, moving each part of creation toward its Creator, it yet remains true that creatures have different capacities for absorbing the presence of God. This varying capacity of different creatures to absorb the light of God was thought to be perfectly illustrated with an analogy to light. Take coal, for example: dark, dirty, greasy coal has little reflective power, but even coal, if you light it on fire, can release a burning light as if there were light hidden within. But other types of matter, say a diamond or an emerald, were just made to be filled with brilliant light! They let light flow through them, hardly obstructing its path at all. Topaz can be saturated by heavenly light; the dull stone cannot. Similarly, although all creatures seek out God by a kind of internal movement, some created things imbibe more of his light than others. Otto Von Simson, author of the classic *Gothic Cathedral*, summarizes the teaching in this way:

> According to the [thinkers] of the Middle Ages, light is the most noble of natural phenomenon. . . . Light is the creative principle in all things, most active in the heavenly spheres, whence it causes all organic growth here on earth, and weakest in the earthly substances. But it is present even in them, for, asks St. Bonaventure, do not metals and precious stones begin to shine when we polish them, are not clear windowpanes manufactured from sand and ashes, is not fire struck from black coal, and is not this luminous quality of things evidence of the existence of light in them?[7]

All of this helps us understand that first terzina of *Paradiso*: "The glory of Him who moves all things / pervades the universe and shines / in one part more and in another less" (*Par.* 1.1–3). God, then, is present to every creature, but he is closer to some on account of the fact that they can be more present to him.

Dante, Words, and the Unspeakable Beauty of God

Modern Christians often do not think about mysticism or negative theology as proper to Christianity. Mysticism seems like some vaguely Eastern phenomenon, something that belongs to Hinduism or Buddhism. But the truth is that Christianity inherited its mysticism from both the Greek and Jewish traditions, and ever since the church fathers (such as Gregory of Nyssa), the doctrine of the "unknowability" of God has been a cornerstone of Christian life. There are even hints of such teaching on God's "unknowability" within Scripture. For instance, in 2 Corinthians 12:2, 4, Saint Paul modestly alludes to a mysterious vision he was given:

> I knew a man in Christ . . . (whether in the body, I cannot tell; or whether out of the body, I cannot tell, God knoweth;) such an one caught up to the third heaven. . . . He was caught up into paradise, and heard unspeakable words, which it is not lawful for a man to utter.

Paul's word for "unspeakable" is *arrhētos*, the equivalent of the Latin *ineffabilis*, from whence we get our own English "ineffable."

A sixth-century Byzantine theologian by the name of Dionysius the Areopagite picked up on this passage in Saint Paul and purported to explain what this mysterious vision was and how we too can come to enjoy it ourselves. His writings were translated into Latin in the early ninth century, after which time they influenced numerous theologians, such as Hugh and Richard of St. Victor (both mentioned in Dante), as well as the great Thomas Aquinas. In fact, if you consult the latter's *Summa theologiae*, you will find that Dionysius is cited more times than any other author within the first thirteen questions (that is, those questions that deal with how human intellects can know God).

Needless to say, "negative theology" is not explained easily or quickly, but I at least want to provide some background for mystical theology before we return to the opening of *Paradiso*. In particular, I will refer to a short, five-page treatise by Dionysius the Areopagite, *The Mystical Theology*.[8]

Dionysius states it simply: God is the cause of all, and "the Cause of all is above all."[9] Because God is above all, the language we routinely use about this world—this lower world of creatures—is radically deficient when we use it in reference to him who is not a creature but the cause of creatures. For example, take the word "is." We can say that there *is* no such thing as a unicorn, but there *is* such a thing as a man called Trevor. When we say "Trevor *is*," we mean that this creature lives and has being. Trevor doesn't necessarily have to exist. We could imagine a world without horses or a world without Trevor. And so, although Trevor "exists" or "is," what we mean by that is simply the following: this creature has being, but not of necessity. Its being is on loan for a short time.

Now, when we turn back to talking about God, we begin to realize the radical limitations of our words. If we utter the seemingly straightforward sentence "God is," we think we know what we mean; but the problem is that we are using the same word ("is") that we use for creatures of dust, and we are trying to apply that to the Being who cannot *not* be! Thus, when we try to use our ordinary language to talk about God, we run the risk of imprisoning his majesty within the cage of our own speech. Dionysius makes this same argument, but he employs a rhetoric full of paradox and mystery: "[The more I climb in my speech] the more language falters, and when it has passed up and beyond the ascent, it will turn silent completely."[10] Dionysius says, then, that the closer we get to God, the less our words mean anything when applied to him. We are left feeling that our words are babble and chatter. We are reduced to silence. Or, in the words of Dionysius, "The fact is the more we take flight upward, the more our words are confined to the ideas we are capable of forming; so that now as we plunge into darkness which is beyond intellect, we shall find ourselves not simply running short of words but actually speechless and unknowing."[11] In this way, Dionysius, using the image of Moses climbing Mount Sinai, says you have to strive to leave everything behind, to recognize the radical limitations of your words for talking about God, and plunge into divine darkness: "[The good cause of all] is on a plane above all this, and it is made manifest only to those who travel through foul and fair, who pass beyond the summit of every holy ascent, who leave behind them every divine light, every voice, every word from heaven, and who plunge into the darkness where, as scripture proclaims, there dwells the One who is beyond all things."[12]

We can now turn back to Dante. In the opening lines of *Paradiso*, the poet refers to precisely this getting lost within God, plunging into his darkness:

> That heaven that draws in more of his light:
> I was there, and I saw things that one who has come down
> from there cannot—nor does he even know how!—tell.

> Because drawing itself near to its desire,
> our intellect is immersed, so profoundly,
> that memory cannot follow up after it from behind. (*Par.* 1.4–9)

Here in *Paradiso* Dante finds himself making up words unheard of before. So strange and shockingly new is his experience that old, tired verbs and nouns will no longer do. His term I translated above as "immersed" is actually *si profonda*—that is, to "profound oneself" or perhaps "our intellect is so in-profounded." Later Dante invents another term, *trasumanar*: "To signify in words 'going-beyond-mere-human': / it cannot be done" (1.70–71).

Throughout the opening verses of *Paradiso*, we see Dante adopting Saint Paul as the patron saint of his journey. Dante alludes to the Pauline passage quoted above: "Whether I was there merely by that part of me you created / last, O Love who rule the heavens, / you know" (*Par.* 1.73–75). Thus, as a pilgrim, Dante follows the example of Saint Paul and Dionysius's description of Moses climbing Mount Sinai. What he saw and experienced is beyond the ability of language to capture.

But all of this—that is, Dante's claim to have gone to a place beyond intellect, beyond memory, and beyond language—presents a major problem for a *poet*, a problem more intense than any Dante has faced so far. Poets are wordy, and they are supposed to talk about things. And thus, to our surprise, we find that Dante not only claims that his subject is ineffable and that he takes Saint Paul as the patron of his journey, but at exactly the same time, he also turns to the classical and epic tradition for inspiration to speak about what he saw. At the beginning of *Paradiso*, then, we see two long-standing traditions collide: that of the mystic whose vision ends in silence and that of the classical poet whose craft of language culminates in eloquence. In addition to being a Saint Paul, Dante also wants to be Orpheus, the legendary poet who could tame beasts and bend trees through the sweetness of his verse. And finally, Dante will lay one more layer on top of all this: he depicts himself also as a great classical hero who goes and steals something of great worth and then brings it home again, like Jason and the Golden Fleece. We hear all of the strands of these interweaving traditions in his opening invocation. Having just mentioned the failure of memory and words, Dante continues:

> Truly, as much of the holy kingdom as
> I could treasure up in my mind
> shall now be the matter for my song. (*Par.* 1.10–12)

Dante makes himself out to be some adventurous hero from a fairy tale who climbs a ladder and steals a miniscule part of the giant's treasure; or perhaps he is like Prometheus, who stole just a spark, banked it, and brought it back home to earth. But Dante is convinced that, given the extraordinary nature of the treasure of this kingdom, if he could get just one single tiny spark from this ocean of fire, and somehow get it back home to earth and into his poem, then the whole world would be consumed with the flame of love. Or as he says, "Poca favilla gran fiamma seconda" ("Great flames leap from the smallest spark," *Par.* 1.34). It is for this reason that Dante prays and begs with such urgency. Dante invokes God, he invokes the Holy Spirit, he invokes the ancient Muses, he calls upon Apollo, as if calling upon anyone who will listen, to enable him to capture just a glimmer of the heavenly kingdom:

> Truly, as much of the holy kingdom as
> I could treasure up in my mind
> shall now be the matter for my song.
>
> O good Apollo, for this final task
> make me into a vessel of your power.
> This you require before you give your laurel, so much loved.
>
> Up to this point, one peak of Parnassus
> has been enough for me, but now I need both
> to enter into the arena that remains for me.
>
> Enter into my breast! May you breath in me,
> as when you drew Marsyas
> out from the scabbard of his limbs.
>
> O divine virtue! If you lend yourself to me,
> I will show forth the shadow of the blessed realm
> that is stamped within my mind.
> . . . .
>
> Great flames leap from the smallest spark. (*Par.* 1.10–24, 34)

"Poca favilla gran fiamma seconda." And so we have a gap between the ambition of the poet and the "unspeakability" of the place into which he ventures. He wants, like Jason, to steal a treasure, a tiny spark, but he worries that his human faculty to carry it home in language is hardly capable of such an adventurous undertaking. And so, what is the pilgrim to do?

Love as the Vehicle of Ascent

And now we return to that deeper problem: the pilgrim's inability to even see the depths of what he hopes to write about! Dante represents this almost right away in *Paradiso* 1, when the pilgrim, inspired by Beatrice, turns to look at the sun (*Par.* 1.54–58). Indeed, this gazing at the sun is the perfect image for Dante's journey into heaven. Ordinarily, the sun is so bright that it blinds you; if you look at the source of sight too much, then it will take away your vision. And thus, for medieval men and women, who loved so much the splendor of shining gems and the dazzling color of stained glass, it was a shame that human powers were not fully capable of enjoying the most beautiful object in the world: the sun. In heaven (and beginning in Eden), though, you are given more power to see, more power than you have here. We will see that as the pilgrim progresses through the spheres of heaven, his power of sight will grow stronger and stronger, so that in the end he will be able to stare at a light that is one thousand times brighter than the sun.

Dante also gives us a precious hint of an answer to a fascinating question: How is it the case that what blinds the pilgrim and sears his eyes with pain will later delight him? How does his vision get stronger? For Dante, the instrument by which his vision is deepened is love. Love adds to our capacity to see:

> I could not bear it long, yet not so short a time
> as not to see [the sun] sparking within,
> like boiling iron when pulled out of the fire.
>
> And then, all of a sudden, it seemed a day to this day
> was added, as if He who can
> had adorned the heavens with another sun.
>
> Beatrice stood motionless with her eyes
> fixed on the eternal wheels; and I fixed my eyes
> on her, withdrawing them from above.

> By gazing on her I was made into something new within,
> just as Glaucus was when he tasted the grass
> that made him consort of the other gods in the sea. (*Par.* 1.58–69)

Having just withdrawn his eyes from the sun, Dante looks down, but to his surprise he sees a new sun blazing directly next to him. This is, of course, Beatrice, who glows so brightly because she herself is looking at the center point of the wheels of heaven. As we will see, in Dante's cosmos, everything that moves, moves because it is filled with a kind of giddy, childlike energy, a bright happiness to be in existence. Beatrice looks at this love at the center of the universe and is moved with love. And when *she* is moved by love, she becomes moving to Dante. Thus, in the reflection of the radiance of her happiness, Dante himself is able to grow in the ability to see bliss.

Dante also says that he can feel himself being changed from the inside out, in the same manner that Glaucus was transformed, an allusion to Ovid's *Metamorphoses*. Ovid relates the tale of a simple fisherman who one day brought in a good haul of fish, pulled up his net, and laid the fish on the bright grass to dry. But then the fish magically came back to life and started hopping about, until they flopped back into the sea. Glaucus was confused:

> I stood dumbfounded, for a while not believing it, searching for the cause. Had some god done it, or the juice of some herb? . . . Gathering some herbage in my hand, I bit what I had gathered with my teeth. My throat had scarcely swallowed the strange juice, when suddenly I felt my heart trembling inside me, my breast seized with yearning for that other element. Unable to hold out for long, crying out: "Land, I will never return to, goodbye!" I immersed my body in the sea.
>
> The gods of the sea received me, thinking me worth the honour of their company, and asked Oceanus and Tethys to purge what was mortal in me. . . . When later I came to, my whole body was altered from what I was before, and my mind was not the same.[13]

This was the metamorphosis of Glaucus: his transformation from human to god. He began to long for new things, to swim with new speed, and to live in new depths, to say goodbye to the ordinary land that used to sustain him. In a similar way, then, Dante's *Paradiso* will be the tale of what the poet calls *trasumanar*—that is, to go beyond ("trans") the human (*Par.* 1.70). This transformation works from the inside out, and it is love that enters into the heart to make it divine from within.

12

"In His Will Is Our Peace": Individuality and Polyphony in *Paradiso*

(*Paradiso* 3–20)

"Only Man!"

In the previous chapter, we discussed what the heavens meant for the medieval sky gazer, how he imagined it as bathed in warmth and sound and light. He looked up at the heavens wistfully, longingly, as a place of peace. But the same sight that could occasion joy could inspire disgust and melancholy. After staring up at the heavens, vibrantly alive, that paradigm of order full of pure light, the medieval poet dejectedly turned his eyes back down, to lament that the human community could not better resemble the world of the stars: Why can't individuals be content to be grouped in constellations? Don't they know that their beauty would be increased? Don't they know that their erratic, selfish movements ruin the dance? In contrast to the orchestra of the heavens, we on earth have factions, wars, hatred, pride, envy, avarice—the tumult of our interior passions. In the previous chapter, we saw how Boethius basks in the warm music of the universe: "Not even the blowing winds are random," he shouts with glee, because God "observe[s] and order[s] all from [his] high office." But there is one creature who messes things up:

> Only man is endowed with freedom
> That you could constrain but have chosen not to, . . .
> The innocent suffer . . .
> Wicked men sit upon thrones.
> Villains thrive and trample the necks
> Of virtuous men into the mud. . . .
> Look down from on high and impose your correction
> You who bind all the world within your laws,
> Who control the waves and the tides, bring order
> To the surging waves of mankind's follies.[1]

Nature obeys God perfectly; humanity, endowed with the gift of freedom, rarely lives in restful harmony. Boethius ached when he thought about how little human society embodied that beautiful cosmic order.

With this in mind, we are prepared to appreciate the great shock of *Paradiso* 3, where Dante, in the heaven of the moon, gets his first chance not just to look at the beauty of the astral bodies but also to speak to heaven's inhabitants: "Just as through transparent and polished glass / or through tranquil and limpid water . . . / faint traces of our visages are reflected . . . / in this way I saw so many faces ready to speak" (*Par.* 3.10–11, 13, 16). The face that is brightest and most eager to speak to Dante is that of Piccarda Donati, the younger sister of Dante's old drinking buddy, Forese Donati, whom we met in *Purgatorio* 23. In *Purgatorio*, Dante did not at first recognize the face of his old friend on account of how emaciated he had grown through penitential fasting. Likewise here he meets the younger sister, but she has grown so fair that Dante does not recognize her at first. Her face is unrecognizable to him, not because of its gauntness, but because it has been transformed in new splendor (*Par.* 3.58–61). Such beauty, even here, in the lowest of all the heavens! Piccarda then relates her story (3.46–57).

Piccarda became a nun, but her ambitious and machinating older brother Corso (not Forese) had her forcibly removed from the monastery and married off. In the next canto Dante struggles over this point: it seems unfair that Piccarda gets demoted to the basement of heaven because of an act of violence that occurred to her against her will. Beatrice addresses this problem head-on (*Par.* 4.73–80): Piccarda could have walked back to the convent every single day. She could have been like Mucius Scaevola, the ancient Roman hero who, when caught in the enemy camp, stuck his left hand into the fire and let it be burned off in order to demonstrate his inflexible commitment. She could have been like Saint Lawrence, who refused to betray his Christian community and was tortured for it. According to pious legend, while being roasted alive, he said, "Turn me over, because on this side I'm done." Piccarda did not have this irrepressible will, even if she wore the "veil of the heart" her whole life (3.117). Her will didn't have the resolve, like fire that always rises up, to keep returning to the good to which she had committed. Her reflective power is less than that of others because her capacity to choose love was less.

As soon as Dante hears this, he is pricked by a question that would probably occur to almost any of us. If I saw a man, every day on my walk to work, who was three times better looking, two times fitter, and four times wealthier, I admit I would probably dislike him. And similarly Dante, who still has much of his earthly thinking with him, hesitantly asks Piccarda and those around her, "But tell me: you who, here, are happy, / do you not desire a higher place / where you will see more and better make yourselves friends?" (*Par.* 3.64–66). I gotta ask you, Piccarda, is there just a small part of you that envies the others, higher up? And Piccarda makes the most amazing reply:

> Along with the other shades, she smiled a little,
> then answered me. She was so happy
> that she seemed to burn in the first fire of love:
>
> "Brother, our will here rests in tranquility,
> because of the power of love, which makes us want
> only what we have, and it makes us thirst for nothing else.
>
> "If we did long to be more exalted,
> our desires would be discordant
> with the will of the one who appoints us to be here.
>
> "And that doesn't work among these circles, as you will see. . . .
>
> "On the contrary! It is the very essence of this blessed *esse*
> to cling within to the divine will,
> so that our various wills are made one.
>
> . . . .

"And in his will is our peace.
It is that sea toward which all things move." (*Par.* 3.67–76, 79–81,
    85–86)

A human will at peace. A human will that wants nothing more. A
human will that loves what it has and finds itself at rest, moving within
the larger cosmic order. If you think back to the heartbroken plea from
Boethius, then you can see what is so striking about Dante's depiction of
heaven. True, his pilgrim soaks up the beauty of the luminescent bodies
and exalts in their symphonic music; but, most importantly, he finds a
community of human beings, at long last, forming an ordered cosmos
that resembles the symphony of the heavenly spheres. It is for this reason
that I think Piccarda is the most beautiful character in all the *Comedy*:
she is a picture of a soul who is not just a member of the choir but a note
in the symphony.

Piccarda understands that, in a heaven of rubies and diamonds, she's
just an opal. And yet, on a deeper level, she also understands that a jewelry
store that only sold diamonds would be dull. In order to better proclaim
the depth of the beauty of God, a diversity of creatures is needed. Piccarda
is happy to accept her role. Paradise, then, is that place where human
beings, now moving in harmony with one another, have finally joined
the cosmic symphony. At the same time, Dante emphasizes the need for
variety in the universe to express the infinite beauty of God. In this way,
Dante builds his heaven on two competing principles: individuality and
harmony. To see better how these core principles reinforce each other, we
need to be attentive to the poet's use of the metaphor of music.

Polyphony in *Paradiso*

The three canticles of the *Comedy* can be thought of as movements in a
symphony, with each movement written in a different key and tempo. Dante
in fact built into his poem a system of allusions to music to make sure we
hear his poetry with musical overtones. In *Dante's Journey to Polyphony*,
Francesco Ciabattoni points out that every allusion to music in *Inferno*
is to broken song, failed hymns, or warped and perverted parodies of the
liturgy.[2] In *Inferno* 6, there are a few fleeting lines that refer to souls who
sing "hymns," but not real hymns, because those souls can only gurgle,

submerged in mud. In life they were those who allowed their hearts to be plagued by constant sorrow (*tristitia*); in death they sing a pathetic hymn that is choked by the mud in their vocal chords. The final canto of *Inferno* opens with a twisted parody of a Christian hymn, and we also hear about the trumpet of Malacoda—that is, his fart—or how Master Adam's dropsied belly rings like a kettle drum. Hell is full of fragmented music and broken instruments; every attempt to raise the voice into music is marked by its collapse into cacophonous sound.

Ciabattoni goes on. *Purgatorio*, in contrast, is full of references to Gregorian chant, called "monophony" by musicologists. Monophony is that sober music of the monastic choir, in which every voice sings the same melodic line. It is restrained and thus used for chanting during the liturgical hours of the Divine Office. Every one of the eighteen songs the poet alludes to in *Purgatorio* are, we are led to understand, chanted in monophony.

In *Paradiso*, though, Dante specifies that the songs and hymns are polyphonic—that is, made up of varying voices, each of which sustains its own melodic line. The choirs form nesting layers of distinct voices. Thus, in heaven you still have that unity practiced in purgatory, but now each voice, while remaining in harmony with the others, is able to regain its individuality without losing its role in adding to the concord of heaven. This form of music, although developed already by the so-called Notre Dame school in thirteenth-century Paris, found its culmination in the English composer Thomas Tallis. In fact, Tallis wrote a piece (albeit three hundred years after Dante) that I have always thought of as one of the best musical embodiments of Dante's *Paradiso*: *Spem in alium*, a forty-two-part motet!

What we find, then, is that Dante's musical program embodies theological realities. Infernal sinners remain willfully rebellious. In life they broke away from the human community to pursue some good in vicious competition with the rest of the human race. Now, as a community, they fail to achieve concord. Like musical notes that remain independent, their retained individuality is ugly and broken. Repentant sinners in purgatory, on the other hand, now willfully submit their individuality to the community. They learn now what it is like to live as members of a body. And thus they erase their tendencies to erratic individualism, forcing their voices into the unison of the simple plainchant. But with the polyphonic hymns of *Paradiso*, we have not only concord but also a simultaneous expression of individuality: Dante gives us a vision of heaven as a million-part motet. And it is the underlying polyphonic reality of heaven that explains why heavenly souls welcome the pilgrim with such affection, as we shall see now.

"This Is One Who Will Cause Our Loves to Grow!": Erotic Love in Paradise (*Paradiso* 5–9)

When the pilgrim moves into the second heaven (the heaven of Mercury), he is greeted with a joy that astounds him:

> I saw more than a thousand splendors
> bring themselves toward us, and in the midst of this light I could hear:
> "Look! This is one who will cause our loves to grow!"
>
> And as each shade came up to us,
> it struck me as steeped in joy
> on account of the bright radiance that emanated from it. (*Par.* 5.103–8)

It is true that *Paradiso* sometimes lacks drama. And yet it has its own energy and peculiar excitement. Here, the pilgrim is immediately enveloped by a thousand souls who surround him from all directions. Their eagerness to know him is embarrassingly flattering: "Look! This is one who will cause our loves to grow" (5.105). Our pilgrim is surprised by joy, disconcerted to find himself enveloped by such superabundant loving.

In chapter 9 we discussed how Dante brought together epic and lyrical modes of writing for his new Christian epic, but it is only in *Paradiso* that we realize how far Dante went to graft the lyrical into his cosmic epic, a bold move, given that many of Dante's contemporaries thought the lyrical tradition was antithetical to theological discussion of heavenly love. The Sicilian poet Giacomo da Lentini said that although he wanted to go to heaven, he would opt out if it meant being there without his lady.[3] Heaven seemed so far away, whereas earthly love was nearer to me than I am to myself. In another poem, Giacomo described his interior suffering, how his heart was plagued by an aching, burning, and longing so violent as to threaten death:

> There burns within me painful sorrow,
> like unto a man who holds fire within,
> hidden within his breast;
> the more he tries to smother it,
> so much the more does it take hold
> and it cannot remain enclosed.
> In just this way do *I* burn
> when I pass by and do not look
> at You, O Beautiful Countenance.[4]

Giacomo uses the verb *ardere* (to burn) three times in only one stanza, as if obsessively returning to the secret flame. The more he tries to keep it in, the more it threatens to devour, as if he were trying to put out a fire by packing it with dry leaves. We have seen, too, how such burning is enkindled by rays shot forth from a lady's eyes, and how the rays follow the channel down to the heart. It comes as a huge surprise, then, when we hear all this language of "sparks" and "fire," "radiant eyes" and "burning hearts," everywhere in . . . *Paradiso*! How did such earthly love make it to heaven?

As I have said, medieval lyrical poetry was meant to perform in you what is happening in me; that is, by describing my experience of love, I could make it take root in you. And it is my opinion that this "performative" aspect of lyrical poetry unlocked an extraordinary *theological* opportunity for Dante: the portrayal of heaven as a community vertiginously falling in love. In other words, in depicting heaven, Dante conducted a literary experiment: he imagined what it would be like if, in heaven, there were no longer any *donne petrose*—stonyhearted ladies—who remain aloof or coldhearted, coy mistresses who have to be convinced. Indeed, in *Paradiso* there are no longer lover and beloved, but rather all souls have "gentle hearts" and thus are easily enflamed with love. As soon as you begin wooing a soul in heaven, you find that, before you have finished, it is trying to ignite a new flame within you. The dynamism of this vision of reality, in which heavenly souls are all lovers, makes even the vernacular courtly lyric seem staid. Dante portrays a whole community of ardent lovers whose love only fires more love in return.

We have come full circle, then—that is, back to *Paradiso* 5 (surely meant to be read in light of *Inferno* 5, which describes Paolo and Francesca!), where Dante is surrounded and enveloped by the joyful souls who dwell within the heaven of Mercury. Just after they call out to him, "This is one who will cause our loves to grow," Beatrice asks one of the souls to speak: Justinian, the former Byzantine emperor. The pilgrim can't help but notice how bright this soul has grown:

> "I can see well how you nest
> in your own light, and how then you send it forth from your eyes,
> because it comes out like lightning when you smile.
>
> "But I know not who you are, nor why your merit is weighed in the
> balance here." (*Par.* 5.124–27)

Justinian, who has been "first to speak" (*Par.* 5.131), seems delighted that Dante wants to know who he is. He is a little like the father or mother leaning over the crib and speaking first to the infant, but when the parents find that their love solicits love within the tiny heart they address, they are filled with even more love than they had before:

> This I said directly to that light
> that had spoken to me first; but there irrupted from within
> a greater brilliance than there had been before.
>
> As the sun that conceals itself
> through the excess of its own light, once its heat has burned through
> the tempering layers of its vapors,
>
> so, too, did he! Because of his increasing joy he hid himself from me,
> within his radiance, that holy figure!
> Thus, enclosed and concealed, he replied . . . (*Par.* 5.130–38)

There is a fascinating connection here. In a canzone that Dante had written as a young man (the love song performed by Casella in *Purg.* 2.112), the poet referred to how the smile of the beloved "overpowers our intellect as a ray of sunlight overpowers a weak sight."[5] There, Dante used the images of sun and weak eyes to represent how a beautiful person conceals herself within her own radiance of light. In *Paradiso*, Justinian is described as a beloved: he not only conceals himself in his radiance, like the beloved, but he also delights in Dante's desire to know *him*, as the lyrical *lover* would. This is a dynamic exchange.

We find the same dynamic increase of love again, perhaps not surprisingly, in *Paradiso* 8—that is, in the heaven of Venus. Dante is careful to add a narrative detail to make us feel the intensity. In hell Paolo and Francesca were whipped about by a violent windstorm; in *Purgatorio* 26 the lustful lovers are described, humorously, as inching forward to speak to the pilgrim, getting as close as they can while remaining within the fire. Thus, in the first canticle, we have an image of violent but empty motion; in the second, we have love that is finally beginning to yield to moderation. And now in heaven we have a passion for the good that makes the love of Paolo and Francesca seem lukewarm:

> There is no wind that descends from cold cloud
> with such violence—either visible or not—
> as would not seem impeded and slow,
>
> to one who had seen those heavenly lights
> come toward us. . . .
>
> Then one of them neared himself to us and
> alone began: "All of us are so eager
> for your delight, so that you may take joy in us." (*Par.* 8.22–26, 31–33)

Needless to say, the fact that such a surprise party awaits him brings the pilgrim great joy. Dante squeals with delight: "Deh, chi siete?" ("And who are you?," *Par.* 8.44). He is, again, almost infantile in the purity of his glee. His joy comes as a response to the generosity of the first invitation, but then the pilgrim's joy adds even more affection to the heavenly soul:

> And then, what I saw! It became greater, both in size and kind!
> It grew by adding a new bliss
> to its bliss, when I had spoken. (*Par.* 8.46–48)

In fact, the soul grows so joyful that, once again, it becomes hidden to the eyes of Dante.

There's more in the next terzine. When this soul (Charles Martel of Anjou, not the more famous Charles) has finished his speech, Dante says:

> "But since I believe that the deep happiness
> your speaking has poured into me, my lord,
> is seen by you, just as I see it,
>
> "I am pleased all the more. . . .
>
> "You have made me happy." (*Par.* 8.85–87, 89, 91)

The narrative details are important, and their significance easy to miss. What we have is a picture of heaven as a place in which souls are constantly and vertiginously falling deeper in love. Charles Martel's speech brings the pilgrim delight, but when Charles observes that his speech has given joy to the listener, his own joy increases yet again because his listener's has grown. But then it continues: when Dante sees now that his growth in joy has been responsible for Charles's increase of joy, he then grows even happier than before. This process, seemingly, could continue.

In hell Dante had to approach the lethargic souls to induce them by blandishment or force to give up their stories; here in heaven he is bombarded and enveloped by eager souls who keep anticipating his questions. The souls rush down upon and around him to sweep him up into that dynamic communal experience of falling ever deeper in love, an experience of love that has been going on for a long time before the pilgrim arrived: "Look! This is one who will cause our loves to grow!" (*Par.* 5.105). In his pilgrimage Dante experiences a role reversal: the love poet becomes the beloved. And so Dante makes a concerted effort to turn up the temperature of his final canticle by embedding within his poetry the language of "glistening eyes" and "burning hearts," borrowed from the lyric tradition.

Long before (in *Vita Nuova*), Dante related an eerie dream in which Love fed his *core ardendo* (burning heart) to an understandably hesitant Beatrice. But such images of burning do not disappear in *Paradiso*; rather, they grow more abundant! In the circle of the sun, Dante is surrounded by *ardenti soli* (burning suns). Dante will later refer to Cacciaguida's "bow of ardent affection" (*Par.* 15.43); to how *ardente* is the "sweet love" that issues from the Eagle of Justice (20.14–15); to the *ardente amore* of Peter, James, and John (25.108); to how Bernard of Clairvaux turns his eyes "with such affection" to Mary that it makes Dante's eyes *più ardenti* ("more burning," 30.142). In fact, Dante uses the adjective *ardente* eleven times in *Paradiso*, only two times in *Purgatorio*, and not at all in *Inferno*. In our popular imagination we think of the realm of Satan as sultry and hot; but if we follow Dante's insight, we should change the simile to "cold as hell." For Dante, *Paradiso* is not only the place of the more intricate music of polyphony (as opposed to the broken songs and warped instruments of hell); it is also hotter and more radiant. It is within this heat that an extraordinary unity is forged: a paradoxical fusion of diverse individuals within a fully united body.

Diversity and Unity in Human Community (*Paradiso* 10–14)

The higher the pilgrim travels through the heavens, the more shocked and amazed he is by this paradoxical diversity within unity. And thus, as the journey continues, the poet has to reach for more imaginative art to match the pilgrim's ever richer experience. This is particularly true for the heaven of the sun and the Eagle of Justice.

The heaven of the sun (*Par.* 10–14) is often a favorite passage for students, in part because most recognize (for a change!) all three of the speakers within it, as well as the subjects they discuss: Thomas Aquinas (the Dominican) first tells the story of the foundation of the Franciscan order by Saint Francis; then Bonaventure (the Franciscan) praises Saint Dominic; and finally, Solomon praises prudence. The poet structured these canti in a chiastic pattern; that is, the speeches and speakers are delicately woven together in an interlocking, X-like pattern. Even beyond that, Dante goes out of his way to make these canti densely poetic. For instance, when Aquinas describes Francis as the "holy man of God," he cycles through a whole carousel of metaphors: he likens Francis to a sun that rose on the world; he describes him as one of those passionate lovers from a rich family who disobeys daddy's wishes and marries the poor girl; he says that the Saracens were "unripe" for conversion, effectively likening Francis to a gardener; he refers to Peter's ship, likening Francis to a navigator; and finally, he refers to the wayward flock, likening Francis to a shepherd.

In addition to these metaphors, Dante portrays Aquinas engaged in poetic wordplay:

> "Let anyone who used words for this place
> not say *Ascesi*, . . .
> but *Orient*, if he wants to say it properly." (*Par.* 11.52–54)

In other words, we should think of Assisi as the little town in which the world was remade, the place in which the sun was reborn. Thus, let's not call it Assisi, which is close to the Latin for "to ascend," but rather Orient, the place where the sun is "reborn." And so Aquinas, that serious theologian par excellence, has grown uncharacteristically wordy, surprisingly poetic, and linguistically playful. In fact, on two occasions in canto 11, Aquinas has to stop himself, recognizing that his poetic exuberance has gotten out of hand ("But, lest I go on too densely," 11.73; "And so, if my words are not too overcast," 11.133).

It's important to recognize the historical reality behind this poetic artifice: these two religious orders had a lot in common but were rivals in the Middle Ages. Both Franciscans and Dominicans taught in the famous universities of their time, but they emphasized different core principles. Dominicans, thanks to their roots in fighting dualistic heresies, were keen to emphasize how grace works through nature, the power of reason, and the importance of study. They said that without knowledge you can't love, and that "first the bow is bent in study"; that is, knowing is necessary for love.[6] Franciscans were scholars too, but because of their roots in Francis's radical embrace of poverty, they tended to emphasize the importance of the will in the spiritual life and wanted to protect the unknowability of God and his frightening distance. And so, to simplify things, if Dominicans proceeded to love through knowledge, Franciscans got to love through acts of service. It so happens among human beings that, even when they agree on almost everything, if there is one tiny difference in *emphasis*, there (sadly) almost always is divisiveness. In the Middle Ages, we know many Franciscan authors who wrote treatises against Aquinas, and some Franciscan leaders even forbade their followers to read his writings![7]

With these tensions in mind, we can turn back to Dante to see how he poetically hints at those differences in these canti. On the one hand, he (through Aquinas) describes Francis as a lover, a man of poverty, and a shepherd. On the other hand, Bonaventure describes Dominic, the great heresy buster, in terms entirely different: Dominic is not a wide-eyed lover but "the holy athlete" (*Par.* 12.56), like a broken-nosed fighter from Philadelphia. Dominic was born "behind the shelter of the noble shield" (12.53) and was "gentle to his own and savage to his foes" (12.57). The word Dante uses for "savage" is *crudo* (raw). Dominic's marriage to the church is described in terms of courtly love, as if he were a knight (12.64). He is also described as the wheel of a chariot that smashes down the faces of enemies in battle (12.106–8). Finally, he is a torrent that strikes with hurricane-like force (12.97–102). And yet, at the same time, Dante also says that Dominic's work gave rise to "fruit" (12.65); Dante refers to him as one who travels through the vineyard (12.86) and the twenty-four plants (12.95–96); his followers are a garden in which the weeds are overgrown, and he is a spring that watered them when he was alive (12.103–5).

We see what Dante has done: through his use of metaphor he has both brought these saints together and kept them apart. Francis, the wild-eyed lover, is contrasted to Dominic, the Rocky Balboa warrior-athlete-saint; yet both tend their flocks, both are gardeners, both are like the sun. Both make sure their "trees rise with greater vigor" (*Par.* 12.105). Both souls now shine like the sun—shielding themselves in brilliance—because they poured out the radiance of their love on earth. And so the two groups, which had viewed one another with suspicion, now have the delightful opportunity to recognize that they were actually playing for the same team. As if in recompense for their earthly doubts, now every time they hear praise of the other order they are overcome with a joyful recognition. For example, as soon as Aquinas has finished speaking, Bonaventure is moved to return the favor:

> "It is fitting that, when one is, the other should be brought up.
> In this way, just as they went to war as one,
> their glory can shine out together." (*Par.* 12.34–36)

In keeping with the densely poetic structure of these canti, Dante de-scribes how these souls are like parts of a clock. In a clock, if gears and mechanisms are moving in opposite directions, that does not mean the clock is broken or at odds with itself. On the contrary, in a clock, diver-gent movements are necessary for unified function (*Par.* 10.139–48). But there are more similes used—indeed, piled up on top of one another. At the beginning of canto 12, after Thomas has finished his speech, the souls cannot help but break into dance and song, again. They are likened to a turning millstone, then to an orchestra, to a wreath of flowers woven together, and even to twin rainbows (12.1–11). At the end of Bonaven-ture's story of Dominic, all the souls are moved yet again. Dante describes them as when you look up at the nighttime sky and see a bunch of stars shining, but then you recognize that those stars, which you had admired as a collection of individuals, actually form a constellation. But then you zoom out one more time and recognize that even that constellation is the centerpiece of an even bigger constellation (13.1–24).

Example after example makes us see how these individuals have been knitted together, including some individuals who no one, neither Do-minican nor Franciscan, would have ever thought would have made it. For instance, Aquinas mentions Sieger of Brabant—a shocking move by the poet Dante, because he was Aquinas's archenemy in life. They each wrote numerous books to refute one another. And so we have a vision of the heaven of the sun, which would be a little like Notre Dame and Wheaton College deciding to start accepting one another's credits and sharing a faculty; or perhaps as though you went to heaven and found Josemaría Escrivá, Pius XII, Dorothy Day, and Thomas Merton all holding hands. Dante's poetry weaves together a cornucopia of metaphors to show how God weaves together different kinds of people within the history of the church.[8]

The Eagle of Justice

What Dante begins in canto 10—weaving souls together through the artistry of his poetry—he continues throughout all the middle canti of *Paradiso*. He seems completely enchanted by the idea of the diversity and unity of heaven. The universe itself is God's poem. Seen as individual pieces, the cosmos looks like a series of mistakes, a series of erratic accidents and off-axis slants (*Par.* 10.13–21). But taken together, these jagged parts cooperate to make manifest the secret, deep, and hidden plan of the divine mind:

> Lift your gaze, reader, to the wheels on high,
> . . . .
>
> now start to look longingly there, upon the art
> of that master craftsman who loves it within himself
> so much that his eye is never moved off of it. (*Par.* 10.7, 10–12)

Dante is convinced that he who studies the order of the cosmos "cannot but taste of Him" (10.5–6).

What God does on the level of cosmology and physics, he also does among human beings and through time: he providentially gathers up broken bits and pieces of human beings and forms them into the great mosaic of history. In the heaven of Jupiter (*Par.* 18–20), Dante speaks this time not to single representative souls but to all the souls together, who speak to him of providence, taking up the single, mighty voice of an eagle. Dante is shocked to learn that, among the great kings who make up the Eagle, there is not only David but also Ripheus and Trajan. Trajan was a pagan Roman emperor who, according to medieval legend, was prayed out of hell by Gregory the Great. Trajan was given his flesh back for a day, and he used his time well, repenting and thus being allowed to enter into heaven. Ripheus is a character in the *Aeneid*, mentioned in passing in only one line as just some soldier who came to help Aeneas fight in Troy. And that's it; he is left out of the remainder of the *Aeneid* and forgotten by history. Dante, though, lifts this failed character out of Virgil's audi- tion and makes him, literally, one of the stars of heaven. The Eagle asks, "Who would have believed down in the erring world / that Ripheus, the Trojan, would have been fifth in this circle / among the holy lights?" (*Par.* 20.67–69). Dante, alarmed, asks, "What are these things?" (20.82). The Eagle responds that Ripheus

> "through grace—that wells up
> from a fountain, so deep, that never did creature
> thrust his eye down to where it issues at its source—
>
> "he set all of his love there on righteousness.
> And for that, from grace to grace, God opened up for him
> his eyes to our future redemption,
>
> "so that he believed in it. . . .
>
> "Those three ladies were there for him in baptism—
> the ones you saw to the right of the wheel—
> one thousand years before there was baptizing." (*Par.* 20.118–24,
>   127–29)

The poet had made up a backstory: Ripheus grew discontented with the wise of his day, and he trusted that God would reveal a savior. And so, in this way, one thousand years before Christ, Ripheus was saved through implicit faith, like Cato. Dante uses his poetic license to invent a story to illustrate concretely the mysterious way providence works through history. Trying to understand its working would be like expecting you could see down to the ocean's floor (*Par.* 20.72).

In conclusion, throughout all these canti, Dante gives us a vision of a shocking and radical diversity, in which seemingly random souls are unex- pectedly gathered up from foreign lands. Heaven is for Dante, as for John in the Apocalypse, "a great multitude, which no man could number, of all nations, and kindreds, and people, and tongues" (Rev. 7:9). In a certain sense, Dante's heaven is more like Los Angeles than Lincoln, Nebraska. And yet Dante's "diversity" is not the isolated and individualistic pluralism of contemporary society, in which we don't have the goods of diversity because none of those goods are brought together into a meaningful and beautiful whole. Dante has something to say to this as well. While it is true that his heaven has an uncompromising diversity and plurality, it is also true that all these souls live and breathe as one.

Intellectual Fasting and the Test of Love: Saturn, Stars, and the Crystalline Sphere

(*Paradiso* 21–29)

Thinking and Doing

In the modern world we tend to imagine a radical opposition between people who *do* and people who *think*: there are those who get stuff done (leaders, businesspeople, executives) and those, like professors at liberal arts colleges, who don't. Too often, doers have contempt for thinkers, while thinkers have disdain for those who participate in the active life. As we have begun to see, Dante works hard to explode such simplistic categories. In the heaven of the sun, we saw that Dominic was called a "great athlete," a man who vigorously campaigned to destroy the church's opposition—clearly a *doer*. But Dante, through the mouth of Bonaventure, adds that Dominic did so through teaching and learning, and for this reason Dante says that he went forth "with doctrine and with zeal together" (*Par.* 12.97). Dominic could not have arrived at his successful *activity* if it were not for his *learning*.

Most of us can comprehend that some intellectual training is needed to be successful in a practical sphere of life, but Dante, as he always does, takes the next step and, by doing so, reveals one of the blind spots in modern culture. For Dante, it is not just that intellectual work is necessary for shaping successful activity, but also that thinking can actually be productive; thinking can be something, even when it is not primarily directed at solving a problem or building a bridge. Under the right conditions, contemplation is an activity that is valuable, productive, and moving. These ideas on active contemplation are present in the heaven of Saturn, the heaven of the stars, and the crystalline sphere.

The Thinking of Angels

According to Dante's cosmology, there is a heavenly sphere, called the "primum mobile" or "crystalline sphere," that encompasses even the sphere of the stars. It is the most vital, dynamic, energetic thing in the whole universe: it moves faster than anything on earth, bounding forward without ever slowing. It is the chief driveshaft that turns the spheres, allowing energy from heaven to slowly trickle down, from sphere to sphere, until it reaches earth. Or to use an organic metaphor, as Beatrice does, the world is like an upside-down flowerpot, whose roots are in the highest heaven—that is, this crystalline sphere—and whose flowers and fruits show up, down below, on earth (*Par.* 27.106–20).

Dante means for this poetic vision of the crystalline sphere to strike us as dazzling, a kind of medieval equivalent to the images from the Hubble Space Telescope. As so often happens throughout the canti of *Paradiso*, this awe-inspiring view of heaven is so breathtaking that it leads to an outburst of anger. After contemplating this sight, Beatrice warmly abuses the blindness of humankind and our pathetic contentment with the mud and puddles of earth (*Par.* 27.121–26). Greed is the excess that causes the blooms of the flowers to spoil.

But what Dante sees in the midst of this great, rotating wheel is even more breathtaking. He sees a tiny point of light, smaller than any star seen from the earth, emitting a beam of blinding brilliance:

> I saw a point that sent out a ray
> of light so sharp that vision is burned by it and
> must close against it because it is so strong. (*Par.* 28.16–18)

Around this point of light there are nine spinning rings (28.13–45); the closer to the point the ring stands, the faster it moves. As Beatrice explains, these are the nine choirs of angels. According to Dante's source (Dionysius the Areopagite's *Celestial Hierarchy*), the two highest ranks of the choirs of angels are made up of the seraphim and cherubim, who are able to look most deeply into the ocean of fire of God's being (28.100–102). "Moved by flaming love," they occupy themselves almost exclusively with that act of looking; however, something of the warmth of their vision spills over into the next lower tier of the hierarchy, the thrones. And in this way, affection cascades down from choir to choir: dominions, virtues, powers, principalities, archangels, and angels. The two lowest tiers of the hierarchy, the archangels and angels, are chiefly responsible for taking this vision out, communicating it to those on earth.

When we recall, though, that these rings of angels are found within the great turning circle of the crystalline sphere, then we realize that Dante understands this hierarchy of contemplation as responsible for generating the physical motion of the heavenly spheres. Quite literally, the *looking* of angels turns the wheeling of the heavens. Because the vision of God is so stirring, love is enkindled in the heart of the one who sees—the one who contemplates—and this energy is released as a kind of spiritual radioactivity, like the energy that irradiates from an atom when it is split. Thus, for Dante, love literally moves the world. Far from the worthless activity it is sometimes called, contemplation moves all other activities in the cosmos.

Once, when I read these words to one of my students, he immediately responded, "That's a beautiful idea, but how could human beings—with their finite intellects—ever participate in such a profound act of intellectual seeing?"[1] His instinct was correct. One of the most striking features of Dante's vision of heaven is his portrayal of *human beings* participating in this profound gaze of love—a gaze for which they don't seem worthy. In the heaven of Saturn (*Par.* 21–22), the poet gives us a few hints about how this is at all possible.

Saturn and Contemplation

According to ancient and medieval astrological theory, Saturn could have a pernicious influence on people on earth: if you were born under the sign of Saturn, then you are melancholic, irritable, morose, and introverted. Poets and artists are born under the sign of Saturn, as Albrecht Dürer brilliantly captured in an engraving depicting melancholy.[2] In *Paradiso* we find a rather more positive interpretation of what your Saturnine disposition would be like if perfected. That irritable tendency to withdraw, to be alone, that frustrated spirit about everyone's faults, is revealed on Saturn for what it could be: a world of profound peace, a spiritual power to be attentive to and delight in the depths of truth. Throughout these canti Dante makes us feel the profound abyss of tranquility located within their souls.

Canto 20 opens in eerie stillness; there is no smiling, no singing, no sound. The pilgrim is perplexed. All he sees is a giant golden ladder, with thousands of sparks raining silently down (*Par.* 21.28–33). Soon, one of these splendors draws near to Dante: Peter Damian, a reforming Benedictine monk of the eleventh century. Dante's first question to him is about this silence: "Tell me: why has it gone silent within this wheel? / What happened to the sweet symphony of Paradise, / which sounds so devoutly down below?" (21.58–60). Peter responds: "You have mortal hearing, just like your sight, . . . / thus here there is no singing / for the very reason Beatrice has not smiled" (21.61–63). This is not a silence due to inactivity, then; rather everyone is holding back. Earlier Beatrice had explained that if she smiled at the pilgrim, he

> "would be Semele when she was reduced to ash.
>
> "For my beauty . . .
> . . . .
>
> "if it were not tempered, would shine so brilliantly
> that your mortal power, in light of its splendor,
> would be a leaf scorched by lightning." (*Par.* 21.6–7, 10–12)

In other words, behind this veil of silence is a music and joy so powerful and profound that it would destroy a mind too feeble to encounter it. It is like a vast amount of water in a reservoir, which exerts so many tons of pressure that the walls of the dam have to be reinforced.

Throughout these canti, Dante cleverly weaves details in and out to give us glimpses of the spiritual energy that is being held back. When Peter Damian hears the pilgrim's question, for example, he comes alive with an extraordinary force, whirling around "like a millstone" (*Par.* 21.81). And at the end of canto 21, Dante gets just a brief glimpse of what would happen if that pressure did break forth. There, Peter Damian, once a cardinal himself, grows angry and excoriates the greedy cardinals of Dante's day. Their fur-lined mantles, he sarcastically grumbles, hang over their horses' sides, so that both man and beast travel under one cloak (21.133–35). Then all of those justice-loving, melancholic souls on Saturn, listening keenly, affirm his words with a short, confident shout:

> At his cry, I saw more flames
> descend, step by step, and spin.
> With every turn they were becoming more beautiful.
>
> They moved around this flame and stopped,
> and then came a shout of such loud sound
> that nothing here could be likened to it:
> nor could I comprehend it! A thunderbolt so overcame me. (*Par.*
>   21.136–42)

It's almost humorous: the pilgrim is frightened, like a child startled by thunder. From our perspective, we realize that this brief outbreak of voices manifests how much they are holding back:

> Struck down in a stupor, I turned to my guide,
> like a little child who always runs back
> to where he finds the most comfort.
>
> And she, like a mother who immediately consoles
> her son . . .
>
> said: "Didn't you know that you are in heaven?
> And didn't you know that heaven is entirely holy,
> and thus that which is done arises from righteous zeal?
>
> "How the song would have knocked you over!
> And my smile! You can see this now,
> given that their shout so shook you." (*Par.* 22.1–5, 7–12)

Sacred Hunger and the Intellectual Life

But how is it that these contemplatives have reached a vision of such depth? How is it that they became capable of looking down into the abyss of truth, so much so that they are full of power? Dante makes it clear that his contemplatives only arrived at such a depth of spirit by practicing extraordinary spiritual discipline. In fact, the poet here refers to contemplatives as "athletes of God," those who sacrifice everything in a spiritual training program. Thus, although it is true that their pure thinking produces a dynamic movement, it is also true that they had to discipline themselves to get to the point of being able to gaze with such profundity. For Dante, contemplatives are not just people who like to read and think in quiet, but also those with a kind of muscular devotion to the intellectual and moral life. Peter Damian sums up his life in this way:

> "I made myself so firm in the service of God,
>
> "that with simple foods of olive oil,
> I heartily suffered the heats and frosts,
> content in contemplative thoughts." (*Par.* 21.114–17)

In order, that is, to find the liberty to dwell steadfastly in those contemplative thoughts, Peter first had to reach an impressive level of discipline, like that of a Division I athlete who gets up every morning at 5:00 a.m. to go to the gym and eats only what his trainer prescribes to him, whether he is hungry or not. The contemplative, then, is like an athlete with his mind, willing to submit to discipline.

In the next canto, Saint Benedict adds, "Peter began without gold and without silver / and I with prayer and with fasting" (*Par.* 22.88–89). This surprising connection between "fasting" and intellectual activity appears throughout the *Comedy*. In *Paradiso* 25, for example, Dante refers to his "sacred poem, / to which both heaven and earth have put forward a hand / so that it has made me, for many years, lean" (25.1–3). In other words, the very process of studying, reading, thinking, meditating, digesting, and carefully seeking the perfect word to express the conception is likened, by Dante, to a great intellectual fast, to a disciplined eating of words and books. In *Paradiso* 19, the pilgrim asks the Eagle a question, begging the Eagle to free him from his "great fast / that for so long now has kept me hungry / since I could not find any food for it on earth" (19.25–27). At the end of *Purgatorio*, Dante also begged for divine assistance, invoking similar terms: "O sacred Virgins, if fasting, cold, or sleepless nights / I've ever suffered for your sake, / necessity drives me to call for my reward" (*Purg.* 29.37–39, trans. Hollander). Consistently, then, throughout the *Comedy* Dante uses the metaphor of fasting, both because of the inherent property of "hunger"—that is, a longing for things that cannot be easily satisfied by ordinary fare—and on account of the discipline, control, and moderation needed for developing the ability to be nourished by only the best books and the richest ideas. As Paul Griffiths puts it in the opening to his *Religious Reading*, this mentality stands in stark contrast to our contemporary consumerist and entertainment-based approaches to information:

> So far as I can recall, I have always been able to read, to make sense of and be excited by written things. I know, of course, that there was a time when I could not read; it's just that I cannot remember it. But I was never taught, and have still not properly learned, how to read with careful, slow attentiveness; it is difficult for me to read with the goal of incorporating what I read, of writing it upon the pages of my memory; I find it hard to read as a lover, to caress, lick, smell, and savor the words on the page, and to return to them ever and again. I read, instead, mostly as a consumer, someone who wants to extract what is useful or exciting or entertaining from what is read, preferably with dispatch, and then to move on to something else. My habits of reading are mostly like my habits of purchasing: dazzled by the range of things I can buy, I spend all that I can as fast as I can, ecstatic at the excitement of contributing to the market economy and satisfied if I can assure myself of a place in that economy by continuing to produce and consume. I'm not alone in this condition. Most academic readers are consumerist in their reading habits, and this is because they, like me, have been taught to be so and rewarded for being so.[3]

Consumerism feeds you, anticipating any craving long before it arises, keeping you from ever experiencing any meaningful hunger. What a contrast to the slow, patient reading and rereading that leads to greater hunger, to an intellectual leanness, to an alert mind—to that kind of reading needed to absorb and slowly chew on a book like Dante's!

At the end of canto 22, Dante leaves these deeply peaceful souls behind. He approaches the golden ladder of the contemplatives, and as soon as he just sets his foot on the first rung of this electrically charged ladder, he is transported instantly, violently, and swiftly thousands of miles up into the heaven of the stars, an extraordinary image for the act of contemplation. From this vista, Dante looks down and sees the heavens spread out beneath his feet:

> And all seven planets were shown to me:
> how large they are, and how swift, and
> where they are in their distant homes.

And that little patch that makes us so ferocious! . . .

All of it was shown to me: from hills to mouths of streams. (*Par.*
22.148–51, 153)

Indeed, Dante describes his view from this vantage point: "I saw this globe
of ours / and I smiled because it seemed so lowly. / I approve that judgment
as best / that holds this earth as least" (22.134–37). From this height, Dante
can prefer the depth of the gaze to the noisy chatter of earth.

The Test of Love

In canti 24, 25, and 26, just before the pilgrim ascends to the primum
mobile, he is within the starry sphere, where the apostles Peter, James,
and John test him to see if he possesses faith, hope, and charity. The poet
models these examinations, somewhat humorously, on the medieval bachelor of arts exam (*Par.* 24.37–39). And so, while Peter is thinking about
how to phrase his question, the pilgrim gets himself ready: "Just as the
bachelor arms himself and does not speak / until the master proposes the
question . . . / just so I was arming myself with every possible argument"
(24.46–47, 49).

In heaven, though, Dante's pesky professors are difficult to please: they
keep prodding, asking him to go beyond the definition. For instance, Peter
asks Dante, what is faith? The pilgrim dutifully provides his biblical and
catechistic answer: "Faith is the substance of things hoped for, / the evidence of things that are not seen" (*Par.* 24.64–65). But Peter begins to
probe him on particular key words in that definition: And what is "substance"? However, as the examination continues, it starts to take on a
peculiarly poetic tone: "Very well: the money has been well examined /
now in terms of its mixture and weight, / but tell me if you have it in your
purse" (24.83–85).

So, what kind of exam is this? What does Peter really want to know?
It would seem, in the first place, that Peter wants to know not just that
Dante holds the right opinion about faith but also that he possesses it as
his own. The coin, as Dante puts it, is in his pocket. Furthermore, one
of the characteristics of a *virtue* (and faith is a theological virtue) is that
it is not just rectitude of opinion but also a power, an energy, a strength
that brings about effects. For instance, at one point Dante affirms his

faith by stating, "I believe in one God, / one and eternal, who moves all the heavens, / though not moved, with love and desire" (*Par.* 24.130–32). In other words, the pilgrim starts reciting the creed, but in a vernacular, poetic form. The creed is now translated into the rhythm and cadence of poetry! Thus, the real demonstration that Dante possesses the theological virtue is that he can move those around him. At the end of his oral exam, when Peter finally approves of his response, the pilgrim announces it by demonstrating that he has been literally moved:

> As the lord who hears that which pleases him
> and so embraces his servant, congratulating him
> on the news, as soon as the messenger has become silent,
>
> in the same way, while blessing me and singing,
> as soon as I had gone silent, he encircled me three times,
> that apostolic light, at whose command
> I had spoken: I had pleased him so much in my speech! (*Par.*
>   24.148–54)

Thus, the true test has been whether the pilgrim can fit the raw matter of ideas into the shape and order of cosmic poetry. Peter doesn't so much want a definition of faith as he wants the pilgrim to perform faith for him, to perform it within him. Peter wants Dante to describe it, poetically, so that he wants to have it, too. Just as the medieval love poet tries to make the beloved share in his love—to perform in you what is happening in me—so too does Peter want to see Dante's faith working, acting, making new faith. There can't be any parasites in heaven; to make it in, you have to be able to add to its love, not just suck up the love of others.

The culminating moment of Dante's bachelor exam in poetic theology, though—his test of love—comes in *Paradiso* 26. In response to John's question, how did you come to know love?—or to use John's metaphor, with how many teeth does love bite?—Dante answers:

> "All those bites
> that can make the heart turn to God
> have come together in my charity:
>
> "the being of the world and my own life,
> the death of the one he endured so that I live,
> and that which every man of faith hopes for, as do I,

> "along with the living knowledge I mentioned before,
> have drawn me from the sea of twisted love
> and have placed me on the right shore.

> "I love the leaves with which the garden
> of the eternal gardener *enleaves* itself,
> as their good comes from him." (*Par.* 26.55–66)

This, then, is the pilgrim's breathless litany of the loves that are scattered throughout the universe; he looks at the world and sees his existence, the world's being, Christ's death, and eternal life. It's a major moment, in which Dante recognizes love not just in a few people or in a few beloved places, but feels all creatures as somehow unveiling some aspect of the face of God. In light of this confession, we can think back to Paolo and Francesca yet one more time. We realize now how inhibited and confined their little love was. They had one little love that distracted them from an ocean of goodness.

— 14 —

The Canti of Surprise: Garden, Book, and Rose

(*Paradiso* 30–33)

The Final Garden

In *Paradiso* 30–33, Dante enters into the ultimate place of rest, the empyrean heaven, the real garden, as opposed to the temporary garden, Eden. This, the tenth heaven, was for medieval scholars a realm of paradox and mystery, at the outermost recesses of the universe but also most interior to the cosmos, a place that is really no place at all. It is as if Dante goes through a magical door on the edge of heaven and then finds that he has entered back inside into its center. It is a space where the bodies of Christ and Mary dwell, and where all the bodies of the saints will one day be, but it is not a place in time, and it is not a place of extension of space. The best the medieval scholars could do was to call it a place in which bodies are made up of pure intellectual light. It is this paradoxical place where God retains his human body and where human beings become God.

That last sentence rings out so boldly that it almost seems like heresy, but the truth is, it's just Christian orthodoxy. It's worth quoting Christian Moevs on this point: when we encounter medieval thought in a more accurate form, he says, we often "do not recognize it as medieval" because "it seems too daring, too sophisticated, too ideologically unfettered, too nonmedieval. It can even, to those who understand it, come to seem at least as compelling as our own examined or unexamined assumptions about the world."[1] Note that Saint Athanasius, a fourth-century church father, famously declared, "God become man so that man might become God." And this is exactly what we find in the last canto of *Paradiso*: a human being brought so far beyond his natural capacity that he is afraid of being destroyed. As Dante looks at God, he finds that his mind is so rocked by that oceanic and tempestuous power that, paradoxically, if he turned away from that vision, he would surely die. He has become God, in a certain sense, because it is only God who sustains him:

> I believe that, given the brightness I endured, issued by
> that living ray, I would have been lost,
> if my eyes *had* been turned from it.
>
> And I remember that I was emboldened still
> to endure: such that I joined
> my gaze with the infinite worth. (*Par.* 33.76–81)

Later, he adds that it was only because a lightning bolt irrupted in his mind that he was able to see at all:

> But my wings were not suited for this,
> had not my mind been struck
> by a bolt of lightning in which what it desired came. (*Par.* 33.140–42)

How can mere human beings enjoy this kind of vision? Dante's answer is: they can't. It is too great, too far beyond, too bright, too real, too terrifying. It comes only as a gift, a gift for which you constantly feel yourself unworthy, and a gift you have to be made worthy to receive. Here, as Dante looks, he feels the perilous state of his mortal humanity, as if he is about to come unglued, and yet at each instant he notes how God sustains his power so that he is not dissolved but rather is given light in which he can continue to look. Dante shares this idea with Aquinas: the idea that although our minds cannot comprehend God's essence, God is yet willing to provide a gift of understanding, a sort of eye on loan, through which we can see his divine essence. Or, to bring it closer to Aquinas's metaphor, God's light is so bright that it blinds our feeble eyes, but he will give us the gift of a light in which we can see his blinding darkness. In this way, Aquinas provides a lovely interpretation of the psalm text "In thy light shall we see light" (Ps. 36:9). This gift of light needed to see God's light is called "the light of glory," or *lumen gloriae*.[2]

These final canti, as the title of this chapter suggests, are not only canti of paradox but also canti of surprise, and the greatest surprise is that the pilgrim can enjoy this vision without falling to pieces. But there are three more surprises: in these canti Dante is surprised by (1) humans in the heavenly rose, (2) an old man, and (3) the face of God.

Surprised by Humans

In each of the heavens he passed through, Dante met representative souls who acted as the spokespeople for that realm and its virtues. As Beatrice explains in *Paradiso* 4, the souls don't actually occupy these posts but rather reveal themselves to Dante in those places in order to help the pilgrim understand their differing capacities to receive God, as well as the various and complementary ways in which they do so. In the empyrean heaven, Dante finally gets to see them all together, assembled into one great community. And the way Dante describes them assembled is scintillating: now as the members of a vast, ordered, and cosmopolitan city; now as marching in rank and file, like soldiers in an army; now as plants in a garden; now as sparks in a river of fire; and finally as if they were the petals of a flower (*Par.* 30–31). It is this shifting use of imagery—as if the poet were looking through a kaleidoscope—that gives these final canti such a dreamlike intensity: "The river and the topazes . . . / and the laughter of the grass / are shadowy prefaces of their truth" (30.76–78). As Dante gazes, he witnesses once again the convergence of unity and plurality in the heavenly community: at times the saints make up one body, like that of a river or a flower; at the same time, they appear as individual gems, sparks, or plants in a garden. Gazing at the garden/rose is the pilgrim's final stage of preparation for the vision of God, and it is testimony to the extraordinary role Dante assigns to human beings: the human community is necessary for the vision of God. And it is this human element that sets Dante's poem apart from other medieval writings.

Dante wasn't the first medieval writer to imagine a journey that went all the way up into the empyrean. One author by the name of Bernard

Silvestris (early twelfth century), upon whose work C. S. Lewis based *Out of the Silent Planet*, wrote a bizarre story in which an allegorical figure, Nature, travels up into space to find Urania, a personification of heavenly wisdom. Together these two go into what Bernard describes as the "realm of pure and uncontaminated light, far removed and wholly distinct from the physical world."[3] This is, of course, similar to how Beatrice leads Dante into the empyrean heaven:

> "We have exited out of
> the largest body to the heaven that is pure light,
>
> "intellectual light, full of love,
> love of true good, full of delight,
> delight that transcends every sweetness." (*Par.* 30.38–42)

A few decades after Bernard, another poet and theologian, Alan of Lille, reworked some of the major themes of his predecessor in another allegorical story of space travel. In his *Anticlaudianus*, the lead character, Prudence, ascends through the heavens and has conversations with powerful cosmic forces. At one point, she meets Theology, who warns Prudence that she will have to abandon the chariot of Reason to proceed farther (5.243–55). Theology then leads Prudence beyond the starry realm, where she comes into the empyrean, which Alan says has the form of waters of fire (5.307–400). Over the course of one hundred lines, Alan luxuriously describes the empyrean as a crystal of fire, as ice that is not cold and does not melt when warmed. He says it is "purer than purity, clearer than clarity, brighter than gold . . . a harmless fire, lacking in heat but abounding in radiance." It is here that Prudence sees "the gleam of a brimming fountain spreading forth an abundant flow of water . . . which then flows back into the fountain" (6.240–50). The Trinity, then, is the source of this liquid light that pools up in the empyrean and forms the brilliant glory in which the angels and saints dwell.[4]

In Dante, though, the pilgrim doesn't have conversations with cosmic forces or allegorical personifications but rather is continuously surprised by human beings who lived in time and history; human beings who rush down to meet him, surround him, and draw him up; human beings who condescend, like Cacciaguida, to speak to him in a baby talk he can understand. This is what comes as a surprise: that, as Dante nears the end of his book, heaven gets more and more social! Human beings become more and more important for realizing a vision of God. Dante assigns an extraordinary role to human relationships; they are not incidental to my relationship with God. Bernard and Alan had personifications (Nature or Prudence) led by cosmological forces (Urania or Theology) into the heaven of pure light, but our poet has a human pilgrim led by *Beatrice*, and this came as a tremendous surprise for Dante's first readers: How could he cast a simple Florentine girl as the lead actress in this great poem of learning?

As Dante moves into the highest heaven, he is surprised by humans yet again. When he comes into the empyrean heaven, he is overwhelmed by its brilliance. He then looks and sees

> light that took the shape of a river,
> dazzling in its radiance. It rested between two banks, each of which were
> painted with the miracles of spring.
>
> From that rushing river living sparks came out
> and, on either side, they settled themselves onto the flowers,
> like rubies circumscribed in gold.
>
> Then, as though inebriated by the odors,
> they plunged themselves in the depths of the marvelous rapids once again,
> and as one dove in, another came forth. (*Par.* 30.61–69)

At this point, Dante's reader would have recognized that he is rewriting Bernard or Alan, faithfully following them as his guides and predecessors in constructing his *own* poetic description of the river of light. Then comes Dante's surprise: the sparks that leap from the river and become the flowers on the banks turn out to be . . . the souls of people:

> Then, like people who have been behind masks,
> then seem other than they were before, once they remove
> their unnatural semblances in which they were disguised,
>
> thus the flowers and the sparks changed for me into a greater festival
> so that I saw both
> courts of heaven made manifest. (*Par.* 30.91–96)

Alan's river of fire has become Dante's river of flowers and sparks, which are now individual saints. Alan's river is a geographical location; Dante's river is made of human eyes and faces.

This "humanization" of the cosmic forces of space has extraordinary theological implications. Beatrice bids Dante to "drink" in this sight and says that he must do so before his "great thirst" can be satisfied (*Par.* 30.74). Bernard of Clairvaux later says, "Fly with your eyes through this garden, / since looking at it will help season your gaze" (31.97–98). In other words, the *lumen gloriae* of Aquinas—the light that is given so that we may see God's blinding light—is reinterpreted in Dante as the spiritual radioactivity of the loving communion of saints. We now see that all of that dynamic warmth and radiance we read about in an earlier chapter is the light in which they see Love! We also remember that Dante borrowed from the vernacular lyric tradition to construct a dynamic vision of lovers trying to enkindle the flame of love in one another. This helps us see that the heavenly rose is eternally growing in luminescence! As the members of the community increasingly fall in love with one another, the *lumen gloriae* in which God is seen also grows. The *lumen gloriae* of heaven increases on account of the ever-abounding love of the saints, and in this light they are able to see more of God's essence. Knowing more of God's beauty fills them with the hopeful expectation of what is in store for their neighbor, and that ardent desire in turn makes them better lovers. And so, in this dynamic circle, the light of heaven grows, to borrow an image from Dante, like a lightning bolt that flashes but doesn't go out. It just keeps adding to its brightness, eternally growing in its luminescence. In this way, for Dante, human beings are not superfluous additions to your private enjoyment of God. Rather, their love is the light in which you see Love.

The Surprise of the Old Man

At a certain point in *Purgatorio*, Dante turned around to ask Virgil for an explanation, only to find that his guide had disappeared (*Purg.* 30.50–52). Now, here in paradise, Dante turns around to share a moment of joy with Beatrice, only to find that *she* has disappeared. Standing in her place is an old man with a beard! Needless to say, Dante intends the reader to experience a great shock:

> I turned around with a will, freshly enkindled,
> to question my lady on many things
> which kept my mind in suspense.

> I expected one thing but was answered by another:
> I was expecting to see Beatrice, but I saw an old man
> clothed like the people of glory.
>
> A beneficent cheer suffused his eyes and cheeks
> and a reverent manner
> such as is fitting for a gentle father.
>
> And "Where is she?" I asked at once,
> and he: "To bring an end to your desire
> Beatrice moved me from my place.
>
> "If you direct your gaze to the third ring
> from the highest step, you will see her again,
> now on the throne her merits have made her lot." (*Par.* 31.55–69)

How surprising for the love poet! He turns around to share a happy smile with the girl he has loved from his youth and finds an old man, with glowing cheeks, looking back at him. This is, of course, the Cistercian theologian Bernard of Clairvaux. It is rather like a megalomaniac Italian director removing the lead actress in the season finale of his blockbuster show. This surprising removal of Beatrice and substitution of Bernard raises all kinds of questions: Why couldn't Beatrice take Dante all the way home? Why is the old guy needed? Whatever happened to the poet of love? Is beauty insufficient for completing the journey? Dante hints at answers to those questions in his description of Bernard, to which we now turn.

At the end of canto 32, Bernard, noting that Dante's allotted time is running short, asks him to do one last thing to prepare himself for his ultimate vision:

> "Let us direct our eyes to the first love,
> so that, looking toward him, you penetrate,
> as much as is possible, into his effulgence.
>
> "But in truth, lest you fall back
> though moving your wings, all the while thinking you move forward,
> grace, by praying, is needed, and this comes by asking for
>
> "grace from her who can aid you.
> And you shall follow me with affection,
> so much so that your heart does not stray from my speech."
> He then began this holy prayer. (*Par.* 32.142–51)

These are the very last words of the penultimate canto, pointing forward to the final and ultimate moment. Significantly, then, Bernard tells Dante that he can't just fly his way home alone; he can't even make himself use his eyes or mind or intellect in the right way to get what he wants. All he can do is turn toward the center of the universe—which is yet invisible to him—wait, long, and look into that black hole . . . and ask Mary for help. And then, as a gift, whatever is there, if it wishes, will come forth from its invisibility, surround him, seize him, embrace him, and make him its own. For this to happen, Bernard says, Dante will need the assistance of her who sees more deeply into this black hole than any other, because, given her complete and absolute humility, she doesn't obstruct at all the light of God that flows through her. And so Dante and Bernard turn to Mary and utter this prayer:

> "Virgin Mother, daughter of your Son,
> humbler and higher than any creature,
> fixed point of the eternal plan,
>
> "you are the one who made human nature
> noble, so much so that its maker
> did not disdain to make himself through what he made.
>
> "In your womb, love was rekindled,
> through whose heat in the eternal peace
> this flower sprouted from the seed.
>
> "Here you are for us the noonday torch
> of charity, and there below, among mortals,
> you are the living fountain of hope.
>
> "Lady, you are so great and of such worth
> that the one who desires grace but does not run to you
> is one whose desire would fly without wings." (*Par.* 33.1–15)

Bernard's prayer is full of paradoxes and extraordinary praise: the mother is the daughter of her son; humble but exalted; a torch that burns at noon; the fulcrum of the whole universal plan of history. At the same time, Bernard calls her merciful, clement, compassionate, generous, the one in whom all human virtues are found (*Par.* 33.19–21). The whole prayer here uttered by Bernard is written with courtly overtones. For instance, Bernard calls Mary *Donna,* "my lady" (33.13), similar to how a troubadour poet would address his beloved. When Bernard introduces himself a few canti earlier, he says,

"And the queen of heaven, for whom I burn / all over with love, will bring down for us every grace, / since I am her faithful Bernard" (31.100–102). The old Cistercian mystic turns out to be even better than the hot young lover! Bernard of Clairvaux, in life, spent years preaching through the Song of Songs and only got through the first three chapters because he kept digressing so much, trying to explain the spiritual value of the language of "embrace," "kiss," and courtship to understand the soul's relationship to God. Bernard was, then, the theologian of love par excellence. Bernard's knightly devotion to Mary parallels Dante's devotion to Beatrice. He utters praise about Mary, just as Dante wrote about his beloved.

Bernard's tutorial comes at a crucial moment in which Dante's poetry takes a turn: Dante had spent his whole life talking about *his* love, but now he must begin to turn toward *love itself*, and it is soon after praying to Mary and looking upon her brightness, which is greater than that of any other creature, that Dante finds himself, effortlessly and naturally, lifting his gaze to look at the center point of the universe.

The Final Surprise

This leads us to our third surprise. When Dante finally does turn to look deep down into the black hole at the center of the universe, he does, of course, enjoy a vision of God, which emerges out of the depths in which it lies hidden. At first Dante sees just the "universal form": "In its depths I saw what it held within, / bound by love into a single volume, / that which is scattered in leaves throughout the universe" (*Par.* 33.85–87). Imagine that all the moments of time and all the different creatures in the universe are like pages pulled from a notebook and then thrown up into the wind, scattered all over the world.[5] In each one of those pages, the handwriting of God is discernible; that is, in each historical fragment and each historical creature, some aspect of God was fleetingly revealed. Here Dante, in looking at the source, sees "the universal form"—that is, the sap that runs through the veins of the whole world of creatures. Dante sees the deep unity and life that lives in each of them, as if every creature is seen now reflected in that which gave it birth. Dante sees the love that is the secret source of desire and movement in the world.

But for Dante, God is not just a cosmic force; he's not just the ultimate law of physics or the *Logos* of the Stoics. No, Dante's vision deepens as more of the vision of God emerges. And so, from the midst of this cosmic love, the secret source of vitality for the universe, Dante then sees three circles of different colors come forth. They all stand exactly on top of one another, and yet they can be seen as perfectly distinct. Obviously, this is a dynamic image for the unity and diversity of the Trinity; it is an image you can think but could never see.

Then—what is an even greater surprise—as Dante is looking at these overlapping rings, something else comes forth: an image, "painted with our likeness," looking out from within. "I longed," he tells us, "to see how it was possible / that the image fit the circle and how it took its place there" (*Par.* 33.138–39). In other words, Dante sees a human face. His vision of the Trinity has turned into a revelation of the incarnation. These stages of revelation come to Dante a little like how you keep taking off the outer shell of a Russian nesting doll. The pilgrim first sees the secret source of life for the universe; he then looks deeper and sees the rings; but then, as he continues to look, he sees God's human face. And God's eyes look deeply into his.

Dante drew near to mystery, expecting to look down into an abyss or chasm, but then sees that it is actually a person who has been waiting for him. Dante is again surprised by a human, surprised that the cosmic force that turns the universe looks at him and through him and into him, as if it only existed for him. And so Dante has a devastatingly personal revelation, in which he is seen through and known so perfectly that nothing is left out or behind.

Now we can understand the role of Bernard, the old Cistercian mystic who wrote love poetry to Mary. He teaches Dante about the ultimate beloved, the Virgin. Thus, at the apex of heaven, Dante the love poet has to stop writing about and for Beatrice, stop being the lover, and now become the beloved himself, become like Mary who was wooed by the Godhead. It's a gigantic role reversal, and it happens all at once. Dante spent his whole life seeking, striving, working, laboring, pursuing; and what he discovers in the end is that *he* is the beloved, that *he* has been wooed by the divine lover who now emerges out of his darkness to seek him in embrace.

This is the last surprise of the *Comedy*. And the final beautiful verses convey that rapture, that yielding, and that rest. For a brief moment, Dante has the energy of a lightning bolt poured into his mind to sustain this vision of gratitude for being loved, and for a fleeting second he turns in peaceful motion with the source of everything that is. Or as he puts it:

> But mine were not wings fitted for that,
> except that my mind was struck
> by a bolt of lightning, and through this what it longed for came.
>
> And now, even for my high imagination, all power failed.
> Already my desire and my will were being turned,
> just like a wheel that moves in balance, by
> the love that moves the sun and other stars. (*Par.* 33.139–45)

Conclusion

The Wonder of the Comedy

Dante was not the only or even the first writer to record a Christian vision of the world beyond. Well before Dante, there were dozens of written visions of the afterlife.[1] In fact, judging by the hundreds of manuscripts that have survived, such afterlife tales of traversing lands of horror and wonder made up one of the most popular medieval genres of literature. For example, English and Irish monks took up their ancestral poems about seafaring warlords and turned them into stories about intrepid saints who went off in search of the "Blessed Isle," such as in *Saint Brendan's Voyage* (from around AD 900). Late Antique "apocryphal" works also remained popular throughout the Middle Ages, as they purported to relate visions of the afterlife revealed to apostles, as in *Saint Peter's Apocalypse* and *Saint Paul's Apocalypse*. Gregory the Great (sixth century), in his *Dialogues*, told stories of monks who had visions of the penitent and the damned, and several centuries later, an illiterate English farmer, Thurkill, was led by Saint Julian on a trip to the afterlife.

At the same time that such visions were being read and copied, medieval men and women could gaze in horrified wonder at the polychromatic sculptural groups that stood above the main doors to so many European cathedrals (such as at St. Lazarus in Autun and St. Pierre in Moissac). In central Italy, they could look at mosaics and frescoes, such as Pietro Cavallini's *Last Judgment* in Rome or Giotto's *Last Judgment* in the Arena

Chapel in Padua. Standing under these frightening visions of souls being stuffed into the mouth of hell, or wounded with instruments of torture, those same medieval men and women could then enter the church to listen to sermons on the last judgment or the pains of hell. When he was still Cardinal Lotario, the later Pope Innocent III wrote a *contemptus mundi* (contempt for the world) treatise called *On the Misery of the Human Condition*, which gives us a good idea of what they would have heard.[2] In the final chapter of that book, the future pope thunderously invokes for the reader what hell holds for the wicked. Lotario takes Matthew 13:41–42, where Christ says that "there shall be wailing and gnashing of teeth," and turns it into this overwhelming rhetorical masterpiece:

> There will be weeping and gnashing of teeth, as well as groans and cries, lam-
> entations, yelling, and pained sobs; clamor and sharp wailing. There will be
> terror and trembling, sorrow and exhausting labor, heat and stench, darkness
> and fearful anxiety, bitterness and harshness, calamity and need, crampedness
> and sadness, bitterness and terrors, hunger and thirst, extreme cold and heat,
> sulphur and fire burning from age to age to age.[3]

Clearly such passages are meant to frighten you out of your wits. We find other medieval texts in Latin, such as Thomas Celano's *Dies Irae*, that help readers imagine themselves in the position of a soul on the day of wrath.

When we consider Dante's poem against the background of such ser-mons, paintings, carvings, poems, and visionary treatises, we get a better idea of what a stupendous feat the *Comedy* was, and why, after it was written, no one would again be able to write or paint about the subject without reference to the *Comedy* (think, for example, of Signorelli's *Last Judgment* in Orvieto or of Michelangelo's *Last Judgment* in the Sistine Chapel, both of which refer continuously to the Italian poem). And so, to conclude, I want very briefly to set the *Comedy* against the backdrop of what came before, referring to two concrete medieval works (one visionary treatise and one painting), before returning to Dante.

The visionary treatise is the *Vision of Thurkill*, already mentioned, which dates to around 1206. It tells the story of how one evening a simple peasant sees Saint Julian walking across his field. Julian asks Thurkill to lie down, leave his body on his bed, and rise up in his soul to follow him. Thurkill is then shown the mansions of the just and the places of punishment of sinners. Thurkill sees pits of fire, which belch forth stench.

He sees a theater in which the devils force the sinners to re-perform their earthly sins. The proud man is made to walk around with his chest swollen and palms back, praising his own fine clothes. Adulterers are made to perform their sin for the demons, but when they realize that all the demons are laughing at them, they grow angry at the partner who used to be the lover, and bite and tear one another up. In fact, all the plays end in gruesome ways. The demons interrupt the sinners' performances to hack their flesh into bits, frying each piece in a pan of hot oil. Then they shove the reconstituted bodies into a heated iron chair that has nails and screws sticking out of it. Wicked priests have their tongues ripped out for their evil sermons; knights charge at one another, wearing armor that is on fire; lawyers eat burning money and vomit it back up; slanderers eat spears; and so forth. When the plays are done, all the souls are stuffed into big stew pots: one pot has a molten metal, one has salt water to sting open wounds, one is full of cold water, and one is full of sulfur. Every eight days the sinners are rotated to a new pot.

Meanwhile, the penitent but yet unclean have to walk down an alley that is on fire and cross (unclothed) a bridge lined with thorns and briars, which poke their bare feet and tear their naked flesh. Then they are plunged in cold water for months or years. The author of this visionary treatise says that when Thurkill returned to his flesh, he became something of a local celebrity, telling his pious tale on every All Saints' Day: "By his continual narration of the visions seen he moved many to tears and bitter lamentations."[4]

The work of the Roman painter Pietro Cavallini is a more sophisticated artistic composition.[5] He painted it on the western wall of the Church of St. Cecilia, in Trastevere, Rome, just a few years before Dante began work on his *Inferno* (sometime around 1300). Toward the top of this work, alas now only in fragments, is Christ, surrounded by a choir of angels. The lordly twelve apostles sit on thrones, holding the instruments of their martyrdom. On the bottom register, two sets of angels blow trumpets to assemble the souls of the dead. The group on Christ's right rise and are shepherded toward the Judge: they stare, bow, fold hands in prayer. They are going to approach the *Stupor Mundi* (the awe of the world). They have wide-open eyes and solemn expressions. On the other side, souls are also assembled, but they are confused and crowded together, as they are pushed in clumps toward fiery pits and handed over to the dark angels. This is stern stuff. We see one pitiable tonsured monk staring out at us from among the damned, as if he now recognizes the falsity of his previous life.

As I have said, Cavallini's fresco is much more sophisticated than Thurkill's vision of graphic punishments. Thurkill seems to imagine that the gorier the description, the more likely you are to repent. And yet, while Cavallini's fresco is artistically beautiful (ordered, balanced, and colorful—the angels' wings are resplendent with many colors, like the feathers of some tropical bird), it still shares with Thurkill an important feature: both the painter and the writer aim to provoke a narrow set of emotional responses—sobriety, fear, awe, anxiety, and homage. The emotional temperature of each is restrained, sober, and cool.

It is against this background of such emotionally cool medieval works that we can appreciate Dante's subtlety because, in contrast, the *Comedy* invites a rich range of emotional responses. You could say that what Cavallini does on the level of his variegated colors, Dante does on the level of psychology. The medieval writer or artist or preacher did, of course, feel a kind of holy obligation to tell the truth dramatically in order to wake up the lethargic world. And Dante, of course, has many of those same elements present within his work. Time and time again, the poet's voice breaks off the narrative and cries out in impassioned warning. Dante's gate to hell delivers a message of stern judgment, like that found in Cavallini's *Last Judgment* fresco. And like Thurkill's, Dante's hell is also populated by foul and painful punishments: fire scorching feet, swords disemboweling schismatics, the fangs of fantastically scary reptiles biting thieves, diseases causing skin to fall off, and souls suffering from eternal thirst. Like Lotario, Dante's poetry often captures the shrill tones the preacher needed to prick his audience. And yet we can see how emotionally monochromatic the earlier works are in comparison to the great Florentine master. For example, remember how Dante swoons, with deep pity, when he hears Francesca's tale (*Inf.* 5). Dante was the only medieval author to give us Francesca's side! But the pilgrim also experiences pity when he hears Pier della Vigna's sad story, and he piously scatters the leaves of the Florentine suicide (14.1–3). Thurkill has no such response to the souls in hell.

In Dante, then, there is a rich variety of psychological responses. Among the envious, Sapia has a sense of irony when she admits that the cause of her salvation was the street vendor she had contempt for in life. When Dante meets his old drinking buddy, Forese, the two of them share a brief moment of humor as they remember how they were both complicit in incontinent fun. But in *Inferno* 15 we see the pilgrim manifest filial piety toward his old teacher, Brunetto; in *Inferno* 16, admiration for souls among the sodomites; in *Inferno* 4, esteem for the damned pagans in limbo; and in *Purgatorio*, simple delight in discovering that old mates, unlikely prospects for salvation (like Casella or Belacqua), somehow got in at the end. The pilgrim also seems to experience hints of remorse that his first best friend, Guido Cavalcanti, won't make it (*Inf.* 10).

Of course, throughout *Paradiso* the pilgrim experiences visions of Beatrice that make even hot earthly passion seem tepid. Then there's the peaceful spirit of Piccarda (*Par.* 3) and the hilarious exuberance of Peter (24.148–54), who, unlike Cavallini's enthroned and stern judge, giddily dances around Dante the pilgrim, blessing him. There's the gentle devotion of Bernard (*Par.* 33), the overwhelming joy of those on Venus to meet someone who will bring new love (*Par.* 8), and the high-spirited military pride of Justinian (*Par.* 5–6). Within the *Comedy*, then, there is a whole world of gradations of emotion. You find not generic damned or (worse) generic saints but individuals in their historical particularity—as if, to represent the full depth of the human heart, Dante needed the whole cast of humanity from all historical ages.

But Dante's *Comedy* stands out in another way: he shows us that the most painful part of punishment exists on the psychological plane. At one point, Virgil tells a violent sinner (Capaneus) that he is his own punishment (*Inf.* 14.65); in other words, it is not the external punishment of the flakes of fire but the fact that he can't let go of the anger that rages within. That is the true source of pain for Capaneus. We all know the experience of anger, how it makes us momentarily manic so that we cannot think of anything else. Dante gives us a Capaneus who, at no point, will choose, or can choose, to let this anger subside. Similarly, Francesca and Paolo barely notice that they are shaken and rocked by hurricane-like winds. They have what they want; they have what they think they want. In this way, Dante allows freedom to play an extraordinary role throughout the *Comedy*, even in *Inferno*. Sinners continue to "choose" their misery, because they cannot imagine a reality in which this one thing is not the only thing that is desirable.

Dante's poem is also extraordinary because the poet shows us that moral growth is moving from having a cramped soul that loves too little to having a generous, open, porous soul that cannot love too much. For Dante, sin is not so much doing "bad things" as it is loving small goods idolatrously, as if they were the only goods that existed. Thus, sinners in hell are portrayed as loving only one thing: Pier his honor, Farinata his party, Satan his beauty, Francesca her Paolo. In purgatory, however, sinners are helped to break the hold of these addictive loves by being coached to love new things in new ways. God so organizes their spiritual exercises that their neighbors become their good. The envious have to lean on another; those waiting in antepurgatory need prayer to move on; the lustful have to exchange brief kisses of peace, and nothing more. In this way, they add to that solitary love they had on earth. But in heaven, souls begin to love all creatures in the cosmos, because each reveals a facet of the beauty of God that could not be seen otherwise. The more facets the gem has, then the more the brilliance of God is manifest—he who has "made for himself so many mirrors in which he spreads himself out / even while he remains one in himself just as before" (*Par.* 29.143–45). Likewise, the pilgrim confesses his love of *all things*, which together

> "have drawn me from the sea of twisted love
> and have placed me on the right shore.
>
> "I love the leaves with which the garden
> of the eternal Gardener *enleaves* itself,
> as their good comes from him." (*Par.* 26.61–65)

Over the course of his poem, Dante progressively reveals how love is at the center. The poet leaves us with "positive" views of some sinners, exciting our pity without explicitly condemning them, because what they wanted was admirable, even though limited. If they had loved more things and more deeply, they could have been liberated from their narcissistic smallness. If they had just been high enough to get a view from above! But the fact is, their own freedom is what imprisons them; because they tightly grasped one thing, they remained voluntarily anchored in mire.

But Dante is not just a psychologically subtle portraitist: at the same time that he gives us convincing individuals, he also locates them within an imaginary world whose architecture is rigorously constructed on the basis of ancient moral philosophy and Christian ethical traditions. Thurkill saw souls who received punishments that more or less fit their crimes, but it is also true that all the souls are lumped together and suffer generic punishments of mutilation, fire, and demonic torture. But Dante divides his souls in layer upon layer, terrace upon terrace, so that his imaginary world becomes the literary incarnation of the treatises of moral philosophy in his day. In *Inferno* 11 and *Purgatorio* 17, Dante explains that his regions are divided according to the severity of the sin, which itself is based on the hierarchy of human powers. This extraordinary architecture regulates the whole vision of the afterlife, and it is a feature of Dante's poem that no medieval visionary treatise had had before.

And finally, in comparison with the monochromatic visions of the afterlife that came before, Dante's vision has one feature that they did not: it is written as a *poem*. It is in verse, organized into terzine, canticles, and canti. And within this formal, geometric structure, Dante weaves in almost every form of writing imaginable: lowbrow comedic interludes, hagiographies, history, denunciatory sermons, hymns, liturgical songs, scientific treatises, snatches of love poems, theoretical reflections on writing, allegorical dreams, apocalyptic visions, and even epitaphs. He maps onto his visionary treatise all of these genres, so that his poem is not only encyclopedic in terms of the diversity of historical people and creatures but is also an encyclopedia of forms of writing.

And yet, within this diversity, you could say that there are two primary literary poles: the epic and the lyric. In Dante's day, the epic was primarily admired as the genre that gets at everything. Thus, Virgil's *Aeneid* was thought not only to tell a story but also to give lessons on all seven of the liberal arts, teach moral theology, and provide information on scientific phenomena.[6] The lyric, though, was that very intimate poem in which I used my words to make you feel what was happening in me. It was *performative*, the vehicle by which the lover made the beloved return his affection. The *Comedy* weaves the lyrical moments, especially in *Paradiso*, into the larger epic framework, because for Dante it's not enough just to know someone's story; you also have to love it as a revelation of God. This, I think, is Dante's single most powerful addition to the genre of visionary writings about the afterlife. Previous attempts give a rather two-dimensional vision of heavenly bliss, but Dante shows us a heaven of lovers wooing one another, as it were, in a way that causes heaven to be constantly and dynamically deepening in love. For Dante, the *Comedy* is not only a universalizing poem; it also portrays a universe of poets, each of whom is singing his or her own lyric song of praise. Each of those individual melodic lines is folded into the choir of the whole.

Notes

Introduction: Dante as Poet, Prophet, and Exile

1. A note on notes: throughout this book I have included bibliographical references. They are not included for the scholar or specialist (there are many studies, especially in foreign languages, that I have left out). These notes are also not for the general reader, who will be content with what is written in the main text. I designed the book, then, so that it can be read without consulting any notes, if that is preferable. When I wrote the notes, I had in mind students (undergraduates and graduates) who would be arrested by some observation. I want to provide them with a path to continue to pursue that particular inspiring idea.

Throughout this book I have used my own translation, based on the Italian text: *Commedia*, ed. Anna Maria Chiavacci Leonardi, 3 vols. (Bologna: Zanchelli, 2000). For readers who are interested in a full translation of the *Comedy*, I recommend the translations of Robert and Jean Hollander (New York: Doubleday, 2002, 2004, 2008). Some translations are more poetic, such as the ones by Robin Kirkpatrick (Penguin) and Anthony Esolen (Modern Library). There is an older, more literal translation by Charles Singleton (Princeton University Press). However, I like the Hollanders' translation because it balances fidelity to the Italian original with a sense for the music of the poetry. I also appreciate Robert Hollander's notes, although they are sometimes overwhelming for first-time readers.

2. See, e.g., John Demaray, *Dante and the Book of the Cosmos* (Philadelphia: American Philosophical Society, 1987); and Nino Pirrotta, "Dante Musicus: Gothicism, Scholasticism, and Music," *Speculum* 43, no. 2 (1968): 245–57. See also Otto Von Simson's references to Dante in his *Gothic Cathedral* (Princeton: Princeton University Press, 1988).

3. Although scholars now think that his book has limitations, Otto Von Simson's *Gothic Cathedral* is still the best introduction to appreciating the geometrical order of the cathedral.

4. Marc Cogan, *The Design in the Wax: The Structure of the* Divine Comedy *and Its Meaning* (Notre Dame, IN: University of Notre Dame Press, 1999).

5. Roberto Antonelli, "Come (e perché) Dante ha scritto la Divina Commedia?," in *Dante Oggi*, ed. Roberto Antonelli, Annalisa Landolfi, and Arìanna Punzi, special issue, *Critica del Testo* 14 (2011): 3–23.

6. For a fascinating and readable study about how Florence responded to Dante in the centuries after his death, see Simon Gilson, *Dante and Renaissance Florence* (Cambridge: Cambridge University Press, 2009).

7. For more on this, see John Freccero, "The Significance of *Terza Rima*," in *Dante: The Poetics of Conversion*, ed. Rachel Jacoff (Cambridge, MA: Harvard University Press, 1986),

258–74; and Zygmunt Baranski, "The Poetics of Meter: *Terza rima,* 'canto,' 'canzon,' 'cantica,'" in *Dante Now: Current Trends in Dante Studies,* ed. Theodore Cachey (Notre Dame, IN: University of Notre Dame Press, 1995), 3–41.

8. For a beautiful example of how medieval monks realized sacred space in the ritualistic performance of sacred time, see Kristina Krueger, "Monastic Customs and Liturgy in the Light of the Architectural Evidence," in *From Dead of Night to End of Day: Medieval Customs of Cluny,* ed. S. Boynton and I. Cochelin (Turnhout: Brepols, 2005), 191–220. But see also Neil Roy's more accessible "The Galilee Chapel: A Medieval Notion Come of Age?," in *Benedict XVI and Beauty in Sacred Art and Architecture,* ed. D. Vincent Twomey and Janet Rutherford (Dublin: Four Courts, 2011), 143–62; and Margot Fassler, *The Virgin of Chartres: Making History through Liturgy and the Arts* (New Haven: Yale University Press, 2010).

For Dante and "sacred time," see Ronald Martinez, "Dante and the Poem of the Liturgy," in *Reviewing Dante's Theology,* ed. Claire Honess and Matthew Treherne (Oxford: Lang, 2013), 2:89–157.

9. George Duby's assessment, in *The Age of the Cathedrals: Art and Society, 980–1420* (Chicago: University of Chicago Press, 1983), as cited in Demaray, *Dante and the Book of the Cosmos,* 1.

10. For the playfulness of the gothic style, see Mary Carruthers, "Varietas," in *The Experience of Beauty in the Middle Ages* (Oxford: Oxford University Press, 2013), 135–65; and Paul Binski, *Gothic Wonder* (New Haven: Yale University Press, 2014).

11. In total, there are 128 speaking characters in the *Comedy,* and another 236 characters who have some nonspeaking action assigned to them. For other exciting statistics such as these, see Bernard Delmay, *I personaggi della "Divina Commedia": Classificazione e regesto* (Florence: Olschki, 1986). One of the most useful tools for navigating this huge list of characters, in addition to Robert Hollander's notes, is the old but newly reprinted work by Paget Toynbee, *A Dictionary of Proper Names and Notable Matters in the Works of Dante,* revised by Charles S. Singleton (1898; rev., Oxford: Clarendon, 1968). As it is now in the public domain, it is easily accessible. See the first edition (Oxford: Clarendon, 1898) at http://warburg.sas.ac.uk/pdf /enh149b2446413.pdf.

12. There are many good books that give basic biographical information. I recommend Stephen Bemrose, *A New Life of Dante,* rev. and updated ed. (Exeter, UK: University of Exeter Press, 2000); and John Scott, *Understanding Dante* (Notre Dame, IN: University of Notre Dame Press, 2004). I am indebted to these works for the following summary of Dante's life.

13. For the medieval poetic "science" of love, the best place to start is to read the bizarre but influential medieval text by Guillaume de Lorris and Jean de Meun, *The Romance of the Rose,* trans. and ed. Frances Horgan, Oxford World's Classics (Oxford: Oxford University Press, 2009). See also Linda Paterson, *The World of the Troubadours: Medieval Occitan Society, c. 1100–c. 1300* (Cambridge: Cambridge University Press, 1995).

14. For Dante's lyric poetry, I have used an older edition: *Dante's Lyric Poetry,* 2 vols., ed. and trans. Kenelm Foster and Patrick Boyde (Oxford: Oxford University Press, 1967). You can also read Dante's lyric poems in a more recent edition: *Dante's Lyric Poetry,* ed. Teodolinda Barolini, trans. Richard Lansing (Toronto: University of Toronto Press, 2014).

For two brilliant introductions to Dante's lyric poems and their relationship to *Vita Nuova,* see Teodolinda Barolini, "Dante's Lyric Past," in *The Cambridge Companion to Dante,* ed. Rachel Jacoff (Cambridge: Cambridge University Press, 1993), 14–33; and Manuele Gragnolati, "Authorship and Performance in Dante's *Vita Nuova,*" in *Aspects of the Performative in Medieval Culture,* ed. Manuele Gragnolati and Almut Suerbaum (Berlin: de Gruyter, 2010), 125–41. But the most important study on Dante and his lyric poetry is now Tristan Kay, *Dante's Lyric Redemption: Eros, Salvation, Vernacular Tradition* (Oxford: Oxford University Press, 2016).

15. For the text, see Foster and Boyde, *Dante's Lyric Poetry,* 3a.

16. See Ronald G. Witt, *The Two Latin Cultures and the Foundation of Renaissance Humanism in Medieval Italy* (Cambridge: Cambridge University Press, 2012).

17. *Dante's Vita Nuova*, trans. Mark Musa (Bloomington: Indiana University Press, 1973). In this and subsequent citations, I cite the section number from the *Vita Nuova* followed by the page number(s) in Musa.

18. For a discussion of Dante's explanation of the providential nature of his exile, see Albert Ascoli, "Language: *Neminem ante nos*," in *Dante and the Making of a Modern Author* (Cambridge: Cambridge University Press, 2008), 130–74.

Chapter 1 Zooming In and Zooming Out

1. Most notably, Charles Singleton, "In Exitu Israel de Aegypto," *Dante Studies* 118 (2000): 167–87; and Robert Hollander, *Allegory in Dante's* Commedia (Princeton: Princeton University Press, 1969).

2. See Valentina Atturo, "Contemplating Wonder: 'Ad-miratio' in Richard of St. Victor and Dante," *Dante Studies* 129 (2011): 99–124.

3. Mary Carruthers, *The Medieval Experience of Beauty* (Oxford: Oxford University Press, 2013), 148. See also Caroline Walker Bynum, "Wonder," in *Metamorphosis and Identity* (New York: Zone, 2001), 37–71.

4. Carruthers, *Medieval Experience of Beauty*, 142.

5. See Susan McNamer, "The Origins of the *Meditationes Vitae Christi*," *Speculum* 84 (2009): 905–55.

6. Guglielmo Gorni, "Canto I," in *Lectura Dantis Turicensis: Inferno*, ed. Georges Güntert and Michelangelo Picone (Firenze: Cesati, 2000), 27–38 (at 34).

7. Mircea Eliade, *The Sacred and the Profane: The Nature of Religion*, trans. Willard R. Trask (New York: Harper Torchbooks, 1961).

8. For translations of Virgil, I have used A. S. Kline's beautiful and free translation, online at http://www.poetryintranslation.com/PITBR/Latin/Virgilhome.htm.

Chapter 2 The Fear of Hell and the Fear of God

1. My translation slightly modifies that found in Linda Seidel, *Legends in Limestone: Lazarus, Gislebertus, and the Cathedral of Autun* (Chicago: University of Chicago Press, 1999), 2–7.

2. For more on the pagan poet's limitations concerning the Christian afterlife, see Robert Hollander, "Dante's Virgil: A Light That Failed," *Lectura Dantis Virginiana* 4 (1989): 3–9, https://www.brown.edu/Departments/Italian_Studies/LD/numbers/04/hollander.html; and Lloyd Howard, *Virgil the Blind Guide* (Montreal: McGill-Queen's University Press, 2010).

3. Dorothy Sayers, "The Other Six Deadly Sins," in *Creed or Chaos?* (New York: Harcourt, Brace, 1949), 81.

4. For more on the medieval attitude toward the authors of antiquity, see Jan Ziolkowski, "Cultures of Authority in the Long Twelfth Century," *Journal of English and Germanic Philology* 108, no. 4 (2009): 421–48.

5. See Ronald Witt, *In the Footsteps of the Ancients* (Leiden: Brill, 2003). For Dante's relationship to the classical world, see Michelangelo Picone, "Dante and the Classics," in *Dante: Contemporary Perspectives*, ed. Amilcare Iannucci (Toronto: University of Toronto Press, 1997), 51–73.

6. See Teodolinda Barolini, "Dante and Cavalcanti (On Making Distinctions in Matters of Love): *Inferno* V in Its Lyric Context," *Dante Studies* 116 (1998): 31–63, http://italian.columbia.edu/files/italian/pdf/Barolini%20Dante%20and%20Cavalcanti.pdf; and Elena Lombardi, *Wings of the Doves: Love and Desire in Dante and Medieval Culture* (Montreal: McGill-Queen's University Press, 2012).

7. This is what Aquinas calls "swelling of the mind" (*Summa theologiae* II-II, q. 158, a. 7).

8. See Erich Auerbach, "Camilla, or the Rebirth of the Sublime," in *Literary Language and Its Public in Late Latin Antiquity and in the Middle Ages*, trans. Ralph Manheim (Princeton: Princeton University Press, 1993), 181–234.

Chapter 4 White-Collar Criminals and Sins against Words

1. I borrow the terminology of "cold" and "hot" sins from Dorothy Sayers, "The Other Six Deadly Sins," in *Creed or Chaos?* (New York: Harcourt, Brace, 1949), 63–88.

2. Evagrius, "Praktikos," in *Evagrius of Pontus: The Greek Ascetic Corpus*, trans. Robert E. Sinkewicz, Oxford Early Christian Studies (Oxford: Oxford University Press, 2003), 95–96.

3. John Scott, "*Inferno* XXVI: Dante's Ulysses," *Lettere Italiane* 23, no. 2 (1971): 145–86 (at 185–86).

Chapter 5 Icy Hearts and Frozen Souls

1. For more on Dante's controversial relationship with Islam, see Jan Ziolkowski, ed., *Dante and Islam* (New York: Fordham University Press, 2015).

2. See John Freccero, "The Sign of Satan," *Modern Language Notes* 80 (1965): 11–26.

3. See Zygmunt Baranski, "The 'Marvelous' and the 'Comic': Toward a Reading of *Inferno* XVI," *Lectura Dantis* 7 (1990): 72–95.

Chapter 6 Waiting for God

1. For more on the medieval understanding of purgatory, see the classic by Jacques LeGoff, *The Birth of Purgatory*, trans. Arthur Goldhammer (Chicago: University of Chicago Press, 1984).

2. For the nature of medieval affective spirituality, see Dennis Martin, introduction to *Carthusian Spirituality: The Writings of Hugh of Balma and Guigo de Ponte*, Classics of Western Spirituality (New York: Paulist Press, 1997), 1–66. "Various words have been employed by translators: feeling, sentiment, disposition, inclination, movement, devotion. Most of these call for the active voice in their accompanying verbs. 'Movedness' rather than 'movement,' 'devotedness' rather than 'devotion,' or 'disposedness' rather than 'disposition' would better capture the Latin noun's meaning, but they are all extremely awkward. The present translation resorts most often to 'affection' . . . hoping the reader will not forget the intended actively passive thrust of these words—the affective soul has been moved, swayed, impacted toward God" (6–7).

3. See Ronald Martinez, "Dante and the Poem of the Liturgy," in *Reviewing Dante's Theology*, ed. Claire Honess and Matthew Treherne, 2 vols. (Oxford: Lang, 2013), 2:89–155. For Dante and the "spirituality" of monophony, see Francesco Ciabattoni, *Dante's Journey to Polyphony* (Toronto: University of Toronto Press, 2010).

4. Peter of Celle, "The School of the Cloister," in *Selected Works*, trans. Hugh Feiss (Kalamazoo, MI: Cistercian Publications, 1987), 73.

Chapter 7 The People outside the Gate

1. *Shepherd of Hermas*, in *The Apostolic Fathers*, ed. Michael Holmes (Grand Rapids: Baker Academic, 2002), 359.

2. See Jacques LeGoff, *The Birth of Purgatory*, trans. Arthur Goldhammer (Chicago: University of Chicago Press, 1984), 137–38.

3. See LeGoff, *Birth of Purgatory*, chap. 8, "The Scholastic Systematization," 237–88.

4. As cited in John Scott, *Understanding Dante* (Notre Dame, IN: University of Notre Dame Press, 2004), 247.

5. Translation of the English Dominican Fathers, as found on NewAdvent.org.

6. See *Richard of St. Victor: "The Twelve Patriarchs," "The Mystical Ark," "Book Three of the Trinity,"* trans. Grover Zinn, Classics of Western Spirituality (New York: Paulist Press, 1979).

Chapter 8 In Search of Deep Cleansing

1. For a work that traces the historical roots of the seven deadly sins to the desert monastic tradition, see Morton Bloomfield, *The Seven Deadly Sins: An Introduction to the History of a Religious Concept, with Special Reference to Medieval English Literature* (East Lansing: Michigan State University Press, 1967). For Dante in particular, see Siegfried Wenzel, "Dante's Rationale for the Seven Deadly Sins (*Purgatorio* XVII)," *Modern Language Review* 60 (1965): 529–33; Patrick Boyde, *Human Vices and Human Worth in Dante's* Comedy (Cambridge: Cambridge University Press, 2000).

2. See Marc Cogan, *The Design in the Wax: The Structure of the* Divine Comedy *and Its Meaning* (Notre Dame, IN: University of Notre Dame Press, 1999).

3. See Marion Habig, ed., *St. Francis of Assisi: Writings and Early Biographies; English Omnibus of the Sources for the Life of St. Francis*, vol. 1 (Chicago: Franciscan Herald Press, 1983), 128–29.

4. Treherne's lecture "Dante's Theology in Poetry, Practice, and Society" was given at University College Cork, February 2012, and is available on YouTube (https://www.youtube.com /watch?v=vk9z94jyPtM). For David Ford's discussion of the moods of theology, see *The Future of Christian Theology* (Oxford: Wiley-Blackwell, 2011), 68–83. See also Matthew Treherne, "Art and Nature Put to Scorn: On the Sacramental in *Purgatorio*," in *Nature and Art in Dante: Literary and Theological Essays*, ed. Daragh O'Connell and Jennifer Petrie (Dublin: Four Courts, 2013), 187–210.

5. Dante is on the brink of a major social transformation. See Brad Gregory, *The Unintended Reformation: How a Religious Revolution Secularized Society* (Cambridge, MA: Belknap Press, 2015).

6. For Aquinas on anger, see his *Summa theologiae* II-II, q. 158.

7. Mary Carruthers, *The Medieval Experience of Beauty* (Oxford: Oxford University Press, 2013), 147.

8. Evagrius, "Eight Thoughts," in *Evagrius of Pontus: The Greek Ascetic Corpus*, trans. Robert E. Sinkewicz, Oxford Early Christian Studies (Oxford: Oxford University Press, 2003), 79.

9. Ibid.

10. Throughout, I have used my own translation of the Latin text of Guigo's *Scala claustralium* in Patrologia Latina, ed. J.-P. Migne, vol. 184. For another English translation, see *Guigo II: Ladder of Monks and Twelve Meditations*, trans. James Walsh and Edmund Colledge (Kalamazoo, MI: Cistercian Publications, 1981).

11. Francois Petit, *Spirituality of the Premonstratensians: The Twelfth and Thirteenth Centuries*, trans. Victor Szczurek (Collegeville, MN: Liturgical Press, 2011), 281.

12. See *Se Mai Continga . . . : Exile, Politics, and Theology in Dante*, ed. Claire E. Honess and Matthew Treherne (Ravenna: Longo, 2013).

13. Crassus was the third member of the triumvirate with Pompey and Julius Caesar. He was nicknamed "Dives" (wealthy one) and died a gruesome death when the Parthian king poured molten gold into his open mouth. The story of Heliodorus comes from 2 Maccabees. He was ordered to steal the treasure from the temple in Jerusalem but was cut down by a divinely sent horseman. This event is pictured in one of Raphael's rooms near the Stanza della Segnatura in the Vatican Museum.

Chapter 9 Returning to Humanity's First Home

1. See Zygmunt Baranski, "Dante Alighieri: Experimentation and (Self-)Exegesis," in *The Cambridge History of Literary Criticism*, ed. Alastair Minnis and Ian Johnson (Cambridge: Cambridge University Press, 2005), 561–82.

2. Translated by Daniel Stevenson, at http://classics.mit.edu/Virgil/eclogue.mb.txt.

3. As cited in Humphrey Carpenter, *J. R. R. Tolkien: A Biography* (London: Houghton Mifflin, 1987), 64.

4. "Al cor gentil rempaira," in *German and Italian Lyrics of the Middle Ages*, trans. Frederick Goldin (New York: Anchor, 1973), 286–91.

5. For more on this, see Peter Dronke, "Dante's Earthly Paradise: Towards an Interpretation of *Purgatorio* XXVIII," in *The Medieval Poet and His World* (Rome: Edizioni di storia e letteratura, 1984), 387–407.

Chapter 10 As the Heavens Are Higher Than the Earth

1. Zygmunt Baranski, "'New Life' of 'Comedy': The *Commedia* and the *Vita Nuova*," *Dante Studies* 113 (1995): 1–29 (at 1, 4).

2. Rudolf Otto, *The Idea of the Holy*, trans. John Harvey (Oxford: Oxford University Press, 1936), 6.

3. See Peter Dronke, "The Phantasmagoria in Earthly Paradise," in *Dante and Medieval Latin Traditions* (Cambridge: Cambridge University Press, 1986), 55–82.

Chapter 11 Great Fires Come from Tiny Sparks

1. For the technical information, see Patrick Boyde, "Concerning the Heavens," in *Dante: Philomythes and Philosophe; Man in the Cosmos* (Cambridge: Cambridge University Press, 1981), 132–72.

2. Cicero, *The Republic and the Laws*, trans. Niall Rudd, Oxford World's Classics (Oxford: Oxford University Press, 1998), 90.

3. C. S. Lewis, *The Discarded Image: An Introduction to Medieval and Renaissance Literature*, Canto ed. (Cambridge: Cambridge University Press, 2012), 111.

4. Umberto Eco, *Art and Beauty in the Middle Ages* (New Haven: Yale University Press, 1986), 44, 12.

5. Boethius, *Consolation of Philosophy*, trans. David R. Slavitt (Cambridge, MA: Harvard University Press, 2008), 84–85 (metrum 3.9).

6. For more on this, see David Chamberlain, "Philosophy of Music in the *Consolatio* of Boethius," *Speculum* 45, no. 1 (1970): 80–97.

7. Otto Von Simson, *The Gothic Cathedral* (Princeton: Princeton University Press, 1988), 51–52.

8. For the text of the *Mystical Theology* that I cite here, see *Pseudo-Dionysius: The Complete Works*, trans. Colm Luibheid, Classics of Western Spirituality (New York: Paulist Press, 1987), 133–43. For more on this, see Gregory Rocca, *Speaking the Incomprehensible God* (Washington, DC: Catholic University of America Press, 2004). See also the multivolume series The Presence of God: A History of Western Christian Mysticism, by Bernard McGinn: *The Foundations of Christian Mysticism*, *The Growth of Mysticism*, *The Flowering of Mysticism*, *The Harvest of Mysticism in Medieval Germany*, and *The Varieties of Vernacular Mysticism* (New York: Crossroad, 1991–2012).

9. Pseudo-Dionysius, *Mystical Theology*, 140 (trans. Luibheid).

10. Ibid., 139.

11. Ibid.

12. Ibid., 136.

13. Ovid, *Metamorphoses*, trans. A. S. Kline, available online at http://www.poetryintransla tion.com/PITBR/Latin/Ovhome.htm.

Chapter 12 "In His Will Is Our Peace"

1. Boethius, *Consolation of Philosophy*, trans. David R. Slavitt (Cambridge, MA: Harvard University Press, 2008), 19–20 (metrum 1.5).

2. Francesco Ciabattoni, *Dante's Journey to Polyphony* (Toronto: University of Toronto Press, 2010).

3. Giacomo da Lentini, "Io m'aggio posto in core a Dio servire," in *German and Italian Lyrics of the Middle Ages*, trans. Frederick Goldin (New York: Anchor, 1973), 216–17.

4. You can find the Italian text of Giacomo da Lentini's canzonetta "Meravigliosamente" in Goldin, *German and Italian Lyrics*, 210–15: "Al cor m'arde una doglia, / Com'om che ten lo foco / A lo suo seno ascoso, / E quando più lo'nvoglia, / Allora arde più loco / E non pò stare incluso: / Similmente eo ardo / Quando pass'e non guardo / A voi, vis'amoroso." The translation provided above is mine.

5. "Amor che ne la mente mi ragiona," in *Dante's Lyric Poetry*, ed. and trans. Kenelm Foster and Patrick Boyde, 2 vols. (Oxford: Oxford University Press, 1967), 1:59–60.

6. For such Dominican teaching, see Michael Sherwin, *By Knowledge and by Love: Charity and Knowledge in the Moral Theology of Thomas Aquinas* (Washington, DC: Catholic University of America Press, 2011).

7. See Zygmunt Baranski, "Dante and Doctrine (and Theology)," in *Reviewing Dante's Theology*, ed. Claire Honess and Matthew Treherne, 2 vols. (Oxford: Lang, 2013), 1:9–64.

8. See Angela Meekins, "Reflection on the Divine: Notes on Dante's Heaven of the Sun," *The Italianist* 18 (1998): 28–70.

Chapter 13 Intellectual Fasting and the Test of Love

1. Special thanks to Isaac Owen.

2. See, e.g., http://www.metmuseum.org/toah/works-of-art/43.106.1/.

3. Paul Griffiths, *Religious Reading: The Place of Reading in the Practice of Religion* (Oxford: Oxford University Press, 1999), ix.

Chapter 14 The Canti of Surprise

1. Christian Moevs, *The Metaphysics of Dante's* Comedy (Oxford: Oxford University Press, 2008), 5.

2. For Aquinas's thought on *lumen gloriae*, see *Summa theologiae* I, q. 12, a. 11.

3. Bernardus Silvestris, *Poetic Works*, ed. and trans. Winthrop Wetherbee, Dumbarton Oaks Medieval Library (Cambridge, MA: Harvard University Press, 2015), 99.

4. Alan of Lille, "Anticlaudianus," in *Literary Works*, ed. and trans. Winthrop Wetherbee, Dumbarton Oaks Medieval Library (Cambridge, MA: Harvard University Press, 2013), 219–519.

5. See John Ahern, "Binding the Book: Hermeneutics and Manuscript Production in *Paradiso* 33," *Proceedings of the Modern Language Association* 97, no. 5 (1982): 800–809; Piero Boitani, "The Sibyl's Leaves: Reading *Paradiso* XXXIII," in *The Tragic and the Sublime in Medieval Literature* (Cambridge: Cambridge University Press, 1989), 223–50.

Conclusion: The Wonder of the *Comedy*

1. See Barbara Newman, "Latin and the Vernaculars," in *The Cambridge Companion to Christian Mysticism*, ed. Amy M. Hollywood and Patricia Z. Beckman (Cambridge: Cambridge University Press, 2012), 225–39; and Alison Morgan, *Dante and the Medieval Other World* (Cambridge: Cambridge University Press, 2007). For accounts of visions of the afterlife, I have used the anthology *Visions of Heaven and Hell before Dante*, ed. Eileen Gardiner (New York: Italica, 2008).

2. Lotario dei Segni (Pope Innocent III), *De miseria condicionis humane*, ed. and trans. Robert Lewis (Athens: University of Georgia Press, 1978).

3. It's even better in the original. Just read it aloud to get an idea of the intensity of the language: "Ibi erit fletus et stridor dentium, gemitus et eiulatus, luctus et ululatus et cruciatus,

stridor et clamor, timor et tremor, dolor et labor, ardor et fetor, obscuritas et anxietas, acerbitas et asperitas, clamitas et egestas, angustia et tristitia . . ." (ibid., 232–33).

4. Ibid., 236.

5. See, e.g., "Frescoes in Santa Cecilia in Trastevere, Rome (The Last Judgement)," Web Gallery of Art, http://www.wga.hu/html_m/c/cavallin/lastjudg/.

6. See Jason Baxter, "Through the Eyes of Landino: Dante, *Natura*, and the Poetics of *Varietas*," *L'Alighieri* 43 (2014): 65–89.

Index